The Mid-Atlantic Guest House Book

Corinne Madden Ross

The East Woods Press

First Printing

Library of Congress Cataloging in Publication Data

Ross, Corinne Madden.
The mid-Atlantic guest house book.

Includes index.
1. Hotels, taverns, etc. — Middle Atlantic States — Directories. I. Title.
TX907.R587 1983 647'.9474 82-48993
ISBN 0-914788-62-0 (pbk.)

Cover design by Talmadge Moose.

Inside illustrations and photographs provided by the guest houses of the Mid-Atlantic.
Typography by Raven Type.
Printed in the United States of America.

East Woods Press Books
Fast & McMillan Publishers, Inc.
429 East Boulevard
Charlotte, NC 28203

Contents

List of Maps

Introduction

Economically-minded travelers in Great Britain have long been familiar with the distinctive, homey form of overnight lodging known as "bed and breakfast." In the United States, a similar kind of establishment has been available for many years—the guest house, sometimes called a tourist home. Until recently, however, American guest houses remained pretty much a well-kept secret shared only by experienced travelers and those fortunate enough to come upon them by chance. Today the situation is changing. Not only are more people discovering the pleasures of staying at a guest house, but the number of houses—which only a few years ago was waning—is increasing rapidly. Many guest house owners, too, are practicing the hospitable British custom of offering breakfast to their guests, included in the rates or for a modest extra charge.

This book describes 118 guest houses, located throughout the Middle Atlantic states of New York, Pennsylvania, New Jersey, Delaware, Maryland and West Virginia. Also included are descriptions of the various states and regions, their history, and suggestions on places to see and things to do. In addition to the individual houses, I have included several regional "bed and breakfast" reservation services. These organizations and their host members offer lodgings (generally not listed elsewhere) in areas where traditional guest houses are either scarce or non-existent. A fast-growing trend, bed and breakfast services provide a welcome increase in the choices of accommodations available for travelers.

If you have never stayed in one, you are probably wondering what a "guest house" is, exactly, and what it has to offer. With a few exceptions, a guest house is a private home with several rooms available for travelers. Its owners generally offer lodging only or lodging plus breakfast. A small number, usually situated in isolated areas, also offer optional lunch or dinner; others may provide dinner for their guests only during the off season when most of the local restaurants are closed. The rates are often amazingly low, and even the highest-priced accommodations are generally more reasonable than those in most chain motels or hotels.

As a rule, guest houses are located in or near a town; visitors can easily walk to restaurants, antique and gift shops, historic sites, museums and other local points of interest. Parking is provided on the premises or nearby. Even if you come without a car you will be able to get around without much effort. Some hosts will even arrange to meet you at the bus stop, train station or airport. Guest houses are ideal for families; most of them welcome children and their owners will often provide cots or roll-away beds for a small fee. There is almost always a spacious yard, too, where youngsters can play.

The greatest charm of guest houses, however, lies in their surprising individuality—a refreshing change from the impersonal monotony of most motel accommodations. In the Middle Atlantic States they include some of the region's loveliest homes, often centuries old, with fascinating histories and a gratifying range of architectural styles, as diverse as the region itself. You may stay in a beautiful old stone or brick farmhouse dating back to the eighteenth century, or an elegant Federal or gingerbread-ornamented Victorian mansion. Some homes are situated on working farms, where you're invited to share in the daily chores such as milking the cows or bringing in the hay. Other guest houses include historic taverns, rustic contemporary retreats in the mountains or beside a river or lake, and beach cottages large and small. Many offer luxurious, old-world elegance seldom found elsewhere today; others are merely simple, unassuming homes providing clean, comfortable surroundings.

Guest house owners are as individual as their homes: grandmotherly ladies, young couples and older ones, families, and single men and women of all ages. The majority share one agreeable characteristic: they truly enjoy their guests and often form lasting friendships with them. You may, of course, have as much privacy as you wish. But if you can, spend some time with your hosts and fellow guests—you'll find them interesting, congenial people. A number of houses are locally renowned for their unusual architectural features; many are listed in the National Register of Historic Landmarks. In most cases, their owners have worked hard to restore these handsome structures and will be glad to share their experiences with you. Ask your hosts, too, for suggestions as to the best places to eat and shop in the area, and about local attractions. Guest house owners are proud of their homes, cities and towns and want their guests to appreciate them as much as they do. Many proprietors even act as concierges, making dinner reservations for guests at local restaurants, or arranging tours of the area. Personal service and gracious extra touches are the keynotes of guest house hospitality.

As the houses generally are small with only a few rooms, making reservations in advance by phone or letter is a good idea—and sometimes required. Some owners also request an advance deposit; a few ask for a minimum stay of two or three days, especially over holiday weekends. Credit cards are not usually accepted; cash or traveler's checks are preferred. Personal checks, too, are often acceptable, but it's advisable to ask ahead of time. Because rates, like everything else nowadays, tend to increase from time to time, I have not listed specific prices. Instead, the house's rates (for double occupancy) are described as falling into one of three general categories:

Inexpensive	($10–$25)
Moderate	($25–$45)
Expensive	($45–up)

Most guest houses stay open year-round, but some, especially in seaside areas, close for the winter. Others may close for a vacation for a month or so in early spring. Information on dates open has been included for each house. If the guest house offers breakfast it has been so noted, with a description of the food served. The index also indicates which houses serve breakfast, with a star next to their names. Usually the meal is a simple Continental breakfast, but some proprietors provide heartier repasts for their guests. Others, not starred, may offer complimentary wake-up coffee or juice.

The descriptions of the houses included in this book are as accurate as possible. Sometimes, however, situations and/or owners change, and if you should find any of the accommodations not measuring up to your expectations, I would very much appreciate your letting me know. Also, as you travel, if you discover a guest house that you think would make a good addition, write to me about it so that it may be considered for inclusion in the next edition.

A good rule of thumb to use in searching out a new and unfamiliar house—or any guest house, for that matter—is to decide if you like its looks from the road. If you do, it's likely you will find it just as attractive inside. Good proprietors take as much pride in maintaining their yards as they do their houses—indoors and out. If you have any doubts at all, ask to see the house before you settle in; the owner will be happy to show you around. You probably will have the choice of several rooms, if the house is not filled. It should be noted that not all guest houses offer private baths; in many at least some of the accommodations share a bath. Most do not provide a private phone or television set in each room, either. Few visitors, however, find any of these particulars an inconvenience or hardship.

The Middle Atlantic States, although called a "region," do not fall into an easily-definable mold, as do, for example, the New England States or the South. They are all rich in history, cultural events and sports activities, and offer magnificent scenery. They include great cosmopolitan cities, small Colonial towns, picturesque fishing villages and remote mountain hamlets. Regional foods and festivals of all kinds abound. Each state offers excellent highways that will take you swiftly to a given destination, and miles of scenic back-country roads for more leisurely exploration. Yet each of the six—New York, Pennsylvania, New Jersey, Delaware, Maryland and West Virginia—has a character and topography all its own.

Maryland is a fascinating blend of North and South with some of the country's prettiest towns; tiny Delaware includes remnants of its early Swedish colonists and a wealth of outstanding museums; Pennsylvania has Revolutionary and Civil War battlefields, historic Philadelphia, and the distinctive folk culture of the Pennsylvania Dutch. New Jersey offers fine beaches and charming Victorian seaside resorts; New York has vineyards, forests, Niagara Falls and New York City; West Virginia is a region of rugged mountains and whitewater rivers.

The best way, of course, to understand and appreciate a region is to get to know its people—and staying at one of the Middle Atlantic states' delightful guest houses will provide an unequalled opportunity. Your friendly hosts and hostesses will welcome you with genuine warmth and old-fashioned hospitality and will do their very best to make your visit memorable.

New York

New York, to travelers the world over, means New York City. . . . specifically that glittering portion known as Manhattan, or "The Big Apple." To some, the discovery that there is also a New York State comes as a distinct surprise. I recall with delight letting a Midwestern acquaintance in on the news by showing her a map of the entire state; she was literally unaware of its existence! (There are, it might be added, a number of New York City residents who share the same misconception.) Most visitors to the area will, of course, want to spend some time in New York City, experiencing its multiple attractions. But the rest of the state—extending all the way from the Atlantic Ocean to the Great Lakes—offers the traveler an awesome array of exciting places to see and things to do.

New York's spectacular scenery ranges from forested mountains with rugged gorges and glens to sandy ocean beaches, pastoral valleys, vineyards and farmland. There are great rivers, canals, some 8000 lakes and a myriad of waterfalls, including the thundering cataracts of the Niagara. Cultural events, festivals, and all manner of sports activities abound, with something to suit every taste. Countless historic sites invite exploration, as do sleepy, picturesque villages and bustling cities, impressive mansions, wineries, state parks, and a wealth of intriguing museums, art galleries, and craft and antique shops.

Giovanni da Verrazano, the Florentine navigator, was the first European to visit New York. In 1524 he made a brief stopover just long enough to note a broad, deep-mouthed river "below steep little hills." Eighty-five years later, in 1609, the French explorer Samuel de Champlain journeyed down from Quebec to investigate the northern part of the region. In the same year Henry Hudson, an English navigator hired by the Dutch East India Company to find a short-cut to China, sailed his vessel the *Half Moon* up the mighty river

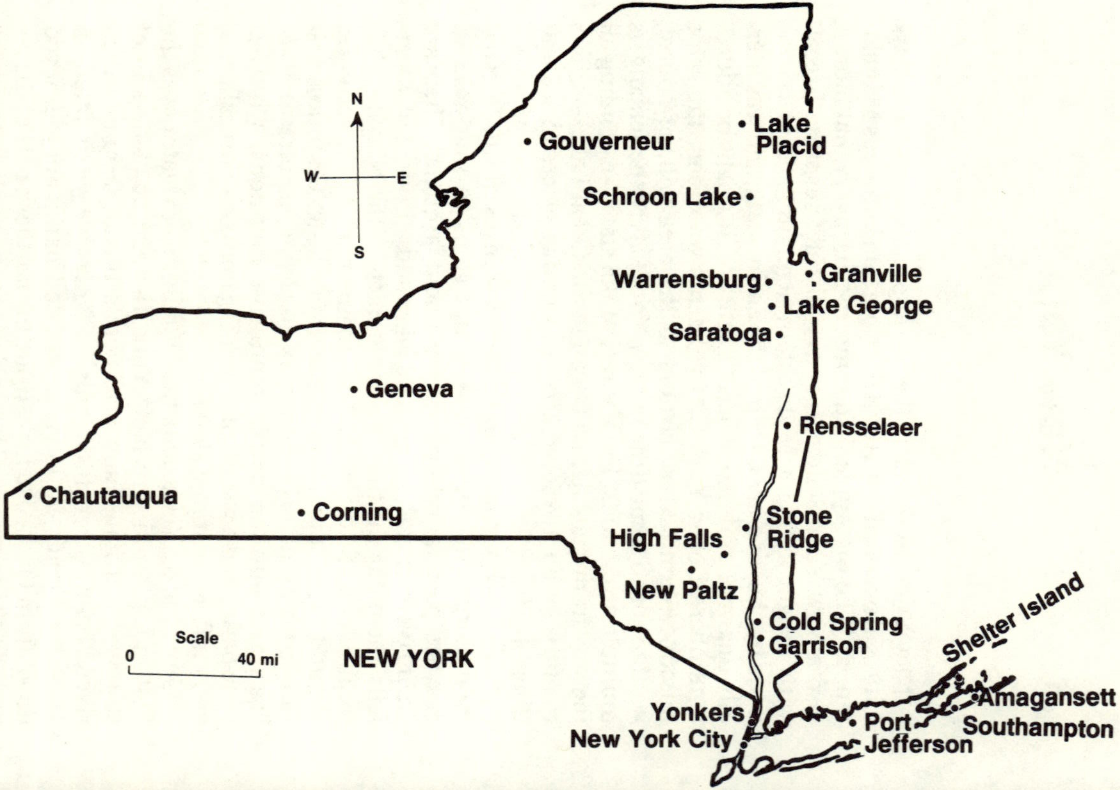
N
W
E
S
Gouverneur
Lake Placid
Schroon Lake
Warrensburg
Granville
Lake George
Saratoga
Geneva
Rensselaer
Chautauqua
Corning
Stone Ridge
High Falls
New Paltz
Cold Spring
Garrison
Shelter Island
Scale
0
40 mi
NEW YORK
Amagansett
Yonkers
Port Jefferson
Southampton
New York City

that now bears his name. Hudson returned to Holland with a favorable report of the territory, including particular mention of abundant furs. Dutch merchants soon dispatched another ship to the region they called New Netherland, and trading posts were established on Manhattan Island and near present-day Albany.

In 1621, the Dutch West India Company was formed to colonize the new territory. The first permanent settlers arrived three years later; others followed in 1625. Many of the earliest families, though, were not actually Dutch: they were Walloons, Huguenots who had fled from France to escape religious persecution. The West India Company's policy of offering enormous tracts of land, called patroonships, soon brought more settlers (who *were* Dutch) to New Netherland, and a governor was appointed to oversee the young colony. He was Peter Minuit, who became forever famous through his purchase of Manhattan Island from the Indians—paying sixty guilders, or approximately $24, worth of trinkets. It may seem an insignificant sum, but as one historian notes, the exchange was one of the very few times that the Indians ever received anything at all for their lands.

The Dutch settlers, unlike the English Puritans up in Boston, were a generally broad-minded lot. Although the Dutch Reformed Church was the established religion, the colonists were not compelled to worship—and New Netherland in the 1630s and 1640s was a haven for religious dissenters from New England. The New Netherlanders also celebrated holidays with gusto, especially Christmas, which the Puritans had banned. St. Nicholas was the colony's patron saint, and the Dutch youngsters believed that St. Nick, or *Sinter Klaas* (forerunner of our Santa Claus), traveled all the way from Holland each year sailing on a special "Christmas Ship."

But Dutch rule in the New World was to last for only 40 years. England vehemently disagreed with Dutch colonial claims to the region. In 1664, King Charles II gave Long Island and all the land between Delaware Bay and the Connecticut River to his brother James, Duke of York, and sent a military expedition to enforce the act. The then Dutch governor, Peter Stuyvesant, reluctantly surrendered the territory to the British. New Amsterdam, the Manhattan Island colony, was renamed New York, and Fort Nassau up river became Fort Albany. In 1673 the Dutch recaptured New York, but lost it once more—for good—a year later. British settlers soon began to arrive and New York slowly turned into a British colony.

France made several attempts to assert a claim of its own to the region in the 1700s. Even though some of the Indian tribes sided with the French in the French and Indian War (1754–1763), their efforts failed. British rule over the colonies, however, was also nearing its end. One of the earliest confrontations of the American Revolution took place in New York on May 10, 1775, when Ethan Allen and his Green Mountain Boys captured Fort Ticonderoga. New York's eastern regions were the scenes of many battles during the Revolutionary years. New York City, first controlled by General George Washington, was recaptured by the British who held it until the end of the war. The city then became the seat of the new federal government and Washington was elected president of the United States.

Important as European colonialism was to the story of New York's early years, the role of the region's native Americans should also be mentioned. Long before the white man arrived New York was populated by a number of Indian tribes including Algonquians, Mohicans and the Iroquois. They weren't at all friendly with one another, and battles for control of the territory were regularly fought until around 1570. At that time two Iroquoian tribal leaders formed a confederacy called The League of the Five Nations (Mohawks, Onondagas, Cayugas, Oneidas and Senecas) and created a code of laws aimed at generating peace. In the early 1700s, the Tuscaroras, an Iroquois tribe which had emigrated from North Carolina, joined the League and it became the Six Nations.

The European settlers, despite occasional run-ins with the Indians, adopted many of their ways. Later Colonial leaders such as Benjamin Franklin and Thomas Jefferson had extensive experience with the Indians' way of life and greatly admired their wisdom. They particularly respected the tribal methods of self-governing and most of the ideas in the Declaration of Independence, including liberty, consent of the governed, protection of human rights and the pursuit of happiness were taken—not from European culture or beliefs—but from the Great Law of Peace of the Iroquois. And both Franklin and Jefferson gave full credit to the source. The Iroquois Confederacy, incidentally, still continues today—the oldest democratic institution on earth.

EASTERN NEW YORK

Long Island

Approximately 100 miles long, with some 250 miles of coastline, Long Island draws hordes of visitors each summer. They are lured by the island's superb swimming, sunning, boating and fishing, elegant shops and galleries, and its wealth of historic sites and impressive mansions. Many people nowadays come in winter, too, when prices are lower and crowds are fewer. In snowy weather, cross-country beach skiing is fun, as is ice skating on the island's ponds.

Most descriptions of Long Island put out by the state's tourist brochures, however, are somewhat deceptive. They tend to make the island sound like a smaller version of Cape Cod—an uncongested area of beaches, Colonial and fishing villages and windmills. In truth, although the island's attractions are many and varied, they are not all immediately evident to the traveler heading out from New York City. To reach the areas of greatest interest, one has to first pass through miles of uninspiring urban and suburban sprawl and—farther out—flat stretches of potato and strawberry farms.

There are inviting exceptions along the way, of course. In Elmont, near the western end of the island, there's beautiful Belmont Park Race Track where thoroughbred horse racing is held mid-May to late July and September to mid-October. Long Island's south shore offers 2000-acre Jones Beach State Park and the famed Westbury Music Theater. Fire Island lies offshore, reachable by ferry, for surf swimming and fishing. Heading east along the north shore you'll find King's Point, home of the U.S. Merchant Marine Academy. Farther along are some of the island's magnificent estates built by turn-of-the-century magnates like Vanderbilt, Guggenheim, Chrysler and Woolworth. Especially notable are Falaise, part of the Guggenheims' estate in Port Washington, and Sagamore Hill, Theodore Roosevelt's home near Oyster Bay.

But the choicest section of Long Island for many visitors is the Hamptons—a string of seven pretty (and very posh) villages at the eastern tip. Interestingly, the Hamptons are the only part of New York not originally settled by the Dutch. They were founded by English Puritans from Connecticut, in the mid-1600s. Today the Hamptons are havens for artists, writers, and the rich. (These are not at all necessarily the same.)

Guest Houses

Southampton is the area's elegant "shopping center." Founded in 1640, it was the first English settlement in New York, and many of its old landmarks have been preserved. East Hampton dates to 1649; note the Mulford Farmhouse, a salt box structure built in the 1650s, and a number of eighteenth-century houses. In nearby Amagansett, the Marine Museum has a fine collection of fishing, whaling and other nautical artifacts. Montauk, Long Island's easternmost point, is a deep-sea fishing center and site of historic Montauk Point Lighthouse, commissioned by George Washington in 1795. In Sag Harbor, the Suffolk County Whaling Museum presents a host of relics from the town's great nineteenth-century whaling days. A ferry will take you from Sag Harbor to tiny Shelter Island in Peconic Bay, with its tranquil atmosphere and miles of white sand beaches. A monument and seventeenth-century graveyard are remnants of the Quakers who—escaping from religious persecution in New England—settled here in 1652.

The Village Latch Inn. Elegant, relaxed and spacious are all fitting adjectives for the Village Latch in Southampton. Situated on five acres of lovely, tree-shaded grounds, the structure was originally the annex to the village's oldest and most luxurious hostelry, the Irving Hotel—long since torn down. Marta Byer-White and Martin White, the Latch's friendly proprietors, have carefully restored the large white clapboard house to its earlier impeccable self, preserving the wide French doors, floor-to-ceiling windows, handsome wainscoting and fireplaces. Marta, an artist, is an innovative decorator and has made the inn into a unique showcase for the Whites' extensive (and always growing) collection of furniture, artifacts and collectibles. She treats each of the guest rooms as an "art box, a canvas on which to be creative."

Accommodations include 25 guest rooms in the main Village Latch building and 10 in the adjacent Terry Cottage. There's also a motel unit behind the main house. Some of the large, charmingly-decorated rooms offer balconies and working fireplaces; all but four have private baths. Guests will also enjoy the comfortable public rooms: a plant-filled sunroom, a large living room and a television den, the latter two with working fireplaces. On weekends, a lavish country buffet breakfast (included in the rates) is served to guests in the inn's pleasant old dining room: fruit, eggs, ham, cheese, bagels and other breads, and coffee or tea. Lunch, sandwiches, snacks and afternoon tea are also available most days, for an extra charge.

There's a tennis court on the grounds, and your hosts will be delighted to arrange for an array of other activities including horseback riding, golf, bicycling, fishing, boating and access to a health club-spa with a pool. They will also direct you to the best antique shops and restaurants in the area. The beach is less than half a mile away; fashionable Job's Lane with its intriguing boutiques and art galleries is a block away.

The Village Latch Inn, 101 Hill St., Southampton, NY 11968; (516) 283-2160. Rates are expensive, lower during midweek and in spring and fall, with a 10 percent discount for longer stays (adults only). American Express, Visa and MasterCard are accepted. Children and pets are discouraged. Parking is available at the house. The house is open April 15–Nov. 29; the annex is open year-round.

Gansett Green Manor. Walter and Connie Brandt welcome guests to this charming establishment in Amagansett, "the Little Hampton." Gansett Green, consisting of a guest house and several small cottages, is of Nantucket-inspired architecture of natural cedar shakes with white trim. The Manor was constructed in 1910 by Mr. James Baker, a direct descendant of Amagansett's 1680 founder. Your hosts of today live in a cottage on the grounds built in 1696.

For guests there are eight twin-bedded and ten double-bedded rooms; fourteen have private baths and four share one bath. Eleven of the rooms, all with private baths, are on the ground floor. Fourteen of the units also offer private living rooms with fireplaces and kitchens. The guest quarters are brightly painted, with some walls of wood paneling or pretty gingham wallpaper. Original paintings of local scenes, done by the resident artist, decorate most of the rooms; many are for sale. A number of the rooms have murals painted on walls and ceilings—with sea gulls, geese and swans. The decor throughout is Colonial, with quilted bedspreads and some antiques.

Gansett Green's several acres of grounds include spacious green lawns, shade trees and shrubs, and a delightful restored antique covered wagon. And—the perfect pastoral touch—there are sheep in the meadow! Benches here and there are nice places to sit, and umbrella-topped outdoor tables may

Gansett Green Manor

be used by guests. Ocean beaches, bicycle and nature trails, museums and galleries, pubs, a farmers' market and many other attractions are within walking distance. The house is easily reached from the bus and railroad station, if you choose to come without a car. No food is served at Gansett Green Manor, but there are plenty of excellent restaurants in the vicinity; ask the Brandts for suggestions.

Gansett Green Manor, Main Street, P.O. Box 799, Amagansett, NY 11930; (516) 267-3133. (On Rte. 27, Montauk Hwy., in center of village.) Rates are moderate (for rooms sharing a bath) to expensive (rooms with private bath, living room and kitchen), lower off season (30 percent less from September 12–November 15), and lower for children. Special rates are available for weekly, monthly and longer stays. Visa and MasterCard are accepted. Well-behaved children are welcome; small pets on leash are also welcome, with a deposit for damages. No large pets, please. Parking is available at the house. Open May 1–Nov. 15.

The Bowditch House. A wonderfully rambling old farm house on secluded Shelter Island, the Bowditch House was built in 1854 as part of the Bowditch estate. The family's best-known member was Nathaniel Bowditch, a mathematician, astronomer and ship's captain who wrote *The New American Practical Navigator,* first published in 1802 and still recognized as the Bible of navigation books.

Nora and Jim Furey are your hosts today at Bowditch House, and they offer guests seven comfortable rooms with double beds and two with two twin-size beds. The rooms share two baths; there's also a guest bathroom on the ground floor. Oak and birds-eye maple furniture, including many antiques, predominate in the individually-decorated rooms, which are graced with fabric walls. Guests are invited to enjoy the entire house, especially the large, pleasant living room with its rocking chairs and wood stove. Breakfast, included in the rates, is served in the Colonial breakfast room or, in season, out on the sunny deck. And the meal is a genuine feast, with fresh fruits, juices, cereals, homebaked breads and pastries, English preserves, and coffee or tea. On weekends the Fureys add a hot dish of bacon and eggs, omelets, French toast or some similar tasty item. In the afternoons, from 5:30 to 7 p.m., wine and refreshments are also offered.

Set on an acre of land with lots of trees, shrubs and flowers, Bowditch House is a short walk from a good selection of restaurants and shops. "The Heights," an area famed for its cluster of Gothic Revival ("Gingerbread") houses, is five minutes away by foot. Golf, tennis, sailing, hiking, fishing and bicycling are all available nearby, as are the island's beautiful beaches. Above all, as your hosts will be sure to tell you, Shelter Island offers a restful haven with a slow, easy-going pace, and an atmosphere reminiscent of an old New England fishing village.

The Bowditch House, 166 N. Ferry Rd. (Rte. 114), Shelter Island, NY 11965; (516) 749-0075. (Take the North Ferry, a shuttle service, from Greenport on Long Island's north shore, or South Ferry from North Haven just north of Sag Harbor on the south shore. On Shelter Island, go one mile on Rte. 114 South; the Bowditch House is on 114, the second building on the left just past the corner of Winthrop Road.) Rates are expensive, lower before the last weekend of June; special rates are also available Sunday through Thursday, and an extra bed in the room is $8. Visa and MasterCard are accepted, but only if reservations are made ahead of time through Western Union. Children over five are accepted, but not encouraged; the Fureys feel that their house does not lend itself to youngsters. No pets, please. Parking is available. Open weekends Memorial Day to mid-June, daily until Labor Day, and weekends again until November.

A Reasonable Alternative, Inc., Bed & Breakfast on Long Island. Kathleen B. Dexter's bed and breakfast organization offers a year-round selection of comfortable, clean, homelike accommodations scattered throughout Long Island's Nassau and Suffolk counties. They are all personally inspected, and as Ms. Dexter says: "We have bounced on innumerable beds, sampled countless cups of tea and coffee, and checked the reading lamps in a myriad of rooms." Lodgings, with complimentary Continental breakfast, are available in a wide variety of settings: one includes a book-lined sitting room overlooking a garden; another offers a private beach. There are accommodations with views of the water, and one host provides lodgings that are *surrounded* by water—on a cabin cruiser!

Contact: A Reasonable Alternative, Inc., 117 Spring St., Port Jefferson, NY 11777; (516) 928-4034. A deposit of $20 is required with reservation; reservations will be confirmed by mail. Rates are moderate to expensive, depending on location, facilities and season. A discount is offered for visits of one week or longer. MasterCard and Visa are accepted. No pets, please.

New York City

First-time visitors to New York City often feel daunted—by its size, its awesome array of attractions, its rapid pace, and its prices. Don't let yourself be cowed. Manhattan, the city's borough most travelers want to see, is really quite manageable. The subway system, buses, taxis and feet will get you around with little effort. Driving your own car is *not* advised; traffic in New York can be harrowing and often impossibly jammed. If you do come with a car, it's best to find a garage where you can leave it for the duration of your stay.

Buy a map of the city. Familiarize yourself with the various areas, and choose which ones you'd like to explore. Begin, for example, with Fifth Avenue, on which you will find the Empire State Building, St. Patrick's Cathedral, Rockefeller Center, Central Park, the Metropolitan Museum of Art, and some of the most elegant shopping in the world. Also note the ubiquitous sidewalk vendors, a peculiarly New York institution. Located right outside the haughty confines of such stores as Saks Fifth Avenue, Tiffanys, Bergdorf Goodman's and the like, vendors will be offering tableloads of, say, gloves, scarves or toys. In cool weather the tempting smell of hot roasted chestnuts pervades the air; all year around other mini-entrepreneurs offer pretzels, hot dogs, hot or cold drinks, and an entire menu of ethnic foods. Another appealing activity along Fifth Avenue is to take a ride in one of the many horse-drawn buggies, the classic old vehicles bright with paint and decorated with flowers.

Once you have explored mid-town Manhattan, strike out to some of New York's other lures: Greenwich Village, Chinatown, SoHo, the United Nations and the Statue of Liberty. A visit to the Cloisters, at the northern tip of Manhattan, shouldn't be missed. The museum includes parts of five medieval cloisters, and has a superb collection of medieval sculpture and painting. The fabulous *Hunt of the Unicorn* tapestries are on view here, too.

If you're interested in seeing how a cathedral is built, stop in at St. John the Divine in uptown New York. It is the largest cathedral in the world, and, next to St. Peter's Basilica in Rome, the second largest church. Construction began in 1892, stopped temporarily in 1941, and was resumed in 1979. There is a stoneyard where apprentice stonecutters learn their craft, and the public is invited to share in the completion of the structure by purchasing numbered hand-cut stones. The price ranges from $100 for an ashlar (the basic block) all the way up to turrets at $500,000 and two major pinnacles at one million dollars!

You will undoubtedly want to see a play or musical during your stay. The theaters of New York are justly famed, many of them concentrated near Times Square. Times Square is a notoriously raffish area, but safe to walk through except possibly in the early hours of the dawn (when no city is without danger). Theater tickets are costly, but preview performances of new productions can be had at lower prices. If you enjoy ballet and opera, the Lincoln Center for the Performing Arts, on Broadway between W. 62 and 66 Streets, offers some of the world's finest.

New York's restaurants, too, are internationally-renowned and often viciously expensive. The visitor can easily spend a small fortune dining at Lutece, for instance. A less-costly (but not cheap by any means) favorite of mine is the colorful Russian Tea Room, next to Carnegie Hall. But travelers on a budget can still discover good food at modest prices in smaller, out-of-the-way restaurants. And families with children along can always find a McDonald's or similar sort of fast-food emporium.

Most hotels in New York are also very high-priced. In the past few years, however, several "bed and breakfast" organizations have appeared on the scene, offering moderately-priced accommodations for travelers. Most lodgings are located right in the heart of the city, near transportation and within easy reach of New York's diverse attractions. Not only will you find a comfortable, quiet place to stay during your visit but you'll have an opportunity to meet some of New York's most interesting and cosmopolitan people—your cordial hosts. The actual rates charged are not included in the following listings, as they vary depending upon the accommodations. Be assured, however, that they will be considerably less than those charged by the average commercial hostelry. And, you get breakfast in the bargain!

Urban Ventures, "Bed & Breakfast In the Big Apple." This service concentrates essentially on New York City, but also has a few rooms outside the city limits. Urban Ventures provides prospective visitors with a map of the city, divided into five areas. You choose the area that suits you best; they will find the best accommodations available at the time you want them. Some 80 apartments, townhouses, lofts and a variety of other city spaces are included in their lists. All accommodations have been inspected, and hosts interviewed, so that you can be assured of clean, comfortable lodgings with pleasant, welcoming people. Typical listings include a twin bedded room with private bath and balcony near Lincoln Center in a building with a doorman, and accommodations with a window view of a church spire, Central Park and skyscrapers offered by an artist-host who will even let you use the living room and kitchen.

Urban Ventures also provides lists of moderately-priced restaurants, current museum and gallery showings, and will get theater or sports events tickets for you. If you like, they'll even arrange a special theater tour that includes bed and breakfast accommodations, top-ranked shows, all dinners, taxes and tips, an escort/guide, entree to classes and rehearsals, and a free morning for museums and shopping. Other tours such as architectural, museum or shopping can be arranged, too, tailored to your particular specifications.

Contact: Urban Ventures, Inc., 322 Central Park West, New York, NY 10025; (212) MO2-1234. You will be sent a reservation form so that you can detail your requirements. Accommodations may be either "Budget Range," most with shared bath, or "Comfort Range," most with private bath. A deposit of $20 per person is required to hold your reservation; balance is due on confirmation. A $25 key deposit will be collected by your host. For a stay of only one night there is a 10%

surcharge and payment in full must be made with reservation. Refunds (less service charge of $15 for placement) are made upon cancellation notice of 72 hours.

The B & B Group (New Yorkers at Home) Inc. Another excellent bed and breakfast referral service, The B & B Group also offers a moderately-priced alternative to hotels and motels. Its more than 60 hosts include artists, actors, writers, doctors, engineers and other professionals who invite guests to share a wide variety of comfortable accommodations in mid-New York. (Lodgings are also available in Queens, Brooklyn, Westchester and other New York locations and in New Jersey.) Mid-city addresses offer easy access to theaters, museums, parks, historic points of interest, shopping districts, business areas and restaurants. All are within walking distance of public transportation. In some instances, even laundry facilities are available. All hosts have been thoroughly screened and their houses or apartments personally inspected to be sure they meet the service's high standards.

Sample listings include a room with private bath in a 1792 Dutch Colonial three-story brick house in Greenwich Village with the use of a kitchen and living room complete with fireplace, and a twin bedroom with shared bath in a duplex apartment on an island in the middle of the East River. A doctor of oncology and his sister offer a large double bedroom with private bath near Central Park West in the 90s; another host has a double bedroom with bath for guests in a duplex apartment in a converted loft—with a Jacuzzi and an upper bedroom reached by a captain's ladder. One charming hostess offers lodging in her two-story brownstone with handsome wainscoting and cherrywood paneling and a private entrance; the house's decor was described in *Redbook.*

Contact: The B & B Group (New Yorkers at Home) Inc., 301 East 60 St., New York, NY 10022; (212) 838-7015. You will receive a guest questionnaire and reservation form; be sure to write at least two weeks in advance of desired visit. Minimum stay is two nights; a deposit of $30/single or $45/double is required, refundable if the service cannot fill your request or if you cancel before completed arrangements have been made. The balance in full for the length of stay is due on arrival to be paid in cash or by traveler's check.

Bantz House. Situated in suburban Yonkers just north of

New York City, this bed and breakfast guest house is owned by Gloria and Norman Bantz. The large brick Federal-style home, in a lovely residential section of Westchester County, is only 30 minutes from Manhattan via car or train. There are three double and two triple air-conditioned rooms for guests on the second floor, sharing three baths. A 32-foot living room with TV and a large fireplace, and a spacious screened porch, are pleasant places to relax and meet some of the other guests. The hearty breakfast, included in the rates, usually consists of eggs, cereal, ham, sausages or bacon, coffee or tea. One of your hosts' hobbies is bee-keeping, and their own honey will be featured as part of the menu, perhaps along with freshly-baked honey pastries. Other meals are served by special arrangement. Restaurants and shops are within walking distance of the house, and the train station with regularly-scheduled service to New York City is only a block away. Mr. and Mrs. Bantz will also arrange airport or bus terminal pick-up.

Bantz House, 82 Vermont Terrace, Yonkers, NY 10707; (914) 779-6411. (Just north of New York City at Exit 8 off Bronx River Parkway, one block from the Crestwood/Eastchester Railroad Station.) Rates are moderate; 25 percent less for stays of one week or more. Children are welcome; no pets, please. There is parking available at the house. Open year-round.

The Hudson Valley Region

The headwaters of the Hudson River are far north, high in the Adirondack Mountains. But from the city of Troy south to the river's mouth the Hudson is a tidal estuary, its banks rising to steep highlands and mountains, including Storm King, 1530 feet above sea level. The beautiful lower valley of the Hudson is rich in historic sites, farms and apple orchards, and picturesque river villages. We'll begin our exploration of the valley at Tarrytown, in Sleepy Hollow Country. Here you can visit Sunnyside, Washington Irving's house, a marvelously gingerbready structure the author called "as full of angles as an old cocked hat." Irving, whose stories include *The Legend of Sleepy Hollow* and *Tale of the Headless Horseman*, is buried at the Old Dutch Church of Sleepy Hollow in Tarrytown. The early-American Phillipsburg and Van Cortlandt Manors, and Lyndhurst, a Gothic Revival mansion, are also open to visitors.

Cross the Hudson via the Tappan Zee Bridge and pay a visit to Nyack. In addition to a group of handsome Victorian edifices, the village has more than 70 craft and antique shops and art galleries. Then follow the Palisades Parkway to Bear Mountain State Park; Rte. 17 West leads you to the Museum Village of Nineteenth-Century American Crafts, at Monroe. In Washingtonville, a few miles northeast, the Brotherhood Winery—America's oldest—offers wine-tasting tours. West Point, home of the United States Military Academy, is just to the east overlooking the Hudson. The view is impressive, and so are the cadets. The Bear Mountain Bridge will take you over the river once again to the charming old villages of Garrison and Cold Spring. The area is antique hunter's heaven, with at least 60 shops to choose from. And be sure to see Boscobel, a restored early nineteenth-century Federal-style mansion with exceptionally fine gardens. There are also several attractive guest houses in the vicinity, any of which would make a good base from which to roam the entire Hudson Valley region.

Farther north you'll come to Hyde Park, the site of Franklin D. Roosevelt's home, library and museum. President Roosevelt and his wife Eleanor are buried here in the Rose Garden. At Rhinebeck, a short distance to the north, air shows with vintage aircraft participating in mock aerial dogfights are presented on summer and fall weekends at the Old Rhinebeck Aerodrome. For the very brave, open-cockpit biplane rides are available, too. And at Old Chatham, the finest collection of Shaker furniture and artifacts anywhere is on view at the Shaker Museum.

The Golden Eagle Inn. Located in Garrison's Landing, the Golden Eagle is a small, elegant "bed and breakfast" inn. The attractive three-story structure dates to 1848, and is set on wooded grounds on the banks of the Hudson River. Formerly the Garrison Hotel, it was selected as the location for the film "Hello Dolly." George and Stephanie Templeton, your hosts, have six double rooms for guests, four with private bath and two sharing a bath. Stephanie, a former interior designer, and George, a former industrial and display designer, have decorated the rooms with great charm and taste, using a blend of antique and contemporary furnishings. Flower arrangements from the gardens, chosen to complement the color scheme of each room, add their own bright touch.

Guest Houses

Guests will particularly enjoy relaxing in the Hudson Room with its antique carved mantel and walls hung with original paintings. In chilly weather a wood fire blazes cheerfully in the fireplace. The paintings and other art on exhibit are for sale, if you'd like a special memento of your stay. Outdoors, a spacious, plant-bedecked veranda offers a perfect spot to watch the river flowing past the 100-foot lawn. The Templetons offer their guests a Continental breakfast of fresh fruits in season, buttery homebaked croissants and coffee or tea. Breakfast, included in the rates, is served on individual trays in your room or—in warm weather—out on the veranda. Your friendly hosts often ask their guests to join them for a glass of wine in the early evening, served indoors or out on the veranda. You may also, of course, have a cocktail (BYOB).

Visitors have a wide choice of things to do in the area including antiquing, touring historic Boscobel or West Point (the latter is directly across the river) and tasting wine at the many local vineyards. Bear Mountain State Park offers hiking, fishing, boating and dancing at the lodge. Guests may play golf at the Garrison Golf Club, go bird-watching, or cruise the river in one of the Templetons' canoes. Guests may even study watercolor painting with George Templeton. In winter, there is cross-country skiing. As for restaurants, ask the Templetons for suggestions; the area is chock-full of excellent places to dine.

The Golden Eagle Inn, Garrison's Landing, New York 10524; (914) 424-3067. (Only 50 miles from New York City, easily reached by car, train from Grand Central Station, or by boat or seaplane mooring at the adjacent Highland Yacht Club. By car, when you reach the junction of routes 403 and 9D and are traveling north, turn left; traveling south, turn right; traveling west, go straight ahead. Follow the road to stop sign, turn left over small bridge, turn left again, go 75 feet and turn right for the inn. The entrance is on the upper veranda.) Rates are expensive, lower for longer stays on request. Your check for payment in full or American Express guarantee must be received within 4 days of your reservations request for room to be held. No pets, please, and no cigar smoking. Children are accepted, but only during the week with prior permission. Parking is available at the house. Open March 15–January 15.

The Antique Mews. This handsome four-story brick townhouse, built in 1805, is in the village of Cold Spring on-the-Hudson. Your host, Jack Kelly, has three double bedrooms for guests, all with private baths. The spacious rooms, each with a sitting area, are individually decorated: one all in Art Deco, one with fabric walls and Eastern art, and one in Early American. Guests may also use the antique-decorated sitting room. A full breakfast is included in the rates, with juice, fruit, eggs or French toast, sausage or bacon, hot breads and coffee. On weekends your host also operates the Coffee

The Antique Mews

House, which features locally-made cakes. Cold Spring, in addition to its nineteenth-century charm, offers visitors some 50 antique, craft and gift shops to explore—including the Antique Mews itself, which presents eclectic antiques from Eastern and Western cultures plus periodic showings of contemporary artists. There are also several good restaurants for lunch or dinner.

The Antique Mews, 73 Main St., Cold Spring, NY 10516; (914) 265-3727. Rates are expensive; special rates are available for stays longer than one week. American Express, Visa and MasterCard are accepted. Children and pets are welcome. Parking is available at the house. Open year-round.

Daley's Antiques. Another striking edifice on Cold Spring's Main Street, Daley's Antiques is a brick Victorian built in 1890. Theodore and Margaret Daley, the house's owners, have decorated the place throughout with antiques. They have one suite for guests, done in old-fashioned decor, with a bedroom, living room, bath and complete kitchen. Breakfast is provided, included in the rates.

Guest Houses

Daley's Antiques, 109 Main St., Cold Spring, NY 10516; (914) 265-2707. Rates are expensive, lower for longer stays. Visa and MasterCard are accepted. Children are welcome; no pets, please. Parking is available at the house. Open year-round.

One Market Street. Philip and Esther Baumgarten own One Market Street, a Federal-style brick townhouse in Cold Spring. Built around 1830, the house boasts a handsome cast-iron staircase, topped with a copper dome, leading up to the entrance. For guests, the Baumgartens have a pleasant suite with private bath. It consists of a bedroom, sitting room and completely-equipped kitchen. Outdoors there's an enclosed, flower-filled yard with umbrella-topped tables for guests' use. Fixings for breakfast (included in the rates) will be found in your suite's kitchen—orange juice, coffee and tea. Coffee buns and a newspaper are delivered each morning. Three restaurants are within walking distance of the house, as well as Cold Spring's many antique and craft shops. Your hosts' own shop, "The Hudson Peddler, A Country Store," is located on the street level of the house and offers antiques, collectibles and gifts. The Hudson River is only a block away; there is swimming at a sandy beach on the river, and the Baumgartens will be happy to direct you to all the other activities in the region.

One Market Street, Cold Spring, NY 10516; (914) 265-3912. Rates are expensive, lower off season (December through March), for weekly or longer stays, and for children. Visa and MasterCard are accepted. Children are welcome; no pets, please. Parking is available at the house. Open year-round.

One Market Street

The Catskills

The mountains called the Catskills are not as impressive as the Rockies. But these ancient, wooded peaks lying just west of the Hudson River have a special beauty all their own. They are laced by numerous picturesque streams, often tumbling through deep gorges (called *cloves* by the Dutch) and falling in spectacular cascades. More than 250,000 acres of the region make up Catskill Park, a protected wilderness area. Covered bridges, a dozen or so throughout the region, appeal to photographers. Fresh-air enthusiasts flock to the area to hike or camp, or for the superb fishing. For the romantic, these mountains are the legendary site of Washington Irving's tale, *Rip Van Winkle.* When thunder rolls over the Catskills it's easy to imagine that the sound really is that of strange, small mountain men—dwarves, perhaps—playing at ninepins. The town of Palenville is thought to have been Rip Van Winkle's home, and a nearby mountain glen the scene of his long sleep.

The Catskills are also renowned for their luxurious resorts, offering a host of amusements including entertainment by top-name performers. An array of summertime festivities, too, attracts visitors by the thousands. At Hunter Mountain there are the German Alps and National Polish Festivals. Narrowsburg presents an Oktoberfest, East Durham an Irish Festival, and there are many more. Historic sites include New Paltz, founded by Huguenots in 1678, with old stone houses to be toured, and Kingston—first capital of New York State—where you can see the Old Senate House, the only building left after the British burned the town in 1777.

Several wineries are located a bit south of Kingston, all offering tours and wine tasting. Woodstock, to the north, has long been a famous artists,' writers' and musicians' colony. Twenty-five miles north of Hunter Mountain, between Cairo and Palenville, the Catskill Game Farm has some 2000 animals and birds to admire—including elephants, giraffes and many endangered species. Stamford, beyond scenic Grand Gorge, is a maple sugar center with a collection of Colonial homes. Whitewater canoe trips are available down the Delaware rapids near Dunraven, and sailplane rides at Wurtsboro.

Ujjala's Bed & Breakfast. "Victorian charm in a country setting" is the way Ujjala Schwartz describes her unique

Ujjala's Bed & Breakfast.

establishment. Located just outside historic New Paltz, the house (circa 1910) sits on 3½ acres of land, with a meadow; apple, pear and quince trees; an old barn and chicken coop; lawn for sunbathing; a vegetable garden and herb and flower beds. Future plans include the installation of a solar hot tub and sauna on the property.

Three charmingly decorated double rooms are available for guests. They share one bath with tub and shower. Upstairs are the Victorian Room, done in rose, beige and light green, with a fluffy comforter on the bed and a basket filled with old lace, and the Country Room in black and beige with patchwork pillows, old jugs and a basket containing hand-dyed and spun wools. The sunny downstairs room is more contemporary with a skylight, leaded handpainted windows, a fireplace, old barn siding on one wall, and a Murphy bed. It is spacious enough, with the bed tucked away into the wall, to act as a sitting room in the daytime. Each bedroom, bright with flowers and plants, has its own tea set.

Guests are invited to make themselves at home in the pleasant living room which opens into the sky-lighted country kitchen, one step down. There is a piano in the living room for guests to play; the kitchen, with brick floors, cabinets of barn siding and lots of plants, has sliding glass doors opening onto an attractive deck. The scenic Shawangunk

Mountains only minutes away offer hiking, jogging, rock climbing, swimming and cross-country skiing. New Paltz with its seventeenth-century Huguenot stone houses is fun to explore, and the area includes a wealth of antique shops, a number of excellent restaurants, and several fine wineries.

In the mornings guests are provided with a complete breakfast including fresh eggs, fruit, homemade muffins or breads, and herbal or regular teas. Breakfast is served in the kitchen, outdoors on the deck in warm weather or, if you like, in your room. Afternoon tea is also offered, with Ujjala's homemade cookies; both breakfast and tea are included in the rates. For an extra charge and upon advance request, your hostess occasionally provides dinners, too. Her specialty is gourmet vegetarian cooking, and she believes that foods should be served as beautifully as possible "with all the colors and textures of a painting."

Ujjala (and this is where the "unique" quality of the place comes in) is very much involved in holistics, the concept of treating the whole human being. Her particular fields are body therapy and stress management; she has given courses at the University College in New Paltz, and for three years she coordinated the Holistic Way program at Mohonk Mountain House. Her bed and breakfast establishment was originally conceived as a holistic retreat for clients, but friends soon persuaded her to expand into a more traditional guest house operation—which it is, with a raft of homey extra touches and a great deal of country charm. Health-oriented guests are still very much welcome, of course, and if you're intrigued by the idea of holistics this is an ideal spot to discover its benefits. Ujjala will accommodate requests for special diet foods, and she also offers sessions in Shiatsu, or deep relaxation massage.

Ujjala's Bed & Breakfast, 2 Forest Glen Rd., New Paltz, NY 12561; (914) 255-6360. (From NY State Thruway take New Paltz Exit 18, go left on Rte. 299 to Rte. 208 South; turn left at the light onto 208 and go 3½ miles. You will see Dressel Farm on the right; Forest Glen is the 2nd road on right after the farm. Turn right on Forest Glen and Ujjala's is the first house on the left corner; go to the second driveway.) Rates are expensive, lower for four-night or longer stay. No children or pets, please. No smoking preferred, but your hostess is not adamant about this. Open year-round, except for Christmas and New Year's.

Guest Houses

House On the Hill. A perfectly delightful place to stay while touring the Catskill region, the House on the Hill is in High Falls, near Kingston. Built in 1825, it is an elegant "eyebrow" Colonial. A stone wall and hand-forged iron fence span the front of the property; apple trees flank the hillside to the right of the house, maple and ash trees line the driveway. Magnificent old locusts surround the house, acting as lighting deflectors, and a stand of evergreens shades a bluestone patio. Guests may play croquet, badminton, volleyball and frisbee or practice putting on the broad green lawn. At the rear of the house are a two-story barn, an old outhouse and a pink-brick smokehouse. Beyond is a large S-shaped pond. The back side of the barn houses a glass porch and screened patio overlooking the pond and a wooded hillside.

Shelly and Sharon Glassman, owners of this appealing country establishment, have five double rooms for guests, with two baths. The rooms, always containing fresh flowers and a bowl of fruit, are decorated in period style with very comfortable brass and iron beds, each with handmade quilts. There is a charming "keeping room," too, for guests to enjoy, with a fireplace that boasts the original andirons and crane. In warm weather, the large front porch with antique rockers and benches is another pleasant place to sit.

The Glassmans really outdo themselves with their breakfast menu. There will be fresh fruit, homebaked muffins, breads or biscuits, cheeses, egg dishes or French toast, blintzes, crepes or a meat dish—all innovatively prepared, delicious, and included in the rates. Depending on the season, breakfast is served by the fire in the keeping room, on the glass porch facing the pond, or outdoors under the trees. Two superb restaurants specializing in international cuisine, described as "extraordinary" by your hosts, are within walking distance of the house. There are also a quaint old saloon for drinks and sandwiches, and a fine Italian restaurant.

House On the Hill, Box 86, Rte. 213, High Falls, NY 12440; (914) 687-9627. (From the N.Y. State Thruway take Exit 18, New Paltz, and go left on Rte. 299 West into New Paltz, right on Rte. 32 North for six miles and left onto Rte. 213 West, then three miles to High Falls.) Rates are expensive. Reservations should be made at least one month in advance, accompanied by a deposit. Children are welcome;

no pets, please. Parking is available at the house. Open year-round.

Baker's Bed & Breakfast. Located just outside of Stone Ridge in the Rondout Valley, two miles from High Falls, Fran and Doug Baker's attractive old house is a welcome haven for travelers. A restored English-style stone farmhouse built in the late 1700s, the structure has the original wide pine floorboards and is furnished with antiques. Five rooms, four with double beds and one with twin beds, are available for guests; a cot can be added. Two bathrooms are shared. The rooms, with covered beams, are decorated in period style; the beds are spread with quilts, coverlets and down comforters. Upstairs on the landing there is a TV area with an antique daybed and wing chair. The house also has a comfortable living room for reading or games, and a solarium with a splendid mountain view.

Breakfast, included in the rates, is served in the charming dining room with its fireplace and old rockers or in the window-walled solarium. The Bakers provide their guests with a lavish spread: juice and fruit, hot muffins or homemade breads, jams, your hosts' own fresh eggs prepared in a variety of ways such as shirred, in timbales, as a puffy cheese omelet, eggs Benedict or to the cook's fancy; ham, bacon, sausage or venison steak, and tea or freshly-ground coffee. For other meals the Bakers will be pleased to direct you to several excellent restaurants not far away. In spring, summer and autumn lunch and soft ice cream are available a short walk from the house.

Golf, tennis and fishing are all easily accessible. Guests may swim in a spring-fed pond right on the property, use one of the Bakers' bicycles, or just sit and admire the views of mountains, fields and woods. In winter visitors can ice skate on the pond and go snowshoeing. Your artist hostess, Fran, offers instruction in watercolor painting, if you'd like to try capturing a bit of the scenery. Lake Mohonk and several state parks are only minutes away by car as are antique shops and historic towns including High Falls, Kingston, Hurley and New Paltz; Woodstock, 20 minutes away, offers a raft of art galleries and shops.

Baker's Bed & Breakfast, RD 2, Box 80, Old Kings Highway, Stone Ridge, NY 12484; (914) 687-9795. (The house is just off Rte. 209 south of Stone Ridge.) Rates are moderate;

with a stay of six consecutive nights the seventh night is free; $15 for a child on cot in room. Children are welcome; no pets, please. Parking is available. Open year-round.

Albany-Saratoga Region

Three and a half centuries ago Albany was a Dutch trading post in the wilderness of the New World. Later, under the patroonship of Kiliaen Van Rensselaer, the young colony attracted settlers from many European countries. Always an important transportation center, Albany really began to expand when the Erie Canal was completed in 1825. The Canal—extending from Albany all the way to Buffalo—opened the way for low-cost conveyance of goods between the Great Lakes and the Hudson River. Today, New York's capital city is a nice blend of old and new. The imposing State Capitol and Robinson Square's nineteenth-century row houses provide visitors with a taste of the past as do the Schuyler, Ten Broeck and Cherry Hill Mansions. The magnificent 100-acre Nelson A. Rockefeller Empire State Plaza, with its splendid marble-faced government buildings, many shops and restaurants, fountains, pools and sculpture, portrays the best of the present.

Saratoga Springs, north of Albany, is a very different scene. Set in the foothills of the Adirondacks, the colorful resort area began as a fashionable nineteenth-century spa. Not quite so glamorous today, the Springs is still a very popular vacation spot, with a remarkable collection of classic architectural styles—Greek Revival, American Gothic, Victorian and Colonial Revival. Thoroughbred racing is one of the major attractions, and has been since the first racetrack was built in 1863. There's harness racing, too, and from June to September the Saratoga Performing Arts Center, set in a beautiful 2200-acre park, presents symphony, ballet, jazz and many other musical events. Visitors may still "take the waters" in the Saratoga State Park Spa Bathhouses.

Washington County, to the east, is Grandma Moses country, immortalized in paintings by America's favorite primitive artist, who lived here for 78 of her 101 years. You'll see old covered bridges, stone walls, historic mills and picturesque small villages all set in lovely, rolling countryside.

Tibbitt's House Inn. Located in Rensselaer just across the Hudson River from Albany, Tibbitt's House is a 127-

year-old farmhouse. It fronts on the old Boston-Albany Post Road, now called the Columbia Turnpike (N.Y. Routes 9 and 20). Once the Turnpike had some twenty guest houses but Tibbitt's House, family-operated for 55 years, is the only survivor. Owners Claire and Herb Rufleth have completely renovated the old place. Flowers—including lilacs, lilies-of-the-valley, petunias, geraniums, iris and violets—bloom

Tibbitt's House Inn

in season, and large maple trees offer cooling shade. An 84-foot enclosed porch is a great place for relaxing, and there are a garden patio and picnic area, too.

The Ruflehs have five inviting rooms for guests, three double and two single, sharing one bath. There are also two efficiency apartments. One, with a private bath, features an old Keeping Room with its original beamed ceiling and corner raised-hearth fireplace—where a cheery blaze will warm you in cold or wet weather. As you climb the stairs to the house's second floor, note the honey-colored walnut banister with ivory mortgage button embedded in the newel post. Braided rugs grace the rooms' glowing, highly-polished fir floorboards. The beds are very comfortable, and each room has been individually decorated.

For a modest extra charge guests may enjoy a large country breakfast, called by the Rufleths "The Hudson River Valley Breakfast," served on the porch or in the family dining room. The meal includes juice, fruit, scrambled eggs and fried potatoes, toast or muffins, and coffee. Or, you may choose a Continental breakfast, also for a small extra fee. Your hosts will be delighted to suggest some good restaurants in the area for other meals. Albany, with all its varied attractions, is only two miles away; a 45-mile-long paved path, also two miles away, parallels the Hudson and Mohawk Rivers and is ideal for hiking and biking.

Tibbitt's House Inn, 100 Columbia Turnpike (Routes. 9 and 20), Clinton Heights, Rensselaer, NY 12144; (518) 472-1348. (If you're traveling west on I-90, the N.Y. Thruway, take Exit B1 and proceed to the East Greenbush Exit, Routes 9 and 20; it is 11 miles from Exit B1 to the house. If you're traveling east on I-90 or north or south on I-87, take Exit 23 and pick up Routes 9 and 20 across the Hudson River and continue up the hill to the house.) Rates are inexpensive; special rates are available for longer stays. No children or pets, please. Parking is available. Open year-round.

The Kimberly. Saratoga's only year-round guest house, the Kimberly is owned by Mrs. Ingrid Downie. It is about 100 years old, and the house may easily be recognized in summer by its splendid display of red and white flowers. The front entrance is also notable, with cut crystal windows and doors. Mrs. Downie has newly decorated her house with wall-to-wall carpeting throughout. She has eight rooms for guests including five doubles, two triples and one single. The single and one double room share a large hall bathroom; the others all have private baths or sink and W.C. One of the guest rooms and a bathroom are located on the ground floor. The rooms are modern, with a few nice pieces of old furniture here and there. No food is served, but each room has a refrigerator and stove or hot plate for guests to use—sort of a "mini-kitchen," according to Mrs. Downie. Your hostess will also be pleased to give you directions to some of Saratoga's excellent restaurants. The house is located three blocks from Congress Park and Canfield Casino Museum, and for those travelers who'd like to visit without a car, the Kimberly is just a block from the bus station.

The Kimberly, 158 S. Broadway, Saratoga Springs, NY 12866; (518) 584-9006. Rates are expensive, lower off season (September–June), and off-season weekly rates are available. No children or pets, please. Parking is available at the house. Open year-round.

Willow Glen Hill. You'll find this charming guest house in New York's Washington County, way over on the Vermont border. Situated two miles from the town of Granville, the big old converted farmhouse overlooks Vermont's Green Mountains to the east and is surrounded by beautiful hilly countryside. Jim and Jo Keats, your hosts, have one single and four double rooms for guests, one with a private bath. The other rooms share a bath. There's a large upstairs foyer-sitting room with a couch, chair, desk and TV for guests' use, too. A Continental breakfast of juice, buns or toast, jelly and coffee or tea is included in the rates; tea and coffee are also available in the afternoon if desired.

Willow Glen offers a host of activities to suit every taste: horseshoes, badminton, tetherball and volleyball, fishing, swimming in lovely Lake St. Catherine or in old-fashioned river swimming holes, birdwatching, hiking, or just relaxing on the Keats's 60-foot-long front porch. In the fall the region is spectacular with flaming foliage, and in winter you can go sleigh riding or ice skating. The town of Granville is noted for its colored slate quarries, which may be viewed for free. Within a 30-minute drive are Lake George, Glen Falls, Lake Champlain and Manchester, Vermont. An hour's drive will bring you to Saratoga Springs for horse racing or concerts at the Performing Arts Center, or several topnotch ski resorts. The Keatses have brochures describing these plus a wealth of other places of interest in the region and will be delighted to tell you about them from their own first-hand experience. They will also suggest some good restaurants in the area.

Willow Glen Hill, Rte. 22, (Box 40, RFD 1) Granville, NY 12832; (518) 642-2079. Rates are inexpensive, lower for additional adult or child in room. Well-behaved children and pets are welcome. Parking is available. Open year-round.

The Adirondack Region

Stretching from Lake Champlain in the east to the Black River in the west, New York's Adirondack Mountain Region is immense. Adirondack Park, established in 1892, covers 8900 square miles; almost 2½ million acres of the park have been set aside as a wilderness forest preserve. Mt. Marcy, at 5344 feet, is the tallest peak in the Adirondacks; before glaciers and time wore them down these ancient mountains were higher than the Rockies. The scenic region also includes thousands of lakes and ponds, 30,000 miles of brooks and streams flowing into 1000 miles of rivers, and just about every form of activity a vacationer could ask for, year-round.

You can climb, backpack, swim, canoe or raft down whitewater rivers. In winter there are ice festivals, skiing, ice skating and tobogganing. Fishing fans will find the waterways teeming with tempting catches, history buffs can roam through old forts, and browsers have a host of craft and antique shops to choose from. Beautiful 32-mile-long Lake George in the region's southwestern corner offers splendid beaches, steamboat excursions, a summertime opera festival and Fort William Henry, a restored French and Indian War site. At Fort Ticonderoga on Lake Champlain to the north, you may watch cannons and flintlock muskets being fired and a Colonial-costumed fife and drum corps. Farther north is Ausable Chasm, a mile-and-a-half flume through which the Ausable River plunges with a spectacular display of waterfalls and rapids.

Inland are Saranac and Tupper Lakes, High Falls Gorge at the base of Whiteface Mountain, and Lake Placid. Site of the 1980 Winter Olympics, Lake Placid offers an array of winter sports, and skating and ice shows year-round. Long, Blue Mountain and Indian Lakes are a bit south; near North Creek east of Indian Lake you can hunt for a keepsake gem at a garnet mine.

And if by some unimaginable quirk of fate you should run out of things to do in the Adirondacks, you can always head back to the shores of 125-mile-long Lake Champlain for a shot at spotting "Champ." The lake's very own Loch Ness Monster, the huge serpent-like creature was first reported by no less a personage than Samuel de Champlain, in 1609. Since then the elusive beast has been sighted many times, and a fairly clear photograph was made of him (her?) in 1977 by a picnicker. Scientists would love to have more photos to study, so take your camera and stay alert!

Corner Birches Guest House. A longtime fixture in the middle of quaint Lake George Village, Corner Birches is a sturdy white clapboard house with green roof and shutters. It sits on a corner lot on a quiet residential street; a fifty-year-old cluster of white birch trees gives the house its name and provides shade for the porch and sideyard parking area. A broad front porch with rocking chairs overlooks the main street, Lake George and a mountain. Ray and Janice Dunklee, your friendly hosts, bought Corner Birches in 1957 when the last of the original owner's family died. Built in the mid-1920s, the house had previously been a private residence and boarding house.

The Dunklees have four guest rooms on the second floor, sharing a bath. Each room has cross-ventilation from two windows, with white ruffled curtains, and a fan. Janice Dunklee loves to decorate and has furnished the rooms with colorful spreads, carpets and drapes, and an appealing collection of furniture, some antique, all guaranteed to make guests feel welcome and right at home. The beds, with pretty patterned sheets, are very comfortable, and the rooms include good reading lamps, chairs and spacious closets. The bathroom boasts the house's original footed tub, to which a shower has been added.

The Dunklees live on the first floor of the house and guests are invited to share their living room and cable TV. The room's free-standing fireplace with electric logs provides a cozy touch in cool weather. There's a collection of games and toys for young guests to enjoy, and a charming wicker child's rocking chair. And a wonderful doll house, filled with Janice Dunklee's handmade furnishings, is fun for everyone to share. A Continental breakfast of juice, toast and coffee is included in the rates. It's served in the sunny dining room at a large table covered with Janice's mother's hand-crocheted tablecloth, under a crystal chandelier. The dining room chairs are covered with your hostess's handcrafted needlepoint. The room also has a small Lowry organ, to be used by anyone who wishes.

You'll like meeting the Dunklees. Jim was born only a block away from Corner Birches, and as a native can offer many tales on "how things used to be" for interested ears. And Janice has this to say: "We and our two grown sons feel privileged to have had the opportunity to meet all types of people from all over the world. We have thoroughly enjoyed our 26 years in the guest house business; it has been interesting, stimulating, educational, sometimes frustrating, confining and hard work—with a bottom line—we wouldn't have had it any differently!"

Corner Birches is within easy walking distance of shops and restaurants; a municipal park with free beach, bathhouse and a bandstand with live entertainment; and lake sightseeing boats. Ask your hosts to tell you more: the entire Lake

George Region offers a wealth of exciting things to do and see.

Corner Birches, 86 Montcalm St. (corner of Helen Street), Lake George, NY 12845; (518) 668-2837. (From Rte. 87 take Exit 21 or 22 to Canada Street, Rte. 9; turn at Rexall Drug Store and go towards Prospect Mountain for three blocks. Corner Birches is on the right.) Rates are inexpensive, lower off season (other than from July 1 through Labor Day, holidays and weekends). Well-behaved children and pets are welcome. Parking is available at the house. Open year-round.

Country Road Lodge. Located near Warrensburg, 15 minutes from Lake George, Steve Parisi's Country Road Lodge offers travelers a delightfully peaceful, rustic haven. The Lodge started out as Steve's summer home, weekender style, which he then improved to create a ski lodge. At first he commuted to an advertising job in New York but then decided it was time to "return to his roots"—he grew up in a house very near the Lodge. So, in 1976, Steve cut his ties and moved permanently into what he considers an idyllic setting. Today he keeps in touch with the world through his guests, but enjoys the rural life of gardening, cutting firewood and clearing trails, and keeping his bees.

The Lodge is set in a clearing at the edge of the Hudson River, surrounded by the Adirondack Mountains. It is a shingled house, built in 1929 as a summer home—for a resident of Warrensburg! Your host describes it as a modest "Adirondack camp" cottage with rather small rooms; modern baths were added in the 1970s. There is also an old outhouse for anyone who really wants to rough it. The simple but comfortable accommodations include one single room, two with double beds, one with twin beds, and one with three twin beds. Two baths are shared. Three of the guest rooms and one bath are on the ground floor. Guests are invited to make themselves at home in the L-shaped lounge with windows on three sides, facing the Hudson River. The room is furnished in local "Sugarloaf Mountain" pieces and includes a number of potted plants and a cheery wood stove. Books and games are available, too.

In summer, a Continental breakfast is included in the rates. For a small extra charge, however, Steve Parisi will cook up a full breakfast that might include juice, toasted homemade bread, eggs, pancakes, French toast (with homemade maple syrup), bacon, cereals, coffee or tea. Tea and coffee are available most any time, and limited use of the kitchen is permitted. In winter, the rates include full breakfast *and* dinner, plus welcoming and apres-ski refreshments. Your host will also provide box lunches for you to take along hiking, sightseeing or skiing, for an extra charge. There are several excellent restaurants in the area, within easy driving distance.

As for things to keep you occupied, Steve suggests hiking in the mountains or along the river; tennis; swimming or canoeing in historic Warrensburg; boat cruises on Lake George; watching old-time fiddling; square dancing and rodeos; Fort Ticonderoga; autumn foliage-watching; wintertime skiing (cross-country trails surround the house and there are three downhill ski areas nearby); or antiquing. The region has scads of antique shops to explore, more than a dozen in Warrensburg alone. And if you don't want to go any farther than the Lodge, your host invites you to pick wild blackberries in season or fresh peas off the vine, play badminton, croquet or horseshoes, or simply laze and commune with nature in the lawn chairs.

Country Road Lodge, Hickory Hill Road, Warrensburg, NY 12885; (518) 623-2207. (From I-87, The Adirondack Northway, take Exit 23 and follow signs to Warrensburg. Turn left off Rte. 9, Main Street, onto Rte. 418—opposite stone church—and go 3½ miles to Hickory Hill Road; Country Road Lodge is the last house in, one-half mile.) Rates are inexpensive and include Continental breakfast, June–October, higher with full breakfast and dinner from November–April. The rates drop after a stay of two days and again after five days. Children are welcome, but only as part of a group of eight people. No pets, please. Open year-round except for month of May.

The Stagecoach Inn. Peter and Sherry Moreau's historic Stagecoach Inn is located just outside the village of Lake Placid. The east wing of the structure, with stone foundations and sills of hand-hewn timber, is thought to date back to the early 1800s. In 1864, a man named Martin Lyon bought the place, added a west wing and proceeded to operate it as an inn. He also opened a general store and post office on the premises. The hostelry quickly became a regular stop on the Elizabethtown–Saranac Lake mail and passenger run, a popular vacation retreat, and the favorite meeting place for local residents. A visitor in 1878 reported: "Here elections were held, people were gathered for sport and horse trading, drank hard cider and sometimes liquids of a more stimulating character." A later owner was James R. Day, president of Syracuse University. Day used the house for a summer retreat until his death in 1923. The Moreaus purchased it in 1977 and turned the grand old place into a guest house—painstakingly restoring it to appear once again much as it did in stagecoach days.

A long, rambling building, the Stagecoach Inn is fronted by a lengthy porch, ideal for scenery-watching. Notable interior features include handsome Georgian pine wainscoting, a cozy, lofty-ceilinged common room and gallery, and five fireplaces. For guests there are seven comfortable double rooms, three with private baths; the others share two baths. Three of the rooms are on the ground floor. A Continental breakfast is included in the rates.

Lake Placid with its restaurants and shops, Olympic winter sports complex and summertime Center for Music, Drama and Art is a mile away. Other nearby attractions include famed abolitionist John Brown's farm and grave, four golf courses, public tennis courts, trout fishing and canoeing on the Ausable River, and Adirondack State Park.

The Stagecoach Inn, Old Military Road, Lake Placid, NY 12946; (518) 523-9474. Rates are moderate, lower for longer stays. Well-behaved children and pets are welcome. Parking is available. Open year-round.

Wood's Lodge. Wood's Lodge is situated on lovely Schroon Lake in the Adirondacks, a bit west of Ticonderoga. The main house was built as a church rectory around 1870; the Wood family purchased the place in 1912. The grandmother of Mrs. Catherine Wood Querns, your present-day hostess, opened the Lodge originally as a boarding house—and the family has now been welcoming guests for more than 70 years.

Accommodations in the Lodge include three two-bedroom family units with private baths, suitable for four, five or six people, and a double room with a bath across the hall. Mrs. Querns describes the house as having a "homey, lived-in look," with many books. Guests enjoy looking through the family scrapbook, too, which includes pictures and memorabilia from 1912 to 1940. A comfortable lobby/

lounge has a fireplace and TV, and the broad front porch provides a fine view of the lake. In 1956 the Woods purchased the adjacent Lake House, built in 1883 as a private summer home. Furnished in antiques, the three-story white gingerbread Steamboat Gothic structure with porches all around offers guests four double rooms, three triples and one room for four, all with private baths. Also on the property are the Chalet annex with four apartments rented by the week during the summer months, and four one-room cabins.

No food is served except for complimentary morning coffee or tea, but guests may use the kitchen and the large dining room, which is also a game room and library. Outdoors on the lawn are picnic tables and grills. Wood's Lodge has its own sandy lake beach for swimming or sunning, canoes and rowboats, and a clay tennis court. There are many hiking trails in the vicinity, and the Schroon River provides fine canoeing. The Lodge is just two blocks from Schroon Lake Village's main street, for shops and restaurants.

Wood's Lodge, Schroon Lake, NY 12870; (518) 532-7529. (From the center of the village, turn towards lake.) Rates are expensive, lower from May 15–June 25 and Labor Day–October 15; special weekly or longer rates are available. Children are welcome; no pets, please. Parking is available. Open May 15–October 15.

Thousand Islands–St. Lawrence Seaway Region

You'll find this New York region—which follows along the St. Lawrence River—just west of the Adirondacks. The "Thousand Islands" actually number 1834, according to the latest count. Dotted along the course of the river, these fir-covered islands range in size from some several miles long down to others which most people would call large rocks. The best way to explore the region is to drive the Seaway Trail (which leads eventually to Buffalo) as far as Oswego, just northwest of Syracuse. At Massena, where the Trail begins, stop at the Dwight D. Eisenhower Lock, six miles north of town. There you can watch great ships lifted and lowered, on their way along the vast inland waterway designated by the U.S. Congress as the nation's "Fourth Seacoast." Continue down to Ogdensburg, founded in 1749, where the Ogdensburg-Prescott International Bridge connects New York and Canada. Here you'll want to visit the Remington Art Museum, containing the largest single collection of paintings, bronzes and sketches by the famed artist of the Old West. Frederick Remington came to the town as a child and returned here to paint and sculpt after his Western journeys.

South, at the resort area of Alexandria Bay, visitors can spot at least 200 of the islands from the Thousand Islands International Bridge. If you're interested in fishing, boats with guides may be hired at Alexandria Bay. Sightseeing boats or a ferry will take you to Boldt Castle, a replica of a Rhineland castle situated on Heart Island. George Boldt, a one-time dishwasher who later became owner of New York City's Waldorf-Astoria Hotel, planned the place as a gift for his wife. She died before the castle was completed, however, and her grieving spouse abandoned the project in mid-construction. A jog inland takes you to Gouverneur, named for statesman and diplomat Gouverneur Morris. He was a member of one of our first congresses, American minister to France prior to the French Revolution, and a United States senator. Morris was also known as "The great lover with the wooden leg"! The town of Gouverneur was the center of a thriving marble-quarrying industry in the late 1800s and early 1900s; many of its marble sidewalks and buildings may still be seen today. Back on the Seaway Trail again, continue down to Pulaski, where the Salmon River offers some of the best salmon and trout catches in the country. Oswego, on the shore of Lake Ontario in the region's southwest, is the largest American port on the lake. There you can explore restored Fort Ontario, first fortified by the British in 1775, and watch guards performing military drills.

Hays' Tourist Home. Gordon and Maxine Hay have been welcoming guests to their nice old home for almost 30 years. Located in historic Gouverneur, the attractive house was built around 1900 and boasts high ceilings, solid oak woodwork and oak and inlaid cherry floors. The Hays have four upstairs rooms for guests, three with double beds and one with twin beds, sharing one bath. Roll-away beds can be added to the rooms, if needed. Accommodations are also available on the basement level, fully furnished and with a private bath. Guests may use the reception room and living room (with TV) and a large fenced-in back yard with swings, picnic table and a handsome fireplace/barbecue shaded in season by a flowering tree. No food is served, but there are restaurants within walking distance. The house is 40 miles from

Hay's Tourist Home

the St. Lawrence River and Thousand Islands; swimming beaches and skiing facilities are accessible within 20 to 25 miles, and the Hays will be delighted to tell you about other places of interest nearby such as Beaver Creek State Forest and the Gouverneur Morris "Mansion," an 1809 stone house called a "mansion" because of its contrast to the rude wooden shelters of the first settlers.

Hays' Tourist Home, 275 East Main St. (Rte. 11), Gouverneur, NY 13642; (315) 287-2945. (If you can't locate the house right off, ask for directions at the police station or any gas station.) Rates are inexpensive, lower for longer stays and for children. Children are welcome; no pets, please. If you are traveling with a pet, however, it could stay in the Hays' yard. Open year-round.

CENTRAL NEW YORK

The Leatherstocking and Finger Lakes Regions

Long ago, when central New York was America's westernmost frontier, rugged adventurers wearing protective leggings called "leatherstockings" blazed trails, trapped for furs and fought Indians here. James Fenimore Cooper described those gritty days in his "Leatherstocking" novels, rollicking tales of life in the wilderness that introduced the memorable character of backwoodsman Natty Bumppo.

Cooperstown, where the author lived and is buried, was founded by his father in 1786. The Fenimore House, headquarters of the New York State Historical Association, includes an interesting exhibit of Cooper memorabilia as well as a superb collection of American art. The National Baseball Hall of Fame is in Cooperstown, too; Abner Doubleday is believed by some authorities to have originated the game of baseball here in 1839. Old-time craftspeople ply their trades at the fascinating Farmers' Museum and Village Crossroads; don't miss America's greatest hoax, the Cardiff Giant—a stone figure weighing 2990 pounds, "discovered" in 1869.

East of Cooperstown, Howe Caverns at Howes Cave offers guided tours and boatrides on a subterranean lake. To the north, Canojoharie (Indian for "pot-that-washes-itself") has an excellent art gallery with paintings by Winslow Homer and other American artists. In the Utica area (northwest) kids will enjoy prospecting for "diamonds," actually quartz crystals, at Herkimer or Middleville. And over in the region's northwest corner you'll find the city of Rome and its early nineteenth-century Erie Canal Village—with old buildings to explore and rides on a horse-drawn 1840 packet boat and steam-driven train.

New York's Finger Lakes, geologists say, were gouged out eons ago by glaciers. A more romantic explanation is the ancient Indian legend that claims these finger-shaped lakes were formed by the Great Spirit placing his hand upon the land. Located just west of the "Leatherstocking" Region, the major Finger Lakes include (from east to west): Otisco, Skaneateles, Owasco, Cayuga, Seneca, Keuka and Canandaigua. They are beautiful, long lakes, surrounded by wooded hills, prehistoric rock formations, lush countryside and charming old towns. From Skaneateles (pronounced "Skinny-atlas") you can take a mailboat cruise along the shores of Lake Skaneateles. In Seneca Falls, at the northern tip of Cayuga Lake, tour the Women's Hall of Fame. The town was the site of the First Women's Rights Convention, in 1848, and the birthplace of Amelia Jenks Bloomer. Geneva, at Seneca Lake's northern end, offers gardens, state parks and Rose Hill Mansion, an 1839 Greek Revival house with Empire-style furnishings.

Ithaca is down at Lake Cayuga's southern tip; Cornell University campus and nearby Taughannock Falls—taller than Niagara—are both well worth seeing. Not far away you'll find Watkins Glen on Lake Seneca, where car races are held all summer at the internationally-renowned Grand Prix

Road Racing Track. Here, too, is the entrance to Watkins Glen State Park where stairs and bridges lead upwards through the gorge past caverns, grottoes, rapids and a series of roaring cataracts. If you'd prefer to walk *down* the two-mile gorge, a taxi will take you to the top.

Samuel Clemens (Mark Twain) is buried in Elmira, south of Watkins Glen, in Woodlawn Cemetery. You may visit his study, too—in which he wrote *The Adventures of Tom Sawyer*—on Elmira College Campus. The room is built to look like a Mississippi River pilothouse. In Corning, a few miles west, head for the stunning new Corning Glass Center. Opened in 1980, the Center includes seven museum galleries that tell the story of glass from its beginnings some 3500 years ago to the present. Around 20,000 objects are displayed in chronological arrangement. In addition, you can learn how glass is made and some of its thousands of uses and—in the Steuben Glass Factory—watch molten glass being fashioned into exquisite crystal. There's also a shop with "seconds," offering some fabulous buys.

New York's famed vineyard country, which produces some prize-winning wines, lies between lakes Keuka and Canandaigua. A number of wineries in the Hammondsport area offer tours and wine-tasting. To the west near Castile, Letchworth State Park encloses the Gorge of the Genesee, a 17-mile-long, 600-foot-deep canyon with three major waterfalls. To the north, in Rochester, visitors are invited to explore a host of museums, including the International Museum of Photography at the George Eastman House, the New York Museum of Transportation and Rochester's Museum and Science Center.

The Rosewood Inn. The Rosewood Inn, according to owners Dick and Winnie Peer, offers travelers "sleeping accommodations in the Victorian manner." Located on a quiet, tree-shaded street in downtown Corning, the house was built in the 1860s in the Greek Revival style; around 1910 it was redesigned into English Tudor. There are five attractive guest rooms, each individually decorated, furnished in period style. The Charles Dana Gibson Room and Jenny Lind Room share a bath; each has one double bed. The Herman Melville Room, with twin beds, has a private bath as does the Frederick Carder Room. The George Pullman Room, on the street level, is a large studio with kitchen, color TV, air conditioning and private bath. Guests may also use the upstairs parlor with antique rockers, color TV and reading material describing local attractions. A hearty Continental breakfast including fresh fruits of the season, hot oatmeal, homemade breads or muffins and coffee is included in the rates. Guests share the meal—and good conversation—around a common table in the paneled drawing room. The marvelous Corning Glass Center, the newly-opened Rockwell Museum of Western Art, and restaurants and shops are all within walking distance of the house. Watkins Glen is 30 minutes away by car, and many of the Finger Lakes wineries about 40 minutes.

The Rosewood Inn, 134 E. First St., Corning, NY 14830; (607) 962-3253. (Rosewood Inn is one block south of Rte. 17 as it passes through downtown Corning.) Rates are moderate. Children are welcome: roll-away beds, a crib and highchair are available. Well-behaved pets are also welcome. Parking is available both on the street and off-street at the rear of the house. Open year-round.

The Cecce House. Another fine old guest house in Corning, the Cecce House is just two blocks from downtown Market Street. Your hosts, Margaret Cecce and Florence Ann Gaiser, describe their home—built in 1899—as having "a rich Mediterranean atmosphere." There are four comfortable, individually-decorated double rooms for guests, with rollaways available for a third person. One bath is shared. The Blue, Pink and Gold Rooms offer twin beds; the Master Bedroom (with TV) has a queen-size bed. There's also a

The Cecce House

small third-floor sitting room with a kitchen area where guests may make morning coffee or tea (no other cooking, please). The house is in a quiet residential section, within easy walking distance of Corning's museums, restaurants, shops, churches and theaters.

The Cecce House, 166 Chemung St., Corning, NY 14830; (607) 962-5682. (Chemung Street runs off of Rte. 17 in downtown Corning.) Rates are inexpensive, with a small extra charge for third person in room. Children are welcome; no pets, please. Parking is available at the house. Open year-round.

The Cobblestones. This beautiful nineteenth-century house, standing on an acre of shaded lawns, is located a few miles west of Geneva. The Cobblestones was built in Greek Revival style in 1848; it is fronted by four large fluted columns graced with Ionic capitals. Balancing wings, with smaller versions of the columns, flank the main section. The entire house was constructed of lake-washed sandstone, sorted for size and color. (During the years 1820 to 1850, many mansions using this type of material were built along the southern shore of Lake Ontario.) The Cobblestones is furnished mostly in antiques and period reproductions, with many Oriental rugs; the original old latches may be noted on the upstairs doors, and there's an interesting collection of old deeds preserved under glass. Mr. and Mrs. Lawrence Gracey, your hosts, have three attractive rooms for guests, one with twin beds and two with double beds. One bath is shared. You are most welcome to share the Graceys' gracious living room, too. No food is served at The Cobblestones, but there are several fine restaurants in the area. Geneva, at the northern end of Lake Seneca, offers convenient access to all of the varied attractions of the Finger Lakes Region.

The Cobblestones, R.D. 2, Geneva, NY 14456; (315) 789-1896. (From N.Y. State Thruway take Exit 42 or 44; The Cobblestones is 3½ miles west of Geneva on north side of routes 5 and 20.) Rates are inexpensive. Children and well-trained pets are welcome. Open year-round.

The Inn at Belhurst Castle. Belhurst is also in Geneva, just outside the city limits on a bluff overlooking lovely Seneca Lake. The imposing structure, surrounded by 25 acres of grounds, is not actually a "castle." It is, however, a grand mansion indeed, of the style known as Richardson Romanesque—and fully as romantic a sight as any ancient European medieval stronghold with its arched porte-cochere, balconies and ivy-covered turrets. Indoors, Belhurst is equally impressive with massive fireplaces and fireplace mosaics, tapestries, carved paneling and an elaborate staircase.

Mrs. Carrie Harron Collins, a niece of Henry Clay, built the red Medina sandstone house over a four-year period, from 1885 to 1889. Fifty men worked on the project, using materials mostly imported from Europe; the total cost of construction was in excess of $475,000. When Carrie Collins died in 1926, the mansion passed to a son who sold it in 1933 to Cornelius J. (Red) Dwyer, a colorful and engaging personality with a wide circle of friends throughout the country. Dwyer turned the place into a popular (and illegal) speak-easy and gambling casino. The upstairs gambling rooms were shut down in the early 1950s.

Robert and Nancy Golden, your present-day hosts, purchased Belhurst in 1975. They offer guests a choice of five luxurious double bedrooms and one two-room suite, with handsome woodwork and glowing stained glass windows. Each has an ultra-modern private bath with colored units, including some bidets. Most of the spacious rooms have fireplaces; all are comfortably furnished with antiques, Oriental rugs and 1800–1804 poster beds. There is plenty of old-fashioned closet and cupboard space, too, plus air conditioning and smoke alarms in every room.

Downstairs, guests may relax in the beautifully furnished public rooms, located off the large center hall. If you follow the staircase to the top of the Castle turret you'll discover a grand view of the lake. And ask Bob and Nancy Golden to tell you some of the fascinating Belhurst legends. They include tales of a runaway Spanish Don, secret tunnels and hidden treasures, a ghost wearing green plaid, and "the crashing about of large pieces of furniture." Your hostess says that these last have been quiet of late, so your sleep most likely will be undisturbed!

A Continental breakfast of juice, fresh fruit, rolls and coffee may be enjoyed in your room and a Sunday Brunch Buffet is served in the dining room or out on the terrace—all included in the rates. If you're feeling particularly grand, room service will bring you chilled champagne. Another

The Inn at Belhurst

hospitable touch: there's a spigot on the second-floor landing from which you may draw a glass of white wine. The restaurant at Belhurst Castle is widely renowned, if you choose to dine there; other restaurants are easily accessible within a few minutes' drive. Swimming is available on the grounds, and there is a large dock with boats for sailing or fishing. In addition, the Goldens will give you directions for winery tours, golf, skiing and all the other activities of the Finger Lakes Region.

The Inn at Belhurst Castle, P.O. Box 609, Lochland Road, Geneva, NY 14456; (315) 781-0202. (On Rte. 14, South Main Street at Geneva city line.) Rates are expensive; one day free with six-day stay. MasterCard, Visa, American Express, Diners-Carte Blanche accepted. Children are welcome; no pets, please. Parking is available. Open year-round.

Geneva On the Lake. Bed and breakfast lodgings come in a wide variety of styles, and Geneva On the Lake may be one of the most unusual you'll ever experience! It is expensive, but if you are in the mood for sheer luxury the place may prove irresistible. A ten-acre estate with formal gardens, wooded paths and secluded nooks, terraces, classical sculptures and a magnificent 70-foot-long swimming pool, Geneva On the Lake extends down to the edge of a cliff overlooking Lake Seneca. On the grounds is the Nestor House, a stunning white Italian Renaissance villa—U-shaped with attached wings and a hipped roof covered by red terra-cotta tiles. The three-story structure was modeled on the Villa Lancelotti, a sixteenth-century country retreat in the village of Frascati, near Rome.

Mrs. Minnie Matthews Nestor had the place built in 1911, three years after the death of her husband, Samuel J. Nestor. Samuel was the founder of the Geneva Malt House, one of the largest such operations in the United States. Their son Byron, who later designed the impressive terra-cotta urns which stand on pedestals near the pool, is believed to have had a hand in creating the villa. In 1949 the Nestor House was acquired by the Capuchin Order and was operated as a monastery until 1973; during that period the wings were added as dormitories. In the late 1970s the estate, which had been more or less abandoned for several years, was purchased by the Geneva On the Lake Development Company. Now faithfully restored, the beautiful mansion once again appears in all its original splendor with marble fireplaces, molded woodwork and paneling, terrazzo floors, marble Ionic columns, and gilt coffered and vaulted ceilings.

There are 18 individually-decorated suites for guests, located in the villa and in separate townhouses on the property; each has a living room, one or two bedrooms, full bath or bath and a half, fully-furnished kitchen, and a splendid view. Some of the suites have working fireplaces; others offer private terraces or balconies. The ambiance is one of quiet elegance, yet there is a homey, comfortable feel, too. The beds are covered with colorful quilts, there are lots of books to read, and each suite offers fresh fruit and flowers, plus a chilled bottle of New York State wine. A Continental breakfast, included in the rates, is offered in summertime and served out on the terrace or in the spectacular original "main room." It consists of fresh juices, croissants, jelly and marmalade, coffee or tea. Also included are summer Sunday evening buffets and wine and cheese parties; each week a different local winery supplies the wines. There will often be musical entertainment, too, perhaps by one of the talented staff, a guest, or even the Finger Lakes Symphony Orchestra.

In addition to exploring the landscaped grounds and swimming in the pool or lake, guests will find sailboats and motorboats for rent and bicycles for touring the area's country

Geneva On The Lake

roads. An 18-hole golf course is only five minutes away. Tennis is available nearby, and in winter there are excellent cross-country and downhill skiing facilities not far away. Rose Hill, Sonnenberg Gardens and Mansion, some 29 wineries, the Corning Glass Center, summer theaters, and many more of the area's attractions are within an easy drive. The region also offers a number of fine restaurants; Belhurst Castle is only ½ mile down the road.

Geneva On the Lake, 1001 Lochland Rd. (Rte. 14 South), Geneva, NY 14456; (315) 789-7190. Rates are quite expensive; lower for longer stays, for children and from November 1 to April 30. Children are welcome; no pets, please. There is parking on the grounds. Open year-round.

WESTERN NEW YORK

The Niagara Frontier and Chautauqua-Allegheny Regions

Outstanding among all of New York's multiple attractions is awesome Niagara Falls, located in the state's northwestern corner. America's most-visited natural wonder, the Falls draws sightseers from all over the world, and with good reason. The Niagara River, which runs for 36 miles between Lake Erie and Lake Ontario, drops 326 feet; more than half that descent occurs in one dramatic plunge at Niagara Falls.

There are actually three separate cataracts: the American, Bridal Veil, and Canada's Horseshoe falls. As you approach the area you'll see mist rising high above and hear the falls' mighty roar. To fully experience its impact, take a look at the river *before* it reaches the falls; from Goat Island, dividing the American and Canadian falls, you can watch the water rushing past with terrifying speed. Then head for any one of the several observation points: the sight of the water pouring over the brink is hypnotic—a green, almost gelatinous mass of incredible power.

An observation tower will give you broader views of the spectacle, and at the Cave of the Winds you can put on a slicker and trek underneath Bridal Veil Falls. Or, go for an exciting trip on one of the *Maid of the Mist* boats, which have been taking visitors for close-up views from below since 1846. Helicopter and Viewmobile rides are also available. The best and most spectacular perspective of all is from the Canadian side of the falls. The Canadian park grounds are beautiful, too, with a magnificent array of flowers in the summertime.

The city of Buffalo, just upriver, is often slighted by travelers intent on reaching Niagara Falls. It shouldn't be: Buffalo is full of interesting places to visit, in particular the Albright-Knox Art Gallery. A 1905 Greek Revival-style structure with a handsome modern wing, the museum houses one of the country's finest art collections, including contemporary works, eighteenth- and nineteenth-century European and American masterpieces, and sculpture from 3000 B.C. to the present. The city also offers architectural tours, symphony concerts, a zoo, botanical gardens, the colorful Old-World Broadway Market, and Allentown, Buffalo's large historic preservation area.

In Lewiston, north of Buffalo, visit beautiful Artpark with its summer-long series of musical and dance performances, International Indian Village, and artists at work. The Tonawandas nearby have two excellent historical museums, and at Lockport not far away you can see the Barge Canal Locks and tour a power tunnel. In East Aurora—just east of Buffalo—Millard and Abigail Fillmore's home is now the Millard Fillmore Museum. (President Fillmore is buried in Buffalo's Forest Lawn Cemetery.)

The Chautauqua–Allegheny Region, a lovely area of rolling hills and woods, lies to the south. Here travelers will find vineyards, historic sites, great fishing, and a host of forests including Allegany State Park with 65,000 acres including 70 miles of hiking trails. Visit Dunkirk and Westfield for winery tours; Salamanca, the nation's only city built entirely on an Indian reservation, offers the Seneca–Iroquois National Museum.

Above all, the region includes Chautauqua Village, on the shore of 22-mile-long Lake Chautauqua. The village is the site of the world-famous Chautauqua Institution, a unique center for the arts, education, religion and recreation. Founded in 1874 as a summer camp to train Methodist Episcopal Sunday-school teachers, Chautauqua rapidly became known for its reading circles, correspondence courses, lectures and concerts. Its fame spread throughout the country, carried by tent-show proprietors who crisscrossed the land with their own version of Chautauqua's lectures, music and drama. Today, the "Chautauqua Circuit," as these shows were called, is gone. But the Institution is still very much alive, offering a nine-week summer program that includes symphony and popular concerts, opera, drama, art exhibits and some 200 different courses and workshops. All manner of outdoor activities are also available, including tennis, golf, swimming and boat trips on the lake. It's an ideal place for families, with many programs just for youngsters.

A visit to Chautauqua is like slipping back into another century—into a quaint, pretty Victorian village with tree-lined, winding brick lanes and wooden cottages, old-fashioned hotels and rooming houses with spacious porches and gardens, and a leisurely, friendly atmosphere. In summer the sounds of music and carillon chimes fill the air; visitors may amble along admiring the architecture, attend lectures and concerts, join in street-corner forums, or just sit and watch the passing scene from porch rockers. Even in winter, when snow covers the lacy gingerbread structures and icy winds blow strong, Chautauqua is well worth a visit just to experience its special quality and great charm.

You may come to spend a day, a week or an entire season; admission is by gate ticket, except for Sundays and pre- and post-season periods. Cars are parked near the main gate; they're not allowed inside during the summer season except for one-hour baggage passes on arrival or departure. To get around the 300-acre grounds visitors walk or take one of the free buses that run through the village. Or bicycle—bike rentals are available. Chautauqua has a broad range of accommodations; descriptions of several of its old Victorian houses are included, and any one would make a good base from which to explore the region. Advance reservations are strongly advised. Alcoholic beverages, by the way, were once banned but are now permitted for private consumption.

Cambridge Inn. Situated right in the heart of Chautauqua, the Cambridge Inn is owned by the Luehrs family: Nick, Susan, Bob and Margaret. Susan Luehrs first came to Chautauqua in the 1950s as a college student working in the dining room of the village's large hotel. Twenty years later she returned, this time with her husband and children. They fell in love with the place, and after several years of renting, the family decided in 1978 to invest in the Inn. The Cambridge has 19 pleasant rooms for guests, including six doubles and 13 singles; some rooms have an extra cot. Six baths are shared; all rooms have sinks. Three of the guest rooms and two baths are on the ground floor. The baths are modern, added by the previous owner, and the beds' mattresses are new and comfortable.

The 100-year-old Inn, which Mrs. Luehrs says is of the "Arts and Crafts" period of architecture, has some beautiful old furnishings—of particular note is the original matched wicker furniture on the two enclosed porches. (There are two open porches, in addition.) Books and board games are available for rainy days. Flowerboxes add cheery touches to the Inn's exterior, and the back yard includes a picnic table. All of Chautauqua's activities are within walking distance; your hosts will provide you with a map of the village and will be pleased to point out good antique shops, restaurants and the like. They also keep menus of area restaurants for guests to read over and choose from. No food is served at the Inn. Canoes, small sailboats and bikes may be rented nearby; swimming, golf and tennis are easily accessible. Susan Luehrs says

Cambridge Inn

that some of their guests also enjoy visiting Lily Dale 20 miles away, a spiritualist center where some believe mediums commune with the spirits.

Cambridge Inn, P.O. Box 1010, 9 Roberts Ave., Chautauqua, NY, 14722; (716) 357-3292. (Near Bestor Plaza.) Winter address: 19150 Inglewood Ave., Rocky River, Ohio 44115; (216) 331-6953. Cambridge Inn office hours at Chautauqua are: 8–9 a.m., 12–1 and 6–7 p.m.; Saturday, 8–10 a.m. and 1–6 p.m. (To reach Chautauqua from I-90, take Westfield exit, follow Rte. 17 to Mayville, then Rte. 394 south.) Rates are moderate; 20 percent lower from June 15 to June 26 and August 29 to September 15. Special rates are available for longer stays. Children are welcome; no pets, please, and no smoking. Parking is available at the house only during off season. Open June 15–September 15.

Chautauqua Inn

Chautauqua Inn. Built in 1876, the porch-wrapped Chautauqua Inn is a delight to see. Your hostess, Ms. Bernice J. Lanpher, describes it as having "a storybook atmosphere." For guests there are 12 double, three triple and three single rooms; four have private baths and there are four shared or semi-private baths. All rooms include sinks and three of the rooms are on the ground floor. The furniture is mostly antique, but the beds are new. Guests are welcome to use the large Victorian living room with TV and fireplace. And there are *five* porches, all with rockers; two have views of the lake. Chautauqua's amphitheater for concerts and other events is about 2½ blocks away; bathing beaches, golfing and tennis are all nearby, as are restaurants and cafeterias. Ms. Lanpher suggests that you might want to bring along your own bike or small sailboat, or you can rent them on arrival. After the season of regular Chautauqua programs is over your hostess will provide morning coffee; otherwise no food is served.

Chautauqua Inn, Box 454, 16 N. Terrace, Chautauqua, NY 14772; (716) 357-3085. In winter and spring contact Ms. Lanpher at 10510 Park Lane Dr., Cleveland, Ohio 44106; (216) 795-1388. (To reach the Inn: inside the gate go left to second street, Ramble Avenue. Turn right on Ramble and go to end; take a jog to the right and turn left down Vincent Avenue—halfway down turn left on N. Terrace, and you'll see the sign.) Rates are moderate, lower after Labor Day; special rates are available for longer stays. Children are welcome; no pets, please. Parking is available at the house during the off season. Open last Friday in June to October 15.

Rose Cottage

Rose Cottage. Harry E. Rose is the owner of this rambling Victorian "cottage" in Chautauqua. Built in 1877, the Institution's third year, it is an all-wood structure; the outside boards are the inside walls. There are, of course, porches—four of them, two upstairs and two downstairs. The furniture is antique, with lots of wicker. Guest accommodations include six rooms with double beds, three with twin beds and two with single beds. Two baths are shared and all rooms have running water. Every room except the three upstairs twins open onto porches; two rooms are on the ground floor. Guests may also use the large living room, with TV. The house is conveniently located on Bestor Square, adjacent to shops, cafeterias and the Ampitheater.

Rose Cottage, P.O. Box 102, 2 Roberts Ave., Chautauqua, NY 14722; (716) 357-5375. Rates are inexpensive, lower before and after the Chautauqua season, and there's a 10 percent discount for early payment. Children are welcome; no pets, please. Parking is available only during the off season. Open May–September.

Baldwins' Top O' the Hill. Mr. and Mrs. David A. Baldwin's Victorian house dates back to 1881. Like most of Chautauqua's old buildings, it was constructed on a small lot, set just off the street. The three-story house has a porch on each level, furnished with rockers. As Mrs. Baldwin says, "A favorite Chautauqua pastime is rocking and visiting while watching the world go by." There are nine small double and five single guest rooms, and your hosts will supply roll-away beds or cots for an extra person if needed. Two rooms, located on the ground floor, have private baths; the others share three baths. All rooms are carpeted and the ones without private baths have sinks. There's also a blue-carpeted lounge furnished with wicker on the ground floor for guests to use, with books to read . . . no TV. Everything at Chautauqua is within walking distance—theater, opera house, restaurants, shops, etc. There are two public beaches plus one for small children and another for high school and college ages, docking facilities, playgrounds and parks. The Baldwins have bikes for rent, too. And if you're feeling too lazy even to walk across the street to the Amphitheater you can watch performances from the Baldwins' second- or third-floor porches! No food is served but there's a modern second-floor community kitchen with refrigerator, stove and cooking equipment. Each guest room has its own cupboard with dishes, glasses and flatware, and space for food storage.

Baldwins' Top O' the Hill, P.O. Box 482, 19 Palestine Ave., Chautauqua, NY 14722; (716) 357-5055. In winter: 1252 Hillcrest Rd., Wellsville, Ohio 43968; (216) 532-2535. (From Chautauqua main gate bear right, then turn left at corner; turn right onto Palestine Avenue at corner.) Rates are inexpensive to moderate, depending on room size and location; special rates available for longer stays. Children are welcome if kept under adult supervision. No pets, please. Open approximately June 15–August 31.

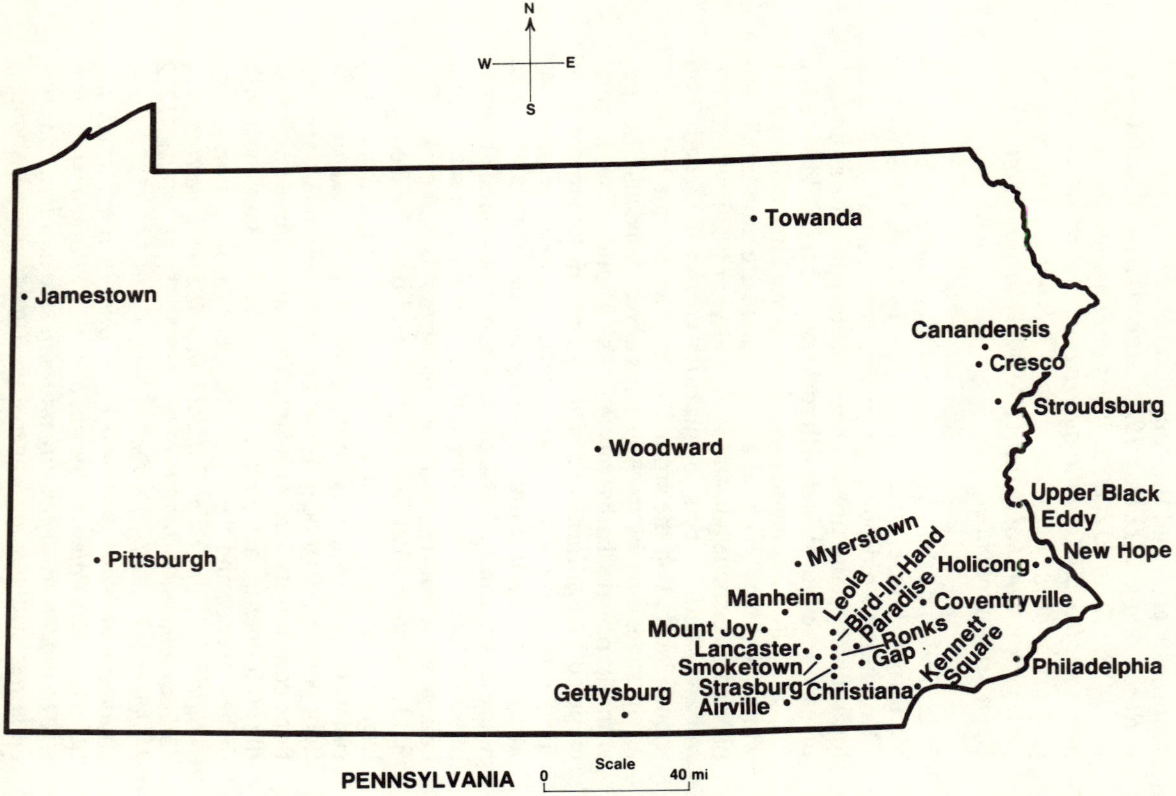
N
W
E
S
Towanda
Jamestown
Canandensis
Cresco
Stroudsburg
Woodward
Upper Black Eddy
Pittsburgh
Myerstown
Holicong
New Hope
Leola
Bird-In-Hand
Paradise
Manheim
Coventryville
Mount Joy
Ronks
Lancaster
Gap
Smoketown
Kennett Square
Philadelphia
Strasburg
Christiana
Gettysburg
Airville
PENNSYLVANIA
0
Scale
40 mi

Pennsylvania

One of America's major industrial states, a leader in the nation's production of coal, steel and oil, Pennsylvania is also richly agricultural. For travelers, the state offers a wealth of attractions, including some of the country's most visited regions—such as colorful Lancaster County with its Pennsylvania Dutch, farmers' markets, horse-drawn Amish buggies, and barns decorated with hex signs. Pennsylvania's Poconos offer glorious mountain scenery abounding with lakes, streams and waterfalls. Bucks County has art, antiques and classic fieldstone houses; history is alive at Gettysburg, Brandywine, Valley Forge and in the three-century-old city of Philadelphia.

Revitalized Pittsburgh to the west proudly shows off its multi-billion-dollar renaissance. There is Hershey, where the air smells deliciously of chocolate, and the streetlights are shaped like chocolate kisses. Vast stretches of the state, even today, are wooded, with rugged wilderness areas for hiking, hunting and camping. In addition, Pennsylvania boasts fascinating old coal mining and oil boom towns, festivals galore, music and museums, and a host of canyons, caverns and picturesque covered bridges.

In the north, Route 6 follows a scenic, meandering course across the state. In the south the 470-mile-long Pennsylvania Turnpike, the nation's first superhighway, is another appealing way to travel from east to west. Far from being a typically boring expressway, the old Turnpike traverses sweeping curves and steep grades, passing through a number of mountain tunnels. But do follow the back roads as much as possible; you'll see so much more. Pennsylvania's beautiful countryside with its prosperous farms and small quaint villages, rolling hills and forested mountains, is well worth investigating.

Nicknamed "The Keystone State" because of its central location among the 13 original states, Pennsylvania has played an important role in our country's history from the start. During much of the early Colonial era ownership of the region was hotly contested by three European nations. The first permanent settlement—on the Delaware River near Chester— was founded by Swedes in 1643. The Dutch, however, had established trading posts along the Delaware a few years earlier and felt that the territory rightfully belonged to them. In 1655 Peter Stuyvesant, governor of the New Netherland colony, marched against the Swedes and took control of New Sweden. Nine years later the British seized New Netherland (renaming it New York) and took over all the Dutch possessions in North America.

In 1681 a young Englishman named William Penn was granted an enormous tract of land west of the Delaware River in payment for a debt owed his father by King Charles II. Penn, a convert to Quakerism, had many times been imprisoned in England for his beliefs. In the New World, he hoped, he could establish a refuge not only for Quakers, but for all religious groups. After sending envoys on ahead to choose the site and begin construction of Philadelphia, the colony's capital, Penn followed. He arrived in Pennsylvania (meaning "Penn's Wood," named in honor of his father) in October, 1682. One of his first actions was to make peace with the Indians. Penn then created a plan of government for the new colony, a remarkable one that included religious tolerance, public education and the right to vote.

More than 3000 settlers, mostly Quakers and Germans, came to Pennsylvania during the following two years, drawn by the promise of religious and political freedom. By 1699 Philadelphia's population was exceeded only by Boston's, and it increased steadily in the early 1700s. "The City of Brotherly Love" attracted many of the best minds in the Colonies, including Benjamin Franklin. Franklin arrived from Boston in 1723; in addition to his countless diplomatic and scientific accomplishments he organized the city's first fire company, improved its streets and lighting, and founded the nation's first public library and hospital.

Pennsylvania's distinctly German character, still very much in evidence today, began with its early Mennonite, Amish and Moravian settlers. In later years new waves of immigrants—Scotch-Irish, French Huguenots, and others from almost every part of Europe—resulted in a colorfully varied collection of ethnic groups and religions. Many of the newcomers moved westward, turning the land into farms.

But life on the frontier did not prove to be as peaceful as in the east. Hostile Indians, resentful of the settlers' claims, harassed them constantly and sided with the French against the British in the French and Indian War.

Although the British won, their rule in Pennsylvania and the other colonies ended with the American Revolution. In 1774, the First Continental Congress met in Philadelphia and the Declaration of Independence was adopted there in 1776. A number of Revolutionary War battles were fought in eastern Pennsylvania, and George Washington's ragged soldiers suffered through a miserable winter at their encampment at Valley Forge. Philadelphia, after the Revolution, became the first capital of the United States.

In the early 1800s came the discovery of the state's immense mineral wealth, and the building of canals and railroads to transport coal and iron ore. Pennsylvania's rapid industrial expansion was halted only by the Civil War, in which the Keystone State played a vital role. Pennsylvanians were the first to answer President Abraham Lincoln's call for troops in 1861. Strategically important to both the North and the South, Pennsylvania was invaded several times by Confederate forces. The last incursion, the most decisive of the War and the only major engagement fought in a northern state, ended in a disastrous defeat for Confederate Gen. Robert E. Lee—at the Battle of Gettysburg.

EASTERN PENNSYLVANIA

Southeastern Region

For history buffs, few areas of the United States offer as much interest as Pennsylvania's southeastern region. It includes Philadelphia (which celebrated its 300th birthday in 1982), Valley Forge, Brandywine Battlefield and Washington Crossing State Park. The region also offers art, music, antiques, sports and a variety of festivals.

Philadelphia, William Penn's "City of Brotherly Love," is a nicely compact metropolis—easy to explore on foot. Go first to Independence National Historical Park with its long mall, cobblestone alleys and historic buildings. At the National Park Service Visitor Center at Third and Chestnut streets you can pick up a brochure that tells about the park and see a film about the American Revolution. Don't miss the City Tavern nearby, built in 1773, called by John Adams "the most genteel tavern in America." Nowadays most of our old Colonial taverns have been turned into museums, but this one still operates as an eating place, serving lunch and dinner! The park also includes Carpenter's Hall, site of the First Continental Congress in 1774, the First and Second Banks of the United States, Library Hall, Old City Hall and Independence Hall—where the Declaration of Independence was adopted and the U.S. Constitution was written. Here too is the famed Liberty Bell, preserved in a glass pavilion, and Franklin Court, the site of Benjamin Franklin's house where he lived while serving in the Continental Congress and Constitutional Convention. In an underground museum visitors will enjoy an entertaining multi-media presentation about Franklin and his remarkable life including his inventions, diplomatic successes and prime witticisms.

Old City, bordering Independence Park, includes Elfreth's Alley, the oldest continuously-occupied residential street in America; Christ Church where Washington, Franklin and other Colonial leaders worshipped, and the Betsy Ross House where (according to legend) the seamstress fashioned the first American flag. Benjamin Franklin and his wife Deborah are buried in Christ Church Burial Ground in Old City, near the United States Mint. Society Hill, also edging Independence Park, is another historic area with several eighteenth-century structures including "A Man Full of Trouble" Tavern. Many of the Hill's hundreds of handsome townhouses have been tastefully restored; the area, dotted with sophisticated boutiques and unusual restaurants, is one of the city's most fashionable.

Philadelphia is a city of museums, more than 100 of them. Several are located on the Benjamin Franklin Parkway: the Franklin Institute, Academy of Natural Sciences, the superb Philadelphia Museum of Art (with the steps made famous by the movie "Rocky"), and the Rodin Museum which contains the largest collection outside Paris of the sculptor's work. In addition to all of these lures, the city offers a fine zoo, the world-renowned Philadelphia Orchestra and a host of colleges and universities. In January, Philadelphia's fabulous Mummers Parade with bands and "Fancies and Comics" struts up Broad Street to City Hall on New Year's Day. In May there's a week-long series of walking and bus tours that includes private homes, gardens and historic buildings in ten of the city's neighborhoods.

Valley Forge National Park, just a short drive from downtown Philadelphia, is the site of Washington's grim winter encampment of 1777–78. Its 2500 acres may be toured by car or on foot. Hopewell Village, located in northwest Chester County, is another intriguing place to visit. A restored eighteenth-century iron-making community, the village is now a National Historic Site. Chadds Ford in Delaware County to the south includes Brandywine Battlefield State Park, scene of one of the most important Revolutionary War battles. Dioramas and audio-visual presentations tell the story of General Washington's defeat by the British on Sept. 11, 1777, and Washington's Headquarters may be explored. There's also the Brandywine River Museum, housed in a restored century-old grist mill, with its collection of Wyeths, Maxfield Parrish and others from the "river school." And Governor Printz Park in Essington is the site of Pennsylvania's first European settlement, founded by Swedish colonists in the mid-1600s.

Bucks County, north of Philadelphia, is famed for its serene rural ambiance, quaint villages, covered bridges and stone barns. The town of New Hope on the Delaware Canal, for half a century the center of a renowned art colony, offers shops, galleries and other amusements; charming Doylestown has the excellent Mercer Museum, housing a unique collection of early Americana. Bucks County is also the site of William Penn's house, Pennsbury Manor, located in Morrisville, and Washington Crossing State Park. Each December Washington's historic crossing of the ice-packed Delaware River on Christmas night, 1776, is reenacted. In Northampton County beyond, travelers will enjoy a visit to Bethlehem to explore its colorful Moravian heritage and, at Christmastime, its famed candlelight and music festival.

Society Hill Hotel. Philadelphia's first bed and breakfast hotel, Society Hill is right in the heart of Independence National Historical Park. Diagonally across the street from the National Park Service Visitor Center at Third and Chestnut, the attractive red-brick structure is within two blocks of Independence Hall, the First and Second Banks, Franklin Court and Penn's Landing. The hotel was built in 1832, and once served as temporary housing for longshoremen from all over the world. Today it is an exceptionally charming small urban inn, in the best European tradition. David DeGraff and Judith Campbell are your hosts.

Society Hill has 12 rooms for guests, including nine doubles and three triples. Six of the rooms are two-room suites. All have private baths and are elegantly furnished with brass beds and lovely antiques. Fresh-cut flowers grace each room. Breakfast, which is included in the rates, consists of freshly-squeezed orange or grapefruit juice, warm croissants with sweet butter and jam, and coffee or tea, served in your room on a wicker tray. Lunches, dinners and Sunday brunch are available in the Hotel Bar/Restaurant. Handsomely done with light woods, stained glass and greenery, the room has huge windows which overlook the park. Philadelphia Cheesesteak is the house specialty; the fabulous Sunday Brunch includes Belgian waffles, eggs Benedict, and fresh fruit and brandied cream.

Society Hill Hotel, 301 Chestnut St. (Third and Chestnut streets), Philadelphia, PA 19106; (215) 925-1394. Rates are expensive. American Express, Visa and Diners Club/Carte Blanche are accepted. Children are welcome; no pets, please. The hotel does not have parking facilities. Open year-round.

Bed & Breakfast of Philadelphia. This bed and breakfast organization offers a very nice selection of overnight accommodations, conveniently located in some of Philadelphia's most interesting areas—including the historic section, Society Hill and Germantown. Others are available in several Philadelphia suburbs and neighboring counties. Each home is personally inspected to assure you of attractive, clean and safe lodgings, and a warm, friendly welcome from your hosts. In Philadelphia itself, typical listings include an apartment in a historic Victorian home with four-poster double bed and a bath with authentic 6-foot clawfoot tub, and a Society Hill townhouse. Another city location offers a large studio with 14-foot ceiling, wood-burning fireplace, and a magnificent collection of art. Previous guests here have included Douglas Fairbanks, Jason Robards, Angela Lansbury and Sir Michael Redgrave. Outside the city the organization's listing include such intriguing offerings as a Colonial stone farmhouse adjacent to the hunt country, a gracious summer home furnished in antiques (with an outdoor pool), and a large contemporary home filled with plants, art, sculpture and crafted pieces. Breakfast, of course, is included.

Contact: Janet B. Mochel, Director, Bed & Breakfast of Philadelphia, P.O. Box 101, Oreland, PA 19075; (215) 884-1084. Send a stamped, self-addressed envelope for a copy of the directory and a reservation request form. You may have three choices of accommodation; the B & B selected for you will either be one of these or a similar one. A deposit of $5 per room per night and at least 10 days' advance notice are required.

Mrs. K's Guest House. The town of Kennett Square, in southern Chester County, is only one mile square. So you won't have any trouble, according to Ms. Charlotte Kanofsky, in finding her house! It is a two-story contemporary home built in 1953 on a quiet residential street, with two screened porches and a large back yard with huge old shade trees. Your hostess has one double and one twin-bedded room for guests, one upstairs and one on the ground floor. Both have private baths, and the house is air conditioned. Guests are welcome to make use of the whole house, its porches and yard. And there are plenty of outdoor chairs, plus a picnic table. Breakfast is included in the rates and will consist of juice, eggs, toast and coffee or something similar. Ms. Kanofsky occasionally bakes, if she knows in advance that people are expected. She will also serve dinner, for an extra fee, upon request. The house is close to a drugstore for a variety of shopping needs; a car is necessary to reach area restaurants, antique shops and the like. Mrs. K's is located five minutes from Longwood Gardens Horticultural Conservatory, one of the country's most extensive botanical gardens; fifteen minutes from Brandywine Battlefield and Brandywine Museum in Chadds Ford; one hour from Philadelphia and Lancaster. Several Delaware attractions are also only minutes away, including Winterthur.

Mrs. K's Guest House, 404 Ridge Ave., Kennett Square, PA 19348; home (215) 444-5559, work (302) 478-5280 ext. 344. Rates are moderate, 10 percent lower for two children sleeping in twin-bedded room. Because your hostess works, she would appreciate advance reservations if possible. Children are welcome but must be toilet trained; there are no cribs so older children are preferred. No pets, please. Parking is available both in driveway and on street. Open year-round except for an occasional vacation.

Coventry Forge Inn Guest House. A charming country retreat, Coventry Forge is just a few miles south of Pottstown, Pennsylvania. It is in Coventryville, a small village in northern Chester County. The white stuccoed guest house, set amidst old shade trees, was built in 1806. Wallis Callahan, proprietor, offers five spacious rooms for guests: four doubles and one triple. Each has an exceptionally large private bath; all have views of the gardens and surrounding countryside. Furnished with antiques, the house also has a pleasant living room for guests' enjoyment. A Continental breakfast, included in the rates, consists of juice, croissants, preserves and coffee or tea. Breakfast is served on the closed-in porch of the adjacent early-eighteenth-century Coventry Forge Inn, a noted dining establishment (rated as one of the country's finest) offering superb French cuisine. Coventry Forge is close to many of Pennsylvania's most scenic and historic areas, including the restored eighteenth-century Hopewell Village. Valley Forge National Park is within easy driving distance, too. There is a swimming pool available for guests, and a map of country walks for hikers who wish to explore the area.

Coventry Forge Inn Guest House, Rte. 23, Coventryville, PA; (215) 469-6222. (1.5 miles west of Rte. 100, 5 miles south of Pottstown.) Mailing address: R.D. #2, Pottstown, PA 19464. Rates are moderate during the week, higher on weekends. Children are welcome; no pets, please. Parking is available at the house. Open year-round.

Pineapple Hill. This inviting guest house in Bucks County reflects the friendly personalities of its hosts, Steve and Mary Darlington. Located just south of New Hope, Pineapple Hill is a spacious stone and frame farmhouse; the oldest part of the house was built in 1800. Now serving as the dining room, it still has the original 18-inch walls, handsome woodwork and large fireplace. Other sections were added to the old farmhouse around 1840. The Darlingtons have four double guest rooms, two on the second floor of one wing and two (with a separate staircase) on the third floor. Each set of two rooms shares a bath and is ideal for two couples traveling together or for families. The rooms are decorated with Victorian and country furnishings; handmade quilts, lace, stenciled designs and wallpaper add coziness and color. The second-floor rooms include a brass and a spool bed, and the third-floor quarters are tucked under straw-colored eave-sloped walls. For guests' enjoyment there are a large parlor with TV and fireplace and a parlor area in the dining room. There's a powder room on the ground floor, too. Throughout the house you will note the pineapple motif, the Colonial symbol of welcome.

Breakfast at Pineapple Hill includes orange juice, croissants, coffeecake or homemade biscuits with preserves, coffee or tea. In the afternoon your hosts offer tea, perhaps with shortcakes, Amish vanilla pie, or homemade cookies. Sherry is proffered in the evenings—and as a special "tuck-in" treat, you'll find homemade fudge! And they are *all* included in the rates.

Five acres of grounds surround the house, with lovely gardens and the ruins of an old stone barn—now enclosing a swimming pool. A quaint restaurant is only ¼ mile away; other restaurants, shops, etc. are reachable by car. Bucks County's many sites of interest include New Hope with its art and craft galleries, the Bucks County Playhouse, Lahaska's antique dealers, and Peddler's Village with an abundance of fine shops. Washington Crossing State Park and Pennsbury Manor are both close by; Philadelphia is an hour's drive. And the Delaware Canal towpath is just around the corner from Pineapple Hill, for walking or jogging. Both canal and river offer canoeing and rafting; in winter there's ice skating on the canal.

Pineapple Hill, Box 34C, R.D. 2, New Hope, PA 18938; (215) 862-9608. (On River Road, Rte. 32, four miles south of New Hope and two miles north of Washington Crossing State Park, across the road from Thorpe Farm sign.) Rates are moderate, lower from Oct. 1 to Memorial Day weekend and for longer stays. Children are welcome; families with small children are asked to make reservations well in advance so that your hosts may plan to make your visit comfortable and to assure the privacy of other guests. No pets, please. Smoking is limited to the parlor area. Parking is available. Open year-round.

The Wedgwood Inn. Situated in New Hope, right in the heart of the Historic District, The Wedgwood Inn—a guest house since 1950—is now owned by Nadine Silnutzer and Carl

Glassman. They purchased the place in 1981 and intend to continue its operation as a bed and breakfast inn, preserving and enhancing its classic nineteenth-century ambiance.

More than two centuries ago the property was the site of "the Old Hiproof House" where, in 1776, Gen. Alexander Lord Stirling stayed during an encampment. The present structure, a 2½-story Victorian with gabled hip roof, was built in 1870 on the foundations of the original house. Nominated for the National Register of Historic Places, the handsome old house, featuring a large veranda with scrolled wood brackets and turned posts, a porte-cochere and a charming gingerbread gazebo, is surrounded by beautifully landscaped grounds.

Hardwood floors, lofty windows and antique furnishings create a warm, comfortable feeling in each of the inn's eight bedrooms. Original artwork and brass ceiling fans add to the rooms' appeal, and guests will enjoy the hospitable touch of complimentary liqueur. Two baths are shared; four of the rooms and one bath are on the ground floor. There's a pleasant parlor, too, where guests can relax with magazines, games or a good book, or join in friendly conversation. Breakfast, included in the rates, is served each morning in the parlor, the kitchen, or—upon request—in your bedroom. The Continental breakfast includes freshly-squeezed orange juice, homebaked hot croissants or muffins, and plenty of coffee. Coffee and tea are always brewing at the Wedgwood Inn.

The house is within two blocks of most of New Hope's restaurants, shops and other historic buildings. You'll enjoy a leisurely walk through the mile-square community exploring its numerous art galleries and craft and antique shops, or along the picturesque canal towpath. Many area shopkeepers, by the way, offer Wedgwood guests 10 to 20 percent discounts on purchases. The placid Delaware River offers swimming, canoeing and tubing, and the countryside is great fun to bicycle or drive around in. Skiing and ice-skating are available nearby in winter. Your innkeepers, Dinie and Carl, will be glad to help you plan activities, make dinner reservations or pack a picnic lunch for you to take on a day's outing.

The Wedgwood Inn, 111 West Bridge St., New Hope, PA 18938; (215) 862-2570. Rates are moderate; lower for weekday accommodations and between January and April. Children are welcome; no pets, please. Parking is available at the house. Open year-round.

Barley Sheaf Farm. Also located in the New Hope area, Barley Sheaf is not merely a guest house—it's a real working farm! Ann and Don Mills raise sheep, pigs and chickens on their 30 acres, and their bees make the honey for your breakfast toast. The oldest section of the comfortable stone farmhouse was built in 1740, and Barley Sheaf Farm is now a National Historic Site. George S. Kaufman, playwright and drama critic for the *New York Times* during the 1930s and '40s, owned the house for 20 years. For guests there are eight double rooms and one suite. Five of the rooms and the suite have private baths; three rooms (on the ground floor) share a bath. There's also a living room with TV and fireplace for guests' use. Breakfast, which is included in the rates, is a typical hearty farm repast with eggs from the Mills' henhouse, home-grown bacon and ham, and homemade jams and breads. Guests can roam around the farm and use the large swimming pool on the grounds. Restaurants, shops, antiques and Peddler's Village are all minutes away. The Delaware River, for hiking and canoeing, is a 10-minute drive, and Washington Crossing State Park is 15 minutes away.

Barley Sheaf Farm, Box 66, Rte. 202, Holicong, PA 18928; (215) 794-5104. Located just off Rte. 202 between New Hope and Doylestown; ask your hosts for precise directions.) Rates are moderate to expensive, 10 percent off for a week's stay. Children over 8 are welcome; no pets, please. Parking is available. Open March 1–December 22.

Guest Houses

Driftin' Del. "Driftin' Del" is in Upper Black Eddy, in northern Bucks County. Situated on 30 beautifully landscaped acres, it offers bed and breakfast, a swimming pool, tennis court, riding stables, boating, a pond and pretty lanes for walking or cycling. The house is a long, rambling structure; its original section was built in 1830, with many additions since then. Bob and Ilse Weinbel, innkeepers, have six bedrooms for guests, each with its own staircase, some with fireplaces. (The house boasts four working fireplaces in all.) All but one room have private baths; five have double beds and one has single beds. Two of the guest rooms are on the ground floor. All are furnished with antiques, including several canopy beds, some handsome period oak pieces, and antique brass. Guests may use the recreation/sitting room with large-screen TV, wood stove and player piano. There are also a library, porch and second-floor balcony.

In wintertime breakfast is served in the large country kitchen, with a fire cheerily crackling in the fireplace. In summer it's served out on the porch, with a view of flowers and hummingbirds. The lavish meal (included in the rates) consists of juice, freshly-baked sweet rolls with homemade jams and jellies, eggs—perhaps "Eggs Ilse," the house specialty—and bacon or sausage, or creamed beef and home fries. For other meals there is Tara (which also has overnight lodging), located on the premises within walking distance. A car is needed for other restaurants and shopping. Scenic Bucks County offers visitors a wealth of things to do; "Driftin' Del" is close to Ringing Rocks Park, with Bucks County's highest waterfall, and the Delaware River for canoeing, tubing, and fishing. Bethlehem, with its Moravian museums and houses, is also within easy driving distance.

"Driftin' Del," Box 309A, Woodland Drive, Upper Black Eddy, PA 18972; (215) 982-5445. Your hosts will give you directions to the house when you make reservations. Rates are expensive. No children or pets, please. Parking is available. Open year-round.

NORTHEASTERN REGION

Pennsylvania's northeastern region is best known for the Poconos. These rounded, green-forested mountains are a four-season resort area,covering 2400 square miles. In summer visitors can swim, boat, fish, water-ski, hike, camp and climb. In winter there's excellent skiing, with more than 50 downhill facilities and miles of cross-country trails. Hunting and foliage watching are popular in the fall; spring brings masses of blooming mountain laurel, the state's official flower. The Poconos, with their great natural beauty and abundance of lakes, streams, waterfalls, wooded slopes and peaceful valleys, are also known—romantically—as "The Honeymoon Capital of the World." The area is dotted with luxurious resort hotels, some designed only for newlyweds and featuring such novelties as heart-shaped beds and bathtubs.

Not so well known, except to Pennsylvanians, are the region's other hills to the west of the Poconos: the Endless Mountains. Seeming to roll on forever into the distance, this wild and rugged terrain was named by early explorers. Here the Susquehanna River twists like a snake as it flows swiftly between the mountains; there are state forests for camping and hiking and miles of back-country roads to follow. In September, the Luzerne County Folk Festival presents an ethnic celebration of food, folk dancing, music and arts and crafts.

Pennsylvania mines most of America's anthracite coal, and in several of the northeastern region's counties visitors can explore old coal mining towns and coal museums. Down in the southern part of Carbon County you'll find the town of Jim Thorpe. When the great Indian athlete died in 1953 his family wanted to bury him in Oklahoma, his birthplace, but could not afford the kind of memorial they wished. The two Pennsylvania mining towns of Mauch Chunk and East Mauch Chunk offered to combine and rename themselves Jim Thorpe in his honor, and build a 20-ton red granite mausoleum. Although Thorpe had never even visited the area, his family accepted. Nestling in a narrow gorge on the Lehigh River between two towering mountains, the town was first settled in 1815 and still retains much its nineteenth-century appearance with a fine collection of period architecture. At the historic restored Railroad Station you can visit a museum and acquire information about a walking tour of the town.

In Scranton the Anthracite Museum Complex offers a group of partially-restored anthracite-fired iron furnaces dating from 1840 and the Anthracite Museum itself, which presents the history of the area. Down near Hazleton, south of Wilkes-Barre, the nineteenth-century miner's village of

Eckley portrays life as it once was in the anthracite region. Now a part of the Museum Complex, Eckley was the site of the filming of "The Molly Maguires."

Pennsylvania's northeastern region also offers exciting whitewater rafting through the Lehigh River Gorge near Hazleton and some 28 covered bridges, scattered through western Columbia and Montour Counties. In the east, Bushkill attracts visitors with its seven waterfalls and the Pocono Indian Museum. Towanda, in the Endless Mountains to the northwest, is the site of French Azilum. In 1793, during the French Revolution, the Asylum Company purchased a million acres in this wilderness region. It was meant to be a refuge for Marie Antoinette, if she managed to escape from France. A thriving colony of French noblemen existed here for a number of years, and today five reconstructed log cabins and a museum may be explored. Nearby, the LaPorte house, built in 1836 by the son of one of the colony's founders, represents the elegant French influence of that long-ago period.

LaAnna Guest House. La Anna is a pretty little village set in the scenic Pocono Mountains. And LaAnna Guest House offers some of the best scenery around right on its own property, including woodland walks, many waterfalls and a pond! The house is just as appealing as the grounds, a century-old Victorian with a broad porch and 10-foot ceilings, entirely furnished with period antiques. Kay and Julie Swingle, your friendly hosts, have four spacious rooms for guests: two doubles with cots and two triples. Two baths are shared. There are also a pleasant living room with TV and a library for relaxation or rainy-day amusement. A Continental breakfast of homemade rolls, juice, coffee or tea is included in the rates. You'll need a car to reach restaurants and shops; swimming, fishing, golf and tennis are all available within six miles of the house. In winter there is cross-country skiing on the grounds, and downhill skiing is only a short drive away.

LaAnna Guest House, (Mailing address) R.D. 2, Box 1051, Cresco, PA 18326; (717) 676-4225 or 857-0227. (When you call for reservations, you'll be given precise directions to the house.) Rates are very inexpensive, even lower for longer stays and for children sharing a room. Well-behaved children and pets are welcome. Parking is available. Open year-round.

La Anna Guest House

Nearbrook. You'll find Dick and Barbie Robinson's Nearbrook in Canadensis, another scenic Pocono mountain town. The attractive house was once the private home of the owners of Pinehurst, one of the area's fine old resorts back in the first half of this century. Three single rooms and one double are available for guests, with two shared baths. One room and bath are located on the ground floor,and all rooms include a sink. Guests are also welcome to use the living room, a reading/writing alcove and the porches. For an extra fee the Robinsons will provide you with a hearty "Mountain Breakfast" and will arrange picnic lunches and dinner. Your hosts cordially invite their guests to explore Nearbrook's lovely, wooded grounds—including rock gardens and a pretty path that leads down to a tumbling mountain stream. Barbie Robinson suggests that writers and artists would find the place ideal—but who wouldn't? A nice selection of restaurants and shops are within a short drive, as are many of the Poconos' year-round attractions and activities.

Nearbrook, Rte. 1, Box 630, Canandensis, PA 18325; (717) 595-3152. (Between Buck Hill Falls and Skytop, just one mile north of Canandensis on Rte. 447.) Rates are inexpensive; special rates are available for longer stays and for children using sleeping bags. Well-behaved youngsters and pets are welcome. Parking is available. Open year-round.

Kovarick's. Kovarick's, a rural Poconos retreat in Stroudsburg, is a great place for youngsters. Set amidst 13 acres of lawns, shade trees, flowers and shrubs, it includes a filtered swimming pool, a children's play area with slides and swings, and shuffleboard and horseshoe areas. In addition there are streams and a two-acre lake with rowboats and fine bass and trout fishing. An excellent golf course with moderate greens' fees is close by. Several good restaurants and shopping centers are within a five-minute drive; antique shops, summer theater, winter skiing, tennis, horseback riding, water slides and a variety of other amusements are 15 minutes away. Your hostess will be delighted to tell you more about the region and its many attractions. Kovarick's has 16 rooms for guests including four singles and 12 doubles, all with private baths. Six of the rooms are on the ground floor, and some have their own living/sitting room. They're all carpeted and are furnished in early American motif, with wood paneling. No meals are served but each room has the makings for coffee and tea. Guests are encouraged to use the barbecue grills which are tucked away in secluded areas on the grounds, with patios, lawn chairs and umbrella tables. Cooking utensils and firewood are furnished at no charge; you provide your own charcoal.

Kovarick's, Box 5019, Rte. 5, Stroudsburg, PA 18360; (717) 421-6842. (Take Exit 49 from Rte. 80 to Dreher Ave., No. 1328. Look for sign and turn into driveway.) Rates are expensive, lower from Labor Day to Memorial Day. Special rates are available for longer stays. American Express accepted. Children are welcome; no pets, please. Ample parking is available. Open year-round.

The Victorian Guest House. Situated in Towanda in the midst of the Endless Mountains, the Victorian Guest House is considered one of the grandest houses in the area. Built in 1897, the elegant old structure is classic Victorian with porches, arches, and a host of period architectural splendors. And it's filled with antiques, including Tiffany lamps. Barbara Mower (Mrs. Frederick J.), who took over the operation of the house from her mother, is your gracious hostess. She offers eleven charmingly decorated rooms for guests: one single and ten doubles. Five have private baths, two have semi-baths and four share two baths. The spacious rooms, all furnished in antiques, include color TV (with movie channel) and phones. Barb Mower provides complimentary morning coffee for her guests, and cold drinks for a small extra fee. No meals are served but the house is only six blocks from the center of town with restaurants, shops and the like. French Azilum, the 1793 settlement created by refugees from the French Revolution, is six miles away. Canoeing and fishing are available ¼ mile away in the Susquehanna River, and swimming at nearby Lake Wesauking. Steven Foster once lived in Towanda, and Camptown of "Camptown Races" is 16 miles away.

The Victorian Guest House, 118 York Ave. (Rte. 6), Towanda, PA 18848; (717) 265-6972. Rates are moderate; American Express is accepted. One or two children are welcome; no pets, please. Off-street parking is available. Open year-round.

CENTRAL PENNSYLVANIA

Southcentral Region

Pennsylvania's southcentral region includes many of the state's most popular attractions. Here you'll find the trim farms and old German towns of Pennsylvania Dutch Country; Harrisburg, Pennsylvania's capital city; Hershey; Gettysburg Battlefield, and historic York—just for starters.

Lancaster is the heart of the Pennsylvania Dutch Country. The so-called "Pennsylvania Dutch" are not Dutch at all, however, but the descendants of German *(Deutsch)* Mennonite and Amish settlers who emigrated here in the 1700s. Some of them still speak their unique regional dialect and many, called "the plain people," still live their daily lives much as their ancestors did. The Old Order Amish, in particular, cling to the ways of the past. Their dress is simple: the women wear bonnets and long, unadorned gowns; the men, with flowing beards, wear broad-brimmed hats and black coats. They ride in horsedrawn buggies or carts, farm with horses and mules, and do not have electricity, telephones or television in their homes. The Amish believe in the literal application of the Bible, and visitors are requested not to take pictures (unless permission is asked and granted) as the taking of photographs violates the Biblical commandment, "Thou shalt not make a graven image."

Several Amish farms may be toured, including the Amish Homestead and the Amish Farm and House. At the People's Place, Lancaster County's center for Amish and Mennonite arts and crafts, you can view two fascinating films and visit the Amish Story Museum and book and craft shop. Throughout the region visitors will hear the clip-clop of horses' hooves as the spirited animals trot along the roadsides pulling shiny, black-painted buggies. In Lancaster and in smaller towns like Bird-In-Hand, Paradise, Blue Ball and Mount Joy you'll see the Amish and Mennonite "plain people" doing their shopping or selling their produce at farm markets. You will also find covered bridges, barns adorned with the colorful radial designs called hex signs, fertile fields and sleek cows, and shops offering Pennsylvania Dutch kitchen accessories or locally-made quilts, aprons and bonnets. Restaurants specializing in Pennsylvania Dutch cooking abound, too, offering the traditional "seven sweets and seven sours" along with a raft of hearty items like chicken pot pie, smoked pork chops, *schnitz un knepp* (a boiled ham dish), and noodles in sour cream.

Even though many of these hard-working folk eschew modern farm machinery, Lancaster County's farms are among the most productive in the world. And its farmers' markets are downright spectacular! (They're not open every day of the week so check on schedules to be sure not to miss a visit to at least one.) In addition to marvelous farm produce the market stalls offer mouth-watering displays of sausages, bologna, scrapple and souse, jars of pickled items, jams and apple butter, and homemade goodies such as shoofly pie and funnel cake. There will also be pretzels, a Pennsylvania Dutch specialty.

In Berks County, northeast of Lancaster near Reading, is frontiersman Daniel Boone's homestead, the 1734 birthplace of the famed frontiersman. Also in this area are a large number of factory outlets where you'll find all manner of items sold at a discount. For antique hunters, Adamstown boasts a score of antique markets where on Sundays year-round thousands of antique dealers come to buy and sell. Kutztown, beyond Reading, is the home of the famed Kutztown Folk Festival held each July and featuring traditional Pennsylvania Dutch foods, craft demonstrations, quilt exhibits and Amish pageants. In Cornwall, north of Lancaster in Lebanon County, there's a historic iron furnace where George Washington directed the forging of cannons for his army. Schaefferstown nearby is the site of America's oldest operating distillery; whiskey is still made by the old-fashioned pot still sour mash method.

Harrisburg, Pennsylvania's capital, is a very attractive city with a beautiful Italian Renaissance capitol building, surrounded by gardens. Its dome imitates St. Peter's Basilica in Rome, and its front steps lead down to the Susquehanna River. Within the Capitol complex are the handsome Forum building and the William Penn Memorial Museum with four stories of galleries housing historical documents, Indian and natural history artifacts, fine arts, an antique auto and carriage collection and a planetarium.

In Hershey, just a few minutes from Harrisburg, you can buy a T-shirt that states: "There's a little bit of Hershey in all of us." More likely there's a *lot* of Hershey in *most* of us—and chocolate lovers will thoroughly appreciate the charms of "Chocolate Town U.S.A." The town's two major thoroughfares are named Chocolate and Cocoa avenues and their streetlights are shaped like chocolate kisses. Hershey's Chocolate World will take you via automated conveyance past all the steps of chocolate production from cacao bean plantations to the making of Hershey bars. Adjacent Hersheypark offers a variety of theme rides, a zoo, craft demonstrations, a walking Hershey Bar and a huge (330 foot high) Hershey Kiss. And Hershey Gardens presents 23 acres of spectacularly beautiful displays of flowers, blooming shrubs and trees.

York, south of Harrisburg and west of Lancaster, offers an array of pre-Revolutionary homes and churches. In 1777 the Continental Congress met in York and adopted the Articles of Confederation, using the term "United States of America" for the first time. Historic structures dating from the 1700s include the Friends Meeting House, General Gates' House and the Golden Plough Tavern. Historic Gettysburg lies southwest of York, in Adams County. A tour of Gettysburg Battlefield is, for most visitors, a deeply moving experience. The battle was the greatest (and one of the bloodiest) ever fought on this continent, and one of the most decisive in world history. On July 1, 1863, Gen. Robert E. Lee's Confederate army of 75,000 men met the 97,000-man Northern army of Gen. George G. Meade. The battle lasted three days, ending in Lee's defeat—and 51,000 dead. Although the Civil War raged on for two more years, the Confederacy never recovered from its losses at Gettysburg.

The site of the battle, now the Gettysburg National Military Park, covers 3500 acres through which run more than 35 miles of roads. There are some 1200 monuments, markers and tablets, and 400 cannon. At the Visitor Center you can follow the battle story on a huge electric map before you start out. As the park is so large, a driving tour is recommended. The Gettysburg National Cemetery, adjoining the park, is the site of President Abraham Lincoln's Gettysburg Address in November, 1863. Also adjoining the Battlefield is the late President Dwight D. Eisenhower's farm, now a National Historic Site.

General Lee's Headquarters are located in the town of Gettysburg, as are the Lincoln Room Museum, the National Civil War Wax Museum and—for a 360-degree view—the Battlefield Tower. A few miles away the Gettysburg Miniature Horse Farm boasts more than 50 miniature horses, representing a variety of breeds. The little horses can be petted, and they perform daily during the summer months.

Guest accommodations in the southcentral region of Pennsylvania are many and diverse, particularly in the Lancaster area. Here you'll find an eighteenth-century inn, several mansions, a rustic retreat, contemporary suburban homes, and a large number of delightful old stone or brick farmhouses situated on working farms—where guests are invited to join in the activities or simply enjoy the clean country air. Many of the houses and farms are owned by Mennonite families, who welcome travelers with gracious hospitality and warmth. Their rates, in most cases, are amazingly low. As most of the houses have only a few rooms for guests, advance reservations are strongly recommended, especially during the busy summer season.

Historic 1725 Witmer's Tavern. In the 1700s there were more than 60 tavern-inns along the 66-mile Philadelphia to Lancaster Turnpike. Witmer's, just east of Lancaster, is the only one left intact and still taking in overnight visitors. Now listed on the National Register of Historic Places, the pre-Revolutionary inn is being restored—floor by floor, room by room—to appear and function as it did in the eighteenth century (but with all modern conveniences.) Brant E. Hartung, innkeeper, operates Witmer's with the help of his mother, two sisters and a brother. Hartung, who also remodels homes and restores antiques, delights in sharing the history of the tavern with interested guests.

Records show that in 1722 Benjamin Weitmer (later

spelled Whitmore and finally Witmer), an agent for the London Land Company, was granted a patent for 265 acres, part of which the house sits on today. He built a log cabin, just east of the present building, and then, in 1725, constructed the one story and loft which comprise the eastern end of the structure. Later Witmers added on to the house, to provide more accommodations for the large number of travelers along the busy Pike.

The Hartung family purchased the building in 1969 and embarked on an intensive restoration project. Initial work included removing the white stucco exterior, repointing the limestone walls and rehabilitating the fireplaces and chimney flues. Brant Hartung then proceeded to sand and varnish the wide plank flooring and strip many layers of paint from the wooden doors, chair rails and trim, repainting them in traditional colors. For guests' comfort electric heating, air conditioning and modern bathroom facilities were installed, and the first restored guest rooms opened in 1979.

Presently, the rooms include three with double beds, and the Lafayette Suite with a double bed and 200-year-old trundle bed. Two rooms are on the ground floor. All are furnished with period antiques and have working fireplaces—with popcorn poppers for guests' use! Closets were unknown in the old days, so guests even now hang their garments on pegs or clothing boards. So as not to destroy the original layout the baths have been built across the hall from every two rooms.

Historic 1725 Witmer's Tavern

The original large "keeping room" is now the sitting room, with a server for Continental breakfast and a glistening potbelly stove. Note the double hinged doors, a beautifully-made corner cupboard, the tavern's old brick floor and huge fireplace, enormous beams with mortise and tenon joinings, bubbly window glass and—gems of early eighteenth-century artistry—the handworked main hall staircase and rail. Your host will be happy to point out all of these and much more, including a number of intriguing architectural puzzles.

Breakfast, which is included in the rates, consists of sticky buns, orange juice and tea or coffee sweetened with honey. No other meals are currently served; the Hartungs furnish a list of restaurants in the area, with a description of each. They also provide information on Lancaster County's many places to visit including farmers' markets, the quaint Amish shopping village of Intercourse, and Rockford's host of historic sites. Within walking distance you'll find the Pennsylvania Dutch Visitor Center for information about the area, Anderson's Pretzel Factory, the Amish Homestead, and lots more. Even closer to hand is Pandora's Antiques (another Hartung family business) with old Amish and Mennonite quilts and a variety of other antiques; it's right on the premises.

Historic 1725 Witmer's Tavern, 2014 Old Philadelphia Pike (Rte. 340), Lancaster, PA 17602; (717) 299-5305. (Located 1½ miles east of Lancaster city limits. Traveling on Rte. 30, just east of Lancaster, take exit marked Intercourse, Rte. 340. The inn is ¼ mile on the right.) Rates are expensive; payment in full in advance is required. As there are no TV or planned activities for youngsters, the Hartungs don't recommend the place for children. No pets, please. Parking is available at the house. Open year-round.

Nissly's Olde Home Inns. Esther Nissly and James Henry are the proprietors of these unusual guest accommodations. Conveniently located on a quiet street in Lancaster's historic area, they consist of two handsome mansions and a carriage house. The Menno Fry Mansion, Ms. Nissly's childhood home, was built between 1894 and 1896. Fry, who had amassed a fortune in tobacco by the end of the Civil War, hired a Lancaster architect—Emlen Urban—to design the house in the ornate style of a French chateau. The adjacent Steigerwalt Mansion is almost a mirror of the Menno Fry

Nissly's Olde Home Inns

house; it's not known if it was also built by Urban but the story goes that the same plans were used, only in reverse. Elmer Steigerwalt, who had the "chateau" built around 1897, was a wealthy real estate developer. The Carriage House is behind the Steigerwalt Mansion's gardens.

Guest accommodations in the three structures are varied, and include individual rooms, family-style apartments and suites. Most have private baths; others share. The ambiance of the two main houses is Victorian with stained-glass beaded windows, Oriental rugs, handcarved woodwork, Tiffany-style chandeliers and a mixture of traditional and modern furniture; the Carriage House is simpler in style. Most of the accommodations have kitchenettes where guests may prepare their own breakfast or other meals. Coffee is available in the mornings for guests who don't have kitchenettes. Many of Lancaster's restaurants are close by, as are grocery stores, farmers' markets, walking tours and historic sites. A tour bus to Amish Country and Hershey picks up passengers at Nissly's main office, by advance reservation. Nissly's will also arrange to meet guests at train or bus terminals, if requested ahead of time.

Nissly's Olde Home Inns, 624-632 West Chestnut St. (Rte. 23), Lancaster, PA 17603; (717) 392-2311 or 866-4926. (One block from College Avenue.) Rates vary widely, depending on accommodations. Nissly's will tell you what is available when you call to make reservations and give you exact directions to the house. Children over 12 are welcome; no pets, please. For the sake of other guests, no partying or entertaining is allowed. There is off-street parking in the rear. Open year-round.

Lincoln House Lodging. Mary K. Zook warmly welcomes travelers to her nice Lancaster home, a white stucco stone house with a distinctive hip roof, about 70 years old. Inside note the beautiful oak staircase, oak floors and stained glass. Your hostess has six pleasant rooms for guests: two of the rooms are suitable for two people, two for four, one for two or three, and one for four to six. Four rooms have private baths; two are semi-private. Two of the guest rooms are located on the ground floor. In addition, Mrs. Zook offers separate accommodations which she calls "sweeps"—two bedrooms with complete kitchen facilities, ideal for two couples traveling together or a family. Guests are invited to share Mrs. Zook's living room or relax out on the front porch. There's also a large yard with a swing, picnic table and built-in grill. Your hostess is especially proud of her flower beds with, as she poetically describes them, "the shining faces of roses." No food is served, but restaurants are within walking distance, and guests are welcome to use the grill for hotdog cook-outs. Swimming is accessible a few miles away, and the Lancaster area's many attractions are easily reachable by car or bus. Mrs. Zook is Amish, therefore cannot take a picture of her own home; guests may, however, and she reports: "I have seen it, and it is very attractive, indeed!"

Lincoln House Lodging, 1687 Lincoln Highway East, Lancaster, PA 17602; (717) 392-9412. Rates are inexpensive, lower from Nov. 15 through April 1 and for longer stays (one night free in a week's stay.) Children are welcome; no pets, please, and no alcoholic beverages in the house. Off-street parking is available. Open year-round.

Honeysuckle Hill. An exceptionally attractive country retreat near Lancaster, Honeysuckle hill is a 2½-story rustic structure situated on a wooded 10-acre site adjoining the Conestoga River. Completed in 1980, the house is owned by Don Claussen. Currently he offers guests a choice of five double rooms and one triple; two additional doubles are planned for the future. Each is a suite, with private bath, private key-lock entrance and balcony or patio terrace. Three of the rooms are on the ground floor. The tastefully furnished accommodations are fully carpeted and include in-room refrigerators, TV, smoke alarms, heating and central air conditioning. A buffet Continental breakfast of juice, pastry, coffee or tea, included in the rates, is served in the hallway immediately outside the rooms. There's also a microwave oven in the hall. The peaceful rural setting offers a half mile of country lane for strolling or jogging, picnic tables, and a rowboat for river roaming . . . yet Honeysuckle Hill is only ten minutes from historic Lancaster.

Honeysuckle Hill, 2060 Millersville Rd., Lancaster, PA 17603; (717) 872-6746. (Approximately three miles south of Lancaster.) Rates are inexpensive; special rates are available for longer stays. Children over 12 are welcome; no pets, please. There is ample parking. Open year-round.

The Spangler's. Paul and Elma Spangler's 1½-story green-shuttered Cape Cod house near Lancaster was built in 1950. There are two attractively decorated guest rooms: one with a double bed, the other with double bed and roll-away bed. One large bath, with tub, shower and electric wall heater, is shared. The rooms offer comfortable beds, wall-to-wall carpeting and air conditioning. Guests may share the Spanglers' living room, with TV, and an awninged side porch with chairs for relaxing. The back of the house looks out over meadows and fields. No meals are served but restaurants are just a mile or two away, as are shops and many of the area's attractions.

The Spangler's, 146 Buckwalter Road, Lancaster, PA 17602; (717) 394-8523. (Exit off Rte. 30 at Rte. 340; turn east and go about one mile to Buckwalter Road, opposite food stand; turn right and go about one block.) Rates are inexpensive; special rates are available for longer stays and sometimes for children. Children are welcome; no pets, please—and no smoking, drinking or abusive language. Parking is available at the house. Open year-round.

Smoketown Village Tourist Home. A handsome brick house with a pillared side porch, Smoketown Village Tourist Home, owned by Paul and Margaret Reitz, offers five pleasant, air-conditioned rooms for guests. There are four doubles and one triple; extra cots and roll-away beds are available. One room has a private bath; the others share a bath. Guests may also use the attractive living room with books and magazines or enjoy the porch and large shaded lawn, with picnic tables. No food is served; ask your hosts to direct you to some of the area's excellent restaurants. They'll also tell you about all the Amish Country sightseeing attractions.

Guest Houses

Smoketown Village Tourist Home, 2495 Old Philadelphia Pike (Rte. 340), Smoketown, PA 17576; (717) 393-5975. (Just east of Lancaster.) Rates are inexpensive. Children are welcome; no pets, please. Parking is available at the house. Open year-round.

Leaman's Country Tourist Lodging. Located in Bird-In-Hand, east of Lancaster, Mr. and Mrs. D. Rohrer Leaman's home is a contemporary ranch-style. The 1973 brick house is built on land that was originally a farm, where Mr. Leaman was born. It sits on a rise, offering marvelous views of sunsets (and sunrises) and surrounding Amish and Mennonite farms. From the porch or yard guests can watch Amish farmers working in their fields, horses and livestock in a nearby meadow, and buggies and wagons passing by. The three guest rooms include one with a double bed and two twins, with private bath, and two with a double bed each, sharing a bath. Roll-away beds are also available. Guests are welcome to use the large, bow-windowed living room with piano and fireplace, and the porch and yard. No food is served, but your hosts will be delighted to recommend some good restaurants in the area. Nearby points of interest include the scenic Amish countryside itself, farmers' markets, Ephrata Cloisters, the Strasburg Railroad, old grist mills and covered bridges.

Leaman's Country Tourist Lodging, Box 203, R.D. 1, Bird-In-Hand, PA 17505; (717) 656-7483. (Located along Rte. 772, midway between routes 23 and 222.) Rates are inexpensive. Children are welcome; no pets, please, and no smoking or drinking in the house. Parking is available in the driveway. Open year-round.

Greystone Motor Lodge. Set on two acres of tree-shaded lawns, Greystone Lodge is also located in Amish Country's Bird-In-Hand. A splendid French Victorian mansion, the house was constructed in 1883 from a farmhouse built in the mid-1800s. The converted Carriage House was originally the barn. Your hosts, Jim and Phyllis Reed, have ten charming rooms for guests, including two on the ground floor, each individually decorated. Four are one-room units; six consist of two-room family units. Some suites have full kitchens; all of the rooms offer private baths, TV and air conditioning. Some of the accommodations feature stained-glass windows, cut crystal doors, original woodwork and antique bath fixtures. A spacious Victorian-style living room is available exclusively for guests' use. No food is served; ask the Reeds for suggestions as to good local restaurants and area attractions.

Greystone Motor Lodge, P.O. Box 270, 2658 Old Philadelphia Pike (Rte. 340), Bird-In-Hand, PA 17505; (717) 393-4233. (On the south side of Rte. 340, one block west of Bird-In-Hand's railroad overpass.) Rates are moderate, lower from Sept. 16 to June 14, and for a third person in the room. MasterCard and Visa are accepted. Children are welcome; no pets, please. Parking is available. Open year-round.

The Millers. J. Kendig and Anna Miller have no sign out in front of their attractive home, but they welcome travelers with warm hospitality. Their house, located in Leola, is a 1938 brick Colonial trimmed in green. There are three double guest rooms with double or twin beds, and two shared baths. Roll-away beds for children are available. The firm, comfortable beds are covered with handmade quilts, some very old; the rooms have wall-to-wall carpeting, electric heat (with individually-controlled thermostats), air conditioning and radios (no TV.) Guests are invited to join the family in the evenings in the pleasant living room or back porch, and Mr. Miller is always happy to share his knowledge of the region and its many attractions. For a modest extra fee your hosts will serve a full family-style breakfast of orange juice, cereals, fruit in season, sweet rolls, eggs, pancakes, bacon or sausage, home fries, scrapple, omelets, creamed chipped beef or French toast. Guests have a choice of two hot foods, and are encouraged to eat all they can!

The Millers, 1 Mayfield Dr., Leola, PA 17540; (717) 656-7946. (On Rte. 23, midway between Lancaster and New Holland; corner of Main and Mayfield diagonally across from Memorial Building, two houses west of Tri Town Super Thrift Market.) Rates are inexpensive. Children are welcome; no pets, please, and no drinking. Smoking is permitted, but only on the enclosed back porch. Off-street parking is available. Open year-round.

Kreider's Tourist Farm Home. Lloyd and Ruth Kreider and their two young sons are a Mennonite farming family, and their nice old house is part of an 86-acre farm in rural Ronks, Pennsylvania. Mr. Kreider's family home, the sturdy brick farmhouse was built in 1856. For guests there are four double-bedded air-conditioned rooms: three doubles and one single. Fourteen persons in all may be accommodated, plus extra children if they have sleeping bags, and groups are welcomed. There are two baths. The comfortable rooms are simply furnished, with fresh wallpaper and paint, rugs, and warm handmade covers for the beds. Each room has a different color scheme—yellow, blue, orange, or dusty pink. Sometimes— depending on her schedule—Mrs. Kreider will provide breakfast, for an extra fee, of eggs, pancakes, hot cereals, freshly-baked rolls, coffee, tea or milk from the farm.

Guests are invited to share the parlor, and best of all, the farm's many activities. It is a working farm with almost 50 dairy cows that must be milked every morning at dawn. In season there are hay making and grain harvesting, canning and freezing fruits and vegetables from the garden and putting up apple butter or grape jelly. You're welcome to help if you like, pet the calves and play with the other animals, or just watch and ask questions; the Kreiders want their guests to feel at home. Other things to do in the area include a trip on the delightful Strasburg Railroad just across the field, horseback riding, skiing and touring the pretty countryside.

Kreider's Tourist Farm Home, 77-A Esbenshade Rd., Ronks, PA 17572; (717) 687-7001. (After you pass the Strasburg Railroad on Rte. 741 East, take the second crossroad left on Esbenshade Road; the house is the fourth on the left.) Rates are inexpensive, lower for children and for longer stays. Children are welcome; no pets, please. Advance reservations are requested. Mrs. Kreider does not allow smoking indoors . . . and . . . "Dare not come in with dirty shoes!" Parking is available. Open year-round.

Benner's Country Home For Tourists. David and Elizabeth Benner used to operate a farm and hosted visitors there from all over the world. Then they retired, sold the farm and built this contemporary home in Ronks in 1970. There are four guest rooms, with double beds (one also includes two single beds); one room, on the ground floor, has a private bath. The others are semi-private. The large, airy bedrooms each have two windows, wall-to-wall carpeting, electric heat and central air conditioning. A wide hallway leads to an upper porch that overlooks the surrounding Amish farms; Mrs. Benner says that guests love to sit up there "and so do we!" There's also a spacious living room with TV and books. The lawn outside, with flowers and shade trees, is big enough for children to play ball and run around, and there are tables with benches so that families can picnic if they like. No meals are served, but occasionally your hosts may share a coffee snack with guests in the evening in the kitchen or on one of the three porches or lawn. Guests may also share the kitchen refrigerator, for keeping milk or soft drinks. An excellent country restaurant is only half a mile away, as are a farmers' market and several gift shops. The Lancaster area is full of scenic and historic places, and the Benners will be happy to suggest a few.

Benner's Country Home For Tourists, 206 N. Ronks Rd., Ronks, PA 17572; (717) 299-2615. (One-half mile south of Bird-In-Hand, off Rte. 340 via Maple Ave. The Benners will give you precise directions when you call or write for reservations.) Rates are very inexpensive. Children are welcome; no pets, please. Smoking is allowed outdoors or on the porches. There's plenty of parking available. Open year-round.

Maple Lane Guest House. One hundred acres to explore, with meadows, woods and a winding stream to wade in—Maple Lane offers all of these, plus a working farm with 120 cows! Located in aptly-named Paradise, this very attractive Colonial-style guest house is in the heart of the Amish Country. The original stone farmhouse, built in 1785 by Jacob Stoutzenberger from Germany, is just across the lane. Edwin and Marion Rohrer have four rooms for guests: three triple and one double, sharing two baths. The air-conditioned rooms are pleasantly furnished with antiques, framed needlework and some exceptionally fine quilts. There's also a charming formal parlor just for guests, done in Williamsburg blue and white with Pennsylvania antiques. Complimentary coffee or tea is offered each morning; a full breakfast is available (with advance reservation) for an extra charge. Within a mile of the house are a handful of nice restaurants, many more within five miles. Also not far away are farmers' markets, the Amish Homestead, Amish bakeries, auctions, and lots of other interesting places to see. And you're more than welcome to watch the dairy operation right on the farm.

Maple Lane Guest House, 505 Paradise Lane, Paradise, PA 17562; (717) 687-7479. (Turn south on Rte. 896 off Rte.

30, proceed to Strasburg; turn left on Rte. 896 at traffic light and proceed 1½ miles out of town. Turn at sign for Timberline Lodge, on Paradise Lane; Maple Lane is the first farm on the left.) Rates are inexpensive, lower from November to April, for longer stays and for children. Children are welcome. Pets are not allowed in the house but may stay outdoors on a leash. Parking is available. Open year-round.

Verdant View Farm. Don and Virginia Ranck are your cordial hosts at their lush Pennsylvania farm in Paradise. The Ranck children are the fourth generation of the family on the 94-acre dairy and crop farm. The house, built in 1896, is a typical country frame structure with a front porch and grand views of the fields from the upstairs windows. Huge old trees shade the place, and guests are welcome to roam about at will. There are four comfortable rooms for travelers, one with private bath and sitting room, three with hot and cold running water, sharing a bath. For a modest extra fee the Rancks will start your mornings (except Sundays) with a hearty country breakfast of fruit, eggs, smoked bologna or dried beef from the farm, homemade muffins, pie and jams, coffee, spearmint tea, and all the fresh milk you want to drink. Guests may use the refrigerator for storing soft drinks and snacks, and there is a picnic area on the property. Swimming and horseback riding are available close by; restaurants and shops are within a 15- to 30-minute walk (or a few

Verdant View Farm

minutes' drive), and the Strasburg Railroad passes right by the farmhouse. You are also invited to attend the Rancks' Mennonite Church on Sunday mornings, if you like.

Verdant View Farm, 429 Strasburg Rd. (Rte. 741), Paradise, PA 17562; (717) 687-7353. (Along Rte. 741, one mile east of Strasburg, ¼ mile from the Strasburg Railroad Station.) Rates are inexpensive; one night free for one week's stay. Children are welcome; no pets, please. No smoking is allowed indoors. Parking is available. Open March–November.

The Amos Ranck Residence. Located just outside of Strasburg, Amos and Martha Ranck's nicely-maintained old house was built by Mr. Ranck's father in 1909. The three-story brick structure includes two guest rooms, each with one double bed; an extra cot is also available. One bath is shared. The light, airy rooms are furnished simply, with carpeting and some antiques. There's a balcony on the back of the house, and a living room which the Rancks share with guests. No food is served, but restaurants are within walking distance. Nearby attractions include historic Strasburg, the Strasburg Railroad and Railroad Museum, and the pleasant sight of Amish buggies passing on the roads.

The Amos Ranck Residence, Rte. 896, R.D. 1, Strasburg, PA 17579; (717) 687-7775. (On Rte. 896 East, ½ block from junction of routes 896 and 741 and the Tobacco Shed gift shop; there's no sign at the house, so if you can't find it just ask someone.) Rates are very inexpensive. Well-behaved children are welcome; pets only if well-controlled. There's parking at the house. Open year-round.

Ben-Mar Tourist Farm. Another of the Amish Country's wonderful old farmhouses, Roy and Mary Benner's establishment in Gap offers dairy animals galore, a large lawn and a meadow with a creek to paddle in. The house, built around 1776, has 21-inch stone walls, wide window sills and a splendid curving stairway. The Benners have an old newspaper which suggests that George Washington may have slept here—so you're in good company! Three attractive, nicely-furnished rooms are available for guests, with double beds (one has two double beds) and private baths. Two of the rooms boast marble fireplaces, and some of the beds are covered with quilts. In addition, there is a fully-furnished efficiency apartment on the ground floor. Breakfast is served on request (except on Sundays) for an extra fee and includes juice, ham and eggs, Mrs. Benner's own homemade bread and jellies, home-canned fruit, coffee or tea. Restaurants are accessible within a 10- to 20-minute drive. Public swimming pools are eight miles away and nearly all of the area's attractions are within a short drive. Many horsedrawn Amish buggies pass the house daily, too. Handiest of all, there is the Ben-Mar farm itself to explore.

Ben-Mar Tourist Farm, Rte. 340, RD 1, Gap, PA 17527; (717) 768-8353. (On Rte. 340 at White Horse, 17 miles east of Lancaster, 6½ miles east of Intercourse.) Rates are very inexpensive. Children are welcome; no pets, please. No smoking indoors. There is parking available. Open year-round.

Winding Glen Farm Tourist Home. You'll find Winding Glen in Christiana, about 19 miles east of Lancaster. Mr. and Mrs. Robert Metzler are your hosts on this family-operated dairy farm, with 40 milking cows and many young calves and heifers. Guests are welcome to watch the milking and explore the property, follow a scenic creek to a covered bridge, and visit a nearby automated chicken house with 60,000 chickens, where you can observe the eggs being gathered and packed by machine. The area also includes a number of quilt and handcraft shops and many small stores operated by Amish. The Metzlers' large, roomy house is more than 200 years old, built of stone with 15-inch-thick walls. There are four rooms for guests: two with two double beds, one with a double and a single bed, and one with one double bed. Two baths are shared, and there's a powder room on the first floor. Guests are invited to use the pleasant living room, too. And the Metzlers even provide entertainment—their son has put together a fascinating slide show, with two projectors, taped music and narrative, which portrays their Mennonite history. The show includes area farming scenes and some from Switzerland, where the Mennonite Church was founded. The same talented son has a woodshop on the premises in which he makes all kinds of furniture including Early American. Mrs. Metzler herself makes ceramics, and has quite a few items for sale. She's also a fine cook and serves guests a hearty breakfast of orange juice, eggs, pancakes, hot chocolate, coffee or tea, and delicious family-style dinners. Her specialties include home fries with cheese, and blueberry cobbler. Both meals are extra, not included in the rates.

Winding Glen Farm Tourist Home, Box 160, R-2, Christiana, PA 17509; (215) 593-5535. (Advance reservations are required; when you call or write you'll be given specific directions to the farm.) Rates are inexpensive, lower for children. Children are welcome; no pets, please. No smoking in the house. Parking is available. Open April 1 to the week before Thanksgiving.

Nolt Farm Guest Home. "Guests like our old (early 1800s) brick farmhouse, the big shady lawn, trees and swings," says Mrs. Grace Nolt of Mount Joy. She and her husband Amos operate the farm, more than 100 acres of rolling land, growing corn, wheat, barley and hay, and grazing beef cattle. There are also chickens, guineas and a friendly collie. The farmhouse, with its "nine over six" windows and small panes, Dutch latches, wide windowsills and transoms is a pleasure to explore. You'll also love the big farm kitchen with Mrs. Nolt's pretty flower arrangements, where breakfast is served. Your hostess offers her guests fruit or juice, eggs, French toast or pancakes, coffee, tea or milk and something freshly baked like coffeecake, zucchini bread, blueberry muffins or applecake. She'll also provide a hearty Pennsylvania Dutch dinner if requested; both breakfasts and dinners are extra. Mrs. Nolt really enjoys her guests and nowadays has time to chat with them as her four children are all married and live some distance away. The Nolts have ten grandchildren, too. There are four bedrooms for travelers: two doubles, one for four and another on the third floor suitable for four or five persons. One bath is shared, and there's a powder room on the ground floor. Guests may also use the family room, living room, porch and lawn. The farm is only seven blocks from Main Street in Mount Joy, for restaurants and shops. Nearby attractions include Hershey, Gettysburg and Amish Country; you'll find country markets, historical sites, flea markets, auctions and loads of other interesting things to see and do. You're also most welcome to attend worship services at the Nolts' Mennonite Church.

Nolt Farm Guest Home, S. Jacob Street Farm, Mount Joy, PA 17552; (717) 653-4192. (Mount Joy is west of Lancaster and southeast of Harrisburg. Come Rte. 283 West toward Harrisburg, get off at Mount Joy exit; cross the Chiques Creek Bridge and take second turn to the left, S. Jacob Street, and go straight in to the farm.) Rates are very inexpensive, less for longer stays and for children. Children are welcome; pets are allowed if the owner takes full charge. No smoking, please. Plenty of parking is available. Open year-round.

Rocky Acre Guest Farm. Mr. and Mrs. Galen Benner invite travelers to come and stay awhile with them and their children at their family heirloom-filled 200-year-old stone farmhouse and modern dairy farm in Mount Joy. They promise a friendly welcome and a raft of things to do: enjoy an outdoor barbecue in the meadow by the creek, swim, wade, fish, or just wander through the fields and woods. There are swings, a sandbox and horse rides for youngsters, and guests of whatever age may help feed the calves or milk the cows. Indoors, for rainy days, a family room offers ping pong and air hockey. There are four guest bedrooms with double and single beds, and one with single beds, sharing a bath. The very modest rates include a hearty farmer's breakfast, served daily except on Sunday. Also available, and ideal for families, is a roomy efficiency with fully-equipped kitchen, living room, tiled bath and two bedrooms overlooking the creek and woodlands. The apartment sleeps seven. The Benners' beautiful Mennonite farm is close to both the Lancaster and Hershey areas for restaurants, shops and an array of interesting places to visit.

Rocky Acre Guest Farm, Box 900, RD 3, Mount Joy, PA 17552; (717) 653-4449. (From Rte. 30 West continue onto Rte. 283 West toward Harrisburg, then Rte. 230 West to Mount Joy. Immediately after the first traffic light turn left at "Y" onto Rte. 141 and continue to Pinkerton Road. Turn left on Pinkerton and go about three miles; Rocky Acre is the first farm on the left after you cross the stone arch bridge.) Rates are inexpensive. Children are welcome; no pets, please. There's plenty of parking. Open March–November.

Landis Farm Guest Home. In Manheim, just northeast of Mount Joy, Earl and Evelyn Landis also operate a large dairy farm to which they welcome guests. Their guest quarters are truly unique—a charming small stone house, more than 200 years old, with its original walk-in fireplace, polished wide plank floors and shuttered windows. No one had lived in the little house for about 100 years until the Landises restored it in 1976 and decided to use it as a guest house. Williamsburg colors have been used throughout, and a modern kitchen and bath have been neatly blended into the Colonial setting. It is also heated and air conditioned; all kitchen utensils, linen and bedding are furnished. Each of the two bedrooms has one double bed, and the living room sofa can be converted into a double bed; sleeping bags for youngsters are provided if needed. The house is perfect for a family or two couples traveling together, but is also usually available in its entirety for one couple alone. The Landises' own house, a handsome 200-year-old brick structure with pillared porch, has also been restored; a pretty, curving brick walk leads to both houses. The grounds are lovely, with shade trees and flowers, and the 75-acre farm offers all manner of things to do. Guests are invited to help milk cows, plow the fields, plant crops, make hay, or just relax on the lawn and play with the bashful Boston terrier. There are usually kittens to cuddle, too, and frisky calves to pet. Mrs. Landis does not serve food, but you can buy supplies at some of the marvelous farmers' markets to cook in the guest house kitchen, or dine out at one of the area restaurants. You'll need a car. The farm is in the heart of the Pennsylvania Dutch Country, and Hershey is only a half hour away.

Landis Farm Guest Home, RD 7, Manheim, PA 17545; (717) 898-7028. (Take Rte. 30 to Rte. 283 West to E. Petersburg-Landisville exit; turn on Rte. 722 North, toward E. Petersburg. Go to first crossroad, Colebrook Road, and turn left; after 2/10 mile turn left at the first road, Gochland Road, to the first farm—Landis Farm.) Rates are moderate, lower for longer stays. Please make reservations in advance. Children are welcome; no pets, please. Non-smokers and non-drinkers are preferred. There is plenty of parking available. Open year-round.

Tulpehocken Manor Inn and Plantation—House Tours and Overnight Lodging. Near Myerstown in Lebanon County, travelers will find a remarkable collection of historic houses and outbuildings—now a National Historic Site—situated on a 165-acre working farm. The plantation's history began with Christopher Ley, who arrived in Philadelphia in 1732 with a group of Palatine pilgrims. Ley soon moved west to a 1000-acre grant in the lush Tulpehocken valley. The first house erected on the property was the old cote, or sheep haus; Ley then constructed a one-story stone house (later expanded to two floors) and an arched barn. In 1769, Ley's son Michael, an officer in the Continental Army, built an eight-room stone house on the grounds. George Washington visited the house at least three times, once to rest and fish and later to inspect the locks for the Union Canal being constructed on the property. The Leys contributed heavily to the support of Washington's troops at Valley Forge. Michael Ley's son Christian had to sell the place in later years due to heavy financial losses; it was purchased by Conrad Loos in 1834. His daughter Elizabeth married Cyrus Sherk in 1845, and their daughter Eliza married Samuel Urich. The Uriches enlarged and altered the old Michael Ley house in the mid-1880s to the present 27-room Victorian manor house. The Urich family also acquired some of the neighboring Spangler land and two of its eighteenth-century houses—and all of these many structures now make up the Tulpehocken Manor Plantation. In 1960, the plantation was sold to Esther E. Nissly and James W. Henry, who also operate a cluster of historic houses in Lancaster.

The showcase house on the grounds is the beautifully-restored Michael Ley Mansion, with 13 rooms for guests. Two are on the ground floor. The spacious accommodations are furnished in Colonial and Victorian period pieces, including four-poster beds, Empire chests, marble-topped dressers, Windsor and Hitchcock chairs and a wealth of other treasures, enough to stock a good-sized museum. The hall baths, equally appealing with wicker furnishings, thick towels, lavender soap and some antique fixtures, are shared. A favorite gathering place for guests, according to Ms. Nissly, is the comfortable, informal living room with antiques, Oriental rugs and greenery.

Also offering guest facilities is the restored stone Christopher Ley House with group accommodations for up to 12 people. There are five bedrooms, 1½ baths, a dining-living room combination and a kitchen. In addition, the small four-room Cyrus Sherk Pipe Smoking Haus (built in 1886 for Eliza Urich's father to smoke his corncob pipe in) sleeps six persons. On the first floor are a kitchen, bath and living room-bedroom; the second floor, reached by a steep, narrow old staircase, has two bedrooms. For longer stays there are the Michael Spangler house with a large one-room efficiency attic apartment, and the George Spangler House with five guest apartments, each with its own kitchen and private bath.

Guests are urged to explore the wooded grounds and fascinating variety of buildings, including a 1777 stone smokehouse, the old bakehouse and barn, an elegant Victorian "necessary," greenhouse and bee house, cob house and much more. There are fishing streams and a paddock with horses for riding, too. Morning orange juice and coffee are included in the rates for Manor guests. Area restaurants offer country breakfasts, lunches and dinners; you'll need a car to reach them. Nearby attractions include farmers' markets, the Cornwall Furnace, historic Schaefferstown, and antiques and crafts shops. By the way, if you can't manage to actually stay at Tulpehocken Plantation do try to stop and take a tour; the Mansion is open to the public daily from 10–5.

Tulpehocken Manor Plantation, 650 West Lincoln Ave. (Rte. 422), Myerstown, PA 17067; (717) 866-4926 or 393-2311. (Two miles west of Myerstown and Rte. 501, on south side of Rte. 422; 18 miles east of Hershey and 25 miles north of Lancaster.) Rates are expensive. Children over 12 are welcome; no pets, please. No alcoholic beverages, no smoking, no food or drinks in rooms, house or on the premises, and no parties allowed. Guests may unload luggage at the house, then park car in adjacent parking area. Open year-round.

Spring House. Down in Pennsylvania's lovely southern York County, not far from the border of Maryland, there is a charming eighteenth-century stone house where travelers will find warm hospitality and bed and breakfast. Spring House, built in 1798 by a Pennsylvania legislator, is made of local fieldstone with a slate roof. Ray Constance Hearne, present owner (and historic preservationist), has carefully restored the old structure to its early appearance. She has three double rooms for guests, one with a wood stove; two baths are shared. The rooms are delightfully decorated with country antiques including spool beds and ladderback chairs, handmade quilts, Oriental rugs, delicate old (and some new) stenciling and many original paintings of the area. Guests are invited to enjoy the house's large parlor/dining room, too, furnished with antiques and offering both a fireplace and wood stove. In addition, there's a pleasant porch that overlooks the quaint eighteenth-century village of Muddy Creek Forks. Breakfast, included in the rates, is ample with such re-

Spring House

gional specialties as scrapple or sausage, pancakes, omelets or frittatas, homemade jellies and hot breads. Dinners may also occasionally be arranged. One of her special treats might be Apron Corn Fritters, so named because the corn is picked in the garden, placed in her apron, and rushed into the house for preparation. Another is French apple cake, served warm from the oven. Ray Hearne has lived here for 12 years and knows the region well. She recommends biking or hiking along the unpaved roads and unused railroad bed of the old Ma & Pa Railroad, a visit to the Indian Steps Museum or to some of the renowned local vineyards. You'll want to explore the village, which looks much as it did a century ago with clapboard mill buildings, creamery and country Gothic store. And Muddy Creek, one of Pennsylvania's scenic rivers, offers trout fishing, swimming and canoeing. Historic York is only 30 minutes away, and Lancaster is a 45-minute drive. Your hostess will be pleased to suggest some good restaurants in the area as well.

Spring House, Muddy Creek Forks, Airville, PA 17302; (717) 927-6906. (About 11 miles from Red Lion, 18 from York and 35 from Lancaster. When you call to make a reservation, Ms. Hearne will give you exact directions to the house.) Rates are moderate, lower for longer stays, half price for small children and no charge for infants. Note: the rooms are not large enough to sleep extra children unless very young, so another room would be needed. Children are welcome; no pets, please, and no smoking. Parking is available. Open year-round.

Twin Elms. Located in historic Gettysburg, Estella M. Williams' 50-year-old guest house is shaded by two large elm trees and a variety of other greenery. The two-story brick structure offers two double rooms for travelers, one with two double beds. The clean, comfortable accommodations, sharing a bath, are air conditioned. Guests are welcome to use Mrs. Williams' living room, and—in warm weather—her front porch. No meals are served but restaurants are within walking distance, and your hostess will gladly give you directions. She'll also tell you how to reach the area's many points of interest including Gettysburg Battlefield and other historic sites, public pools, the beaches at Laurel and Fuller Lakes and, in winter, skiing facilities.

Twin Elms, 228 Buford Ave., Gettysburg, PA 17325; (717) 334-4520. (Five blocks west of town center on Rte. 30.) Rates are inexpensive, lower for longer stays. Children are welcome; no pets, please. Parking is available at the house. Open year-round.

Bentons' Lodging. James T. and Virginia Benton welcome travelers to their Gettysburg home, a neat brick house with a nice front porch. The second floor of the house, reserved for guests, has two rooms with one double bed in each, one room with twin beds, and a family room (two adjoining rooms each with a double bed). Baths with shower are shared. Guests may also share the Bentons' living room and porch. No meals are served, but there are plenty of restaurants nearby. All of Gettysburg's attractions are nearby, too—the Battlefield, President Eisenhower's farm, General Lee's Headquarters and much more.

Bentons' Lodging, 33 East Lincoln Ave., Gettysburg, PA 17325; (717) 334-2442. (Three blocks from Circle going north on Rte. 34; turn right at traffic light on Old Rte. 15; Bentons' is third house on right.) Rates are inexpensive. Children are welcome; small pets are accepted. There is parking both on and off the street. Open year-round.

Swinns Lodging. Also in Gettysburg is Swinns Lodging, owned by Clarence M. Swinn Sr. For guests there are eight air-conditioned double, twin-bedded and family rooms. Three baths, two with shower, are shared. The rooms also include TV and running hot and cold water. No food is served, but restaurants and shops are within walking distance. And best of all, you can walk directly from the house onto historic Gettysburg Battlefield.

Swinns Lodging, 31 E. Lincoln Ave., Gettysburg, PA 17325; (717) 334-5255. (Three blocks north of center of town; at first traffic light turn right. Swinns is two houses down—you'll see the sign.) Rates are inexpensive, lower during winter months and for longer stays. Children and pets are welcome. Free parking is available in Mr. Swinn's private lot across the street. Open year-round.

NORTHCENTRAL REGION

Pennsylvania's beautiful northcentral region is one of rugged mountain wilderness, canyon-like gorges and mysterious caves. Hunting and fishing are excellent throughout the area, as are hiking, camping and canoeing. The Allegheny National Forest, which extends into New York State, begins in McKean County to the west. Pennsylvania's own "Grand Canyon" is located near Wellsboro, in Tioga County. An awesome sight, the canyon—formed by the Pine Creek River—is fifty miles long and 1000 feet deep. In Centre County travelers can explore Penn's Cave, a unique all-water cavern, and Woodward Cave, more than 400 million years old.

Northcentral Pennsylvania also boasts Punxsutawney Phil, the nationally-famed groundhog who makes his annual weather prediction each February 2 from Gobler Knob in the Jefferson County town of Punxsutawney. In the same vein but not so much fun (a very personal opinion) is Cross Fork's Annual Snake Hunt. Each June intrepid contestants fan out through mountainous Potter County searching for rattlers and copperheads. Prizes are awarded for the longest and shortest snake, the snake with the most rattles, and the largest snake. More appealing seasonal flings are the Pennsylvania State Laurel Festival, held in Wellsboro each June, and Clinton County's Flaming Foliage Festival in October.

Woodward Inn. Betty E. (Mrs. Richard) Miltenberger would like all of her guests to treat her home in Centre County as if it were their own. Few of us, however, live in houses listed as National Historic sites! The thought is heartwarming, at any rate, and Mrs. Miltenberger's cordial welcome certainly makes visitors feel at home. The comfortable old limestone house with its long, tree-shaded porch has been in your hostess's family since her grandparents bought it shortly after it was built in 1814. Operated as an inn ever since, the house's ambiance is very much as it was in the early nineteenth century; the kitchen boasts an eight-foot cookstove which served many a stagecoach traveler stopping over on the way between State College and Mifflinburg. There are nine guest rooms, including eight doubles and one suitable for up to four persons, with two private and one semi-private baths. There's also a powder room on the ground floor. The cozy lobby and Mrs. Miltenberger's living room may be shared by guests, and the porch offers a plentiful supply of chairs for warm weather relaxing. A Continental breakfast of juice, homemade rolls, jelly, coffee, tea or cocoa is included in the rates. Mrs. Miltenberger will be pleased to recommend a restaurant or two for other meals and offer suggestions on places to see in the area. Swimming, hiking and picnicking are all available at two state parks minutes away by car, and there are three fascinating caves to explore: Penn's, Woodward and Indian Caverns.

Woodward Inn, Rte. 45, Woodward, PA 16882; (814) 349-8118. (Midway between Penn State University at State College and Bushnell University at Lewisburg.) Rates are inexpensive; one night free with seven-day stay. Children and pets are both welcome. Parking is available. Open March–December 15.

WESTERN PENNSYLVANIA

A region of great diversity and contrast, Western Pennsylvania stretches from the cosmopolitan city of Pittsburgh and the scenic Laurel Highlands in the south to the Allegheny National Forest and Lake Erie's sandy beaches in the north. Here visitors can enjoy year-round outdoor activities, regional festivals, museums and visits to historic sites including old forts and a working coal mine.

Pittsburgh, not too many years ago, was well down on the list of places most tourists wished to see. Known as the "Smoky City," it was a smog-polluted, ugly conglomeration of steel mills and urban decline. Due to a three-billion-dollar revitalization project following World War II, however, Pittsburgh is now an exciting, proud metropolis with clean air, some handsome modern architecture and only one remaining steel mill within the city limits.

Take the Incline, a hill-climbing trolley erected in 1877, up to the top of Mount Washington; there's a splendid view of the stunning rebuilt business district, the Golden Triangle, where the Allegheny and Monongahela Rivers meet to form the Ohio. At 36-acre Point State Park, Fort Pitt Museum offers exhibits on early Pittsburgh, Indian and frontier life, and old Fort Pitt's 1764 Block House may be explored. Pittsburgh's Carnegie Institute includes the Carnegie Museum of Natural History and Museum of Art; Phipps Conservatory in Schenley Park has constantly changing flower displays, and the Frick Art Museum includes an outstanding collection of paintings and sculpture. You'll also enjoy a visit to the Pittsburgh Zoo and the Buhl Planetarium. The Pittsburgh Symphony performs from September to May, and in June the Three Rivers Arts Festival at Gateway Center presents a dazzling array of artists, sculptors and craftspeople, music, dance, drama and mime.

In the beautiful mountain region called the Laurel Highlands, east and south of Pittsburgh, travelers can explore Fort Necessity National Battlefield at Farmington. Here, in 1754, Colonial troops commanded by 22-year-old Lt. Col. George Washington were defeated in the opening battle of the French and Indian War. In Ohiopyle State Park, the Youghiogheny River plunges through a narrow gorge providing some of the wildest whitewater rafting in the country. And at Mill Run in Fayette County you can take a guided tour through Frank Lloyd Wright's masterpiece, Fallingwater. The remarkable house, designed in 1936 and now maintained by the Western Pennsylvania Conservancy, sits in the midst of a forest astride the falls of Bear Run. Its slabs of concrete are dramatically cantilevered over the water; the house, the rocky ledge, the trees and water all seem to blend into one.

In Cambria County to the northeast an interesting place to visit is the Johnstown Flood Museum, where the story of the city's many devastating floods is told. And you can ride the Inclined Plane Railway, in cable cars ascending a steep 72 percent grade. (These inclined planes were first developed to haul heavy goods—even canal boats—up and down Pennsylvania's otherwise impassable mountains.) At the Seldom Seen Valley Mine, a working coal mine in St. Boniface, plastic-domed cars take visitors for a half-mile ride inside the mountain. Bedford County below has Old Bedford Village, a re-created eighteenth-century hamlet with some 40 buildings manned by working craftspeople and a fine collection of handmade crafts for sale. Somerset County to the west is the scene of the Annual Pennsylvania Maple Festival and Old Time Fiddlers Jamboree, both held in March; during Fort Ligonier Days in October there's a reenactment of the unsuccessful French and Indian attack on the British. In September, Washington and Greene Counties south of Pittsburgh—with 35 covered bridges—host a Covered Bridge Festival.

Pennsylvania's northwestern region includes Pithole City, a once famous nineteenth-century oil boom town in Titusville, and Fort LeBoeuf Museum in Waterford. The fort was built by the French in 1753 and later occupied by British and American forces; there is a rare statue of George Washington in a British uniform (as a Virginia militia major.) In the busy inland port city of Erie you can see the Flagship *Niagara,* the restored hull of Commodore Perry's famous brig. During the War of 1812, the ship was instrumental in the defeat of the British; it was sunk in Lake Erie's Misery Bay, raised and rebuilt in 1913. Nearby, Presque Isle State Park, a wooded seven-mile peninsula curving into Lake Erie, offers year-round sports including beach swimming, fishing, boating and hunting.

Das Tannen-Lied. Located in Crawford County south of Erie, Das Tannen-Lied ("The Singing Pines") is a delightful country haven for travelers and a fine place to use as a base for exploring the region. Mrs. Marian K. Duecker offers bed and breakfast, woodland and lake scenery, birds and animals to watch, and—in season—raspberries to pick. Her nice old house dates to 1872, built by a farmer who owned 800 surrounding acres of land. He also had three wives (one hopes not all at once) and 18 children; a local story goes that the farmer erected the cupola on top of the house so he could sit up there and watch his children doing the work! Although all the old barns and outbuildings are gone and most of the original acreage sold, the place still offers a welcome taste of country living.

The square house, to which a rear wing was added in 1950, is furnished in a combination of Victorian and Colonial styles. There are three rooms for guests, two with double beds and one with twin beds. Two baths are shared. All of the rooms are newly decorated and nicely furnished. At the front of the upstairs hall there's a cozy sitting area with well-filled bookcases, a fine place to read and rock. Downstairs, guests may use the parlor, living room and library—with floor-to-ceiling books of all types, a desk and comfortable chairs. In Mrs. Duecker's den is a fascinating collection of German World War I lead soldiers, made and painted in authentic colors by her late husband; do ask to see them.

Breakfast, which is included in the rates, varies from a "farm-type" meal to hot homemade blueberry muffins, fruit and coffee. Your hostess, who enjoys gourmet cooking, does all her own baking from scratch. She'll also create a superb dinner for guests, at extra cost, if arranged ahead of time. Breakfast is often served in the kitchen at a table in front of a large window where one can watch the many birds that come to eat at the feeders and sometimes a virtual parade of deer, rabbits, chipmunks and squirrels. An intriguing note: Mrs. Duecker says that while she and her husband were remodeling the kitchen, the ghost of the original owner made himself known—by the smell of pancakes cooking at 5 a.m.!

Behind the house are acres of woods for hiking; across the road in the front are Mrs. Duecker's large garden, vineyard and raspberry patch. Beyond is beautiful 12-mile-long Lake Pymatuning, part of a 15,000-acre state park. You'll find a private dock and places to sun or swim. You can also laze away the hours on the house's big front porch with a fine view of lake and boats. In addition to fishing, sailing, bicycling, picnicking and such, guests may play golf at a nine-hole course 1½ miles away.

Das Tannen-Lied, East Lake Road, Jamestown, PA 16134; (412) 932-5029. (Two miles north of Jamestown, about 22 miles north of I-80 and 16 miles west of I-79.) Rates are inexpensive. At least one week's advance reservation is required. Children are negotiable; youngsters over five are preferred. No pets, please; Mrs. Duecker has a Norwegian Elkhound. There is parking available. Open April–Nov. 1.

New Jersey

New Jersey is a small state, shaped vaguely like an off-centered hourglass. It is bounded on the west by the Delaware River, to the north and northeast by New York and the Hudson River, on the east by the Atlantic Ocean, and on the south by Delaware Bay.

In the early 1600s—when European settlement began in the region—New Jersey was considered part of New Netherland, and Dutch trading posts were established in Hudson County between 1614 and 1621. In 1643 several Swedish settlements were also founded in the territory, along the Delaware River. Sweden's attempt at colonizing the New World, however, was quickly thwarted by the more powerful Dutch. Then, in 1664, England seized the vast New Netherland territory and King Charles II granted it to his brother James, the Duke of York. James in turn, gave the land between the Hudson and Delaware Rivers to two court favorites, John Berkeley and Sir George Carteret. Carteret, who had previously governed the Isle of Jersey, named the colony New Jersey.

In 1674 the colony was divided into East and West Jersey. Berkeley sold his interest in the west to two English Quakers; later William Penn and several of his associates purchased both West and East Jersey. Due to difficulties in managing the colony, however, a royal governor was requested to take over its rule in 1702. But dissension between the colonists and British authority was growing, and in 1775 New Jersey joined the other colonies in the American Revolution.

A number of major battles were fought on New Jersey soil during the war and Morristown was for a time the site of Gen. George Washington's headquarters. Not all of New Jersey's citizens were in sympathy with the rebels, by any means, including its then governor, William Franklin. Despite the fact that he was Benjamin Franklin's son, William remained a staunch defender of the crown. In 1776 he was arrested; six years later he left New Jersey for England and never returned.

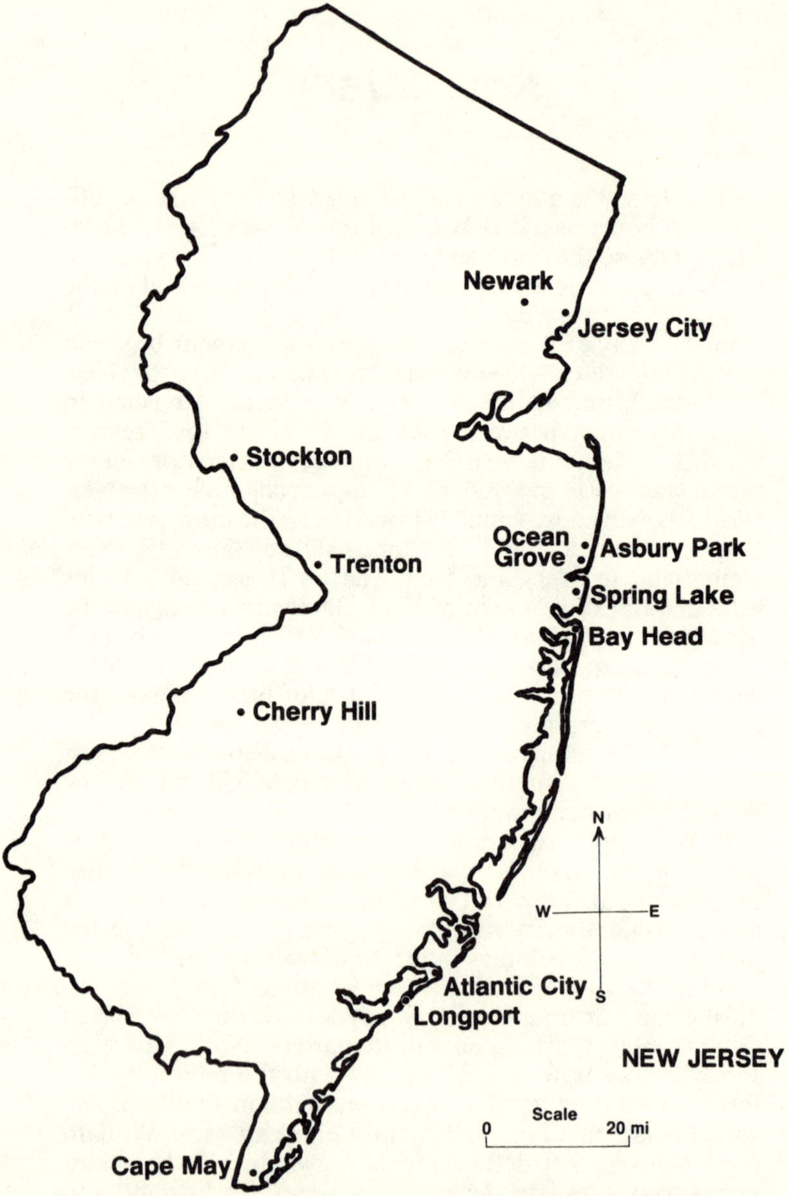
Newark
Jersey City
Stockton
Trenton
Ocean Grove
Asbury Park
Spring Lake
Bay Head
Cherry Hill
N
W
E
S
Atlantic City
Longport
NEW JERSEY
Scale
0
20 mi
Cape May

New Jersey's industrial growth began soon after the end of the Revolutionary War. Secretary of the Treasury Alexander Hamilton saw the possibility of utilizing the power of the Great Falls of the Passaic for industry; in 1791 he formed the Society for Establishing Useful Manufactures, choosing what is now Paterson as its site. Today New Jersey is one of the nation's leaders in manufacturing. Unfortunately, the state's heavy concentration—especially in the northeast—of unlovely industrial cities, factories and oil refineries has given it a less-than-enticing reputation. But there is much more to the state than malodorous petroleum smells and motley commercial sprawl. Trust me: New Jersey will surprise you!

Superb beaches stretch along the Atlantic shore for more than 100 miles, the coastline dotted with resorts ranging in character from flamboyant Atlantic City to Cape May, a Victorian Valentine of a seaside town. In the northwest the scenic Appalachian Highlands resemble New England with wooded hills, lakes and tumbling streams, and picturesque villages.

The central Delaware River region offers remnants of seventeenth- and eighteenth-century Swedish settlements; historic Burlington and Trenton; the attractive university town of Princeton, and the silent, mysterious reaches known as the Pine Barrens. In the south, even today, there are acres of farms growing fruits, vegetables and grain, and grazing cattle. And these are just a sampling of the state's unexpected treasures. All you need do to discover the "other" New Jersey is to head away from the busy expressways and explore. Because it is such a small, compact state you won't have to travel very far.

NORTHERN NEW JERSEY

In the seventeenth century there were two New Jerseys, East and West. In the state's northern portion that division is still there—not by actual boundaries, but certainly by appearance. The northeastern region, New Jersey's most densely populated, is often (and understandably) ignored by tourists. Yet within the area, if you're willing to brave heavy traffic and industry, are a goodly number of interesting sites to visit.

Fort Lee Historic Park at the George Washington Bridge,

for instance, offers reconstructed gun batteries, a Revolutionary War museum, and a panoramic view of the Hudson River and New York skyline. Nearby are the Palisades, impressive cliffs above the Hudson. Near Paterson to the west, the Great Falls Historic District includes old mills and the Great Falls of the Passaic, a roaring 70-foot cascade. Not far away you'll find Lambert Castle at Garrett Mountain Reservation. The 1893 stone structure, built by an immigrant millworker who became a wealthy silk manufacturer, is now a museum housing period furniture and other historic items. Another grand old home in the area is the Dey Mansion in Wayne, where George Washington headquartered in 1780. The beautifully restored Colonial house, with a charming herb garden, is furnished in period style.

In West Orange to the south the Edison National Historic Site is a fascinating place to explore. Thomas Alva Edison's laboratory and library are here, and a museum of his inventions. You may also tour the famed inventor's mansion, Glenmont. At Liberty State Park on the waterfront in Jersey City you'll discover a splendid view of the New York skyline, and ferries will take you out to the Statue of Liberty and Ellis Island. Historic Elizabeth, oldest English settlement in New Jersey, has a marvelous collection of pre-Revolutionary buildings ranging from the 1682 Bonnell House to Boxwood Hall, the Boudinot House, built in 1750. And if you chance to be in the area in mid-April, Newark's Branch Brook Park offers a glorious sight—3500 blooming cherry trees.

Over in New Jersey's northwestern region the traveler will discover a totally different world—a rolling landscape of hills, low mountains, crystal streams, state parks and more than 80 lakes. You might catch glimpses of deer or see a colorful fox hunt coursing cross-country looking like an old English print come to life. Picturesque, historic towns invite the visitor, and there are year-round sports activities of all kinds.

In the late 1700s Morristown's many forges provided ammunition for Gen. George Washington's troops, and Washington and his army spent two miserably cold winters here. In the 1600-acre Morristown National Historical Park you can visit the handsome Ford Mansion, built in 1774 by powdermill owner Col. Jacob Ford, Jr. Washington and his wife Martha lived in the house during the winter of 1779–80. Directly behind is the Museum, with Washington memorabilia and other intriguing items. The park also includes Fort Nonsense, constructed in 1777. It got its odd name many years later, after the local people had forgotten its real name and purpose. At Jockey Hollow, where the Continental Army camped in 1779–80 and 1781, visitors will find log huts typical of the Revolutionary era and signs indicating the locations of various brigades.

In Morristown itself the Schuyler-Hamilton House, built in 1760, may be toured. Macculloch Hall, a restored 1810 mansion, is also open to the public. Inside are period antiques, regional artifacts and an exhibit of Thomas Nast drawings. Nast, a nineteenth-century political cartoonist and one-time Morristown resident, introduced the Democratic Party donkey and Republican Party elephant; he also created a famous series of drawings of Santa Claus. At Frelinghuysen Arboretum, 127 acres of forest, fields and gardens, visitors may attend concerts in summertime. Also in Morristown is Speedwell Village, a cluster of nineteenth-century buildings including the Vail house and a gristmill. The village is the site of Samuel Morse's and co-inventor Alfred Vail's first public demonstration of the telegraph.

To see muskrats, turtles and frogs in their own natural marshy habitat, head for the Great Swamp National Wildlife Refuge south of Morristown. Chester, to the west, is a charming pre-Revolutionary town with antique shops and galleries; to the north you'll find Waterloo, a historic village on the Morris Canal, and Lake Hopatcong, largest of New Jersey's lakes with excellent swimming and fishing. Farther north, at Beemerville, youngsters will enjoy Space Farms with its large collection of wild animals and birds and a petting zoo. High Point State Park, way up at the top of the state, offers a grand view and is the highest point in New Jersey—at 1803 feet.

The Delaware Water Gap National Recreation Area in Warren County to the southwest provides swimming, canoeing, hiking, the historic Old Mine Road and Peters Valley, an old farming village now the center for local crafts. Flemington, in Hunterdon County farther south, offers a host of things to see and do. There is Turntable Junction, an old brickyard now encompassing more than 30 Colonial-style shops, the Black River & Western Railroad which still offers excursion rides on an old steam train, and Liberty Village, a re-created eighteenth-century village with craftspeople working at their trades. In addition, there are Fleming Castle, a Colonial house built in 1756, the Raggedy Ann Antique Doll and Toy Museum, and a number of glass and pottery factory outlets.

The Woolverton Inn. An elegant, antique-filled stone manor house, the Woolverton Inn is in Stockton, on the Delaware River. Ideal as a base for exploring northern and central New Jersey, the gracious bed and breakfast establishment is also just across the river from Pennsylvania's beautiful Bucks County. Flagstone patios and wide porches, including a graceful second-floor balcony, offer cool, restful places to sit and admire the grounds with their broad lawns and formal gardens. An old orchard invites roaming, and you can follow the river towpath. Sheep graze contentedly in a field behind the inn.

John Prall, a local quarry owner, built the house in 1793. The Italianate mansard roof and porches were added in 1876 by Maurice Woolverton, whose family held the property from 1850 to 1939; a later owner, Whitney North Seymour, planted the lovely gardens. George and Ann Hackl purchased Woolverton in 1972 and turned it into the inviting guest house it is today. Deborah Clark, innkeeper, is your friendly hostess.

Guest accommodations include seven doubles, one single, and a two-bedroom suite, sharing 4½ baths. The rooms are charmingly furnished with family antiques, including a variety of wonderful old beds, crocheted bedspreads, Oriental rugs and original oil paintings and prints. Guests are also wel-

The Woolverton Inn

come to enjoy the spacious formal living room with a baby grand piano, the well-stocked library with fireplace, dining rooms and country kitchen.

A Continental breakfast, included in the rates, consists of home-baked croissants or other hot breads, fresh orange juice, fruit in season, and coffee or tea. Afternoon tea with freshly-baked goodies is also included, and the kitchen refrigerator contains wine, cheese and fruit for late-evening snacks. As if all this attention to guests' comfort weren't enough, you'll find your beds turned down at night, and a foil-wrapped chocolate mint on the pillow.

Activities—in addition to exploring the grounds and porch-sitting—include playing croquet on the lawn or canoeing on the river, visiting a covered bridge not far away (the last remaining in New Jersey) and browsing through the area's many antique and craft shops. For lunch and dinner you'll find a raft of excellent restaurants in the region, three within walking distance.

The Woolverton Inn, Woolverton Road, R.D. 3, Box 233-A, Stockton, NJ 08559; (609) 397-0802. (From Rte. 202 South take Lambertville exit before Delaware River bridge and Rte. 29 North to Stockton, then Rte. 523 for 1/8 mile and left on Woolverton Road. The Inn is the second drive on the right.) Rates are expensive; weekday discount for stays over 5 days. American Express accepted. Children are welcome; no pets, please. Parking is available. Open year-round.

DELAWARE RIVER REGION/CENTRAL NEW JERSEY

History buffs will enjoy this attractive section of New Jersey, beginning with Washington Crossing State Park just northwest of Trenton. The park is in several sections on both sides of the Delaware River and commemorates George Washington's famous crossing on Christmas night, 1776. After Washington and his soldiers landed on the New Jersey side they marched to Trenton, where they surprised the unwary Hessians and captured the city. The McKonkey Ferry House, restored as a Colonial inn, is said to have sheltered Washington and some of his men on that fateful night.

Princeton, not far away, is the home of renowned Princeton University. The University Art Museum houses a fine collection of paintings and sculpture, and on display throughout the campus are sculptures by Picasso, Calder,

Moore, Noguchi and other noted artists. George Washington and his troops fought a major battle in Princeton in 1777, soundly defeating the British—and from June to November, 1783, the town served as the capital of the new nation. During that period the Second Continental Congress convened in the University's Nassau Hall. Other interesting places to visit are Princeton Cemetery where Aaron Burr and Grover Cleveland are buried, and Morven, built in 1701 by Richard Stockton, one of New Jersey's five signers of the Declaration of Independence. Now the official residence of the Governor of New Jersey, the house was briefly used by Cornwallis in 1776; Washington and Lafayette both visited Morven later on.

Trenton, New Jersey's capital city, was first settled in 1679. Visitors may explore the State Capitol Complex which includes an excellent museum and planetarium and the Old Barracks, constructed in 1758 and 1759, where British, Hessian and—later—Continental troops were quartered during the Revolution. The William Trent House, the city's oldest, is a superb example of Queen Anne architecture. The house was built in 1719 by Trenton's founder, and includes handsome period furnishings and a Colonial garden.

Joseph Bonaparte, Napoleon's brother and exiled king of Spain and Naples, settled for a time in the early 1800s in Bordentown, south of Trenton. The town is also famed for the invention by a couple of its citizens of "mechanical kegs" during the Revolutionary War. They intended to use the kegs—filled with gunpowder—to blow up the British fleet in Philadelphia. The idea was laudable but it didn't work; the ships were undamaged. Farther south is New Jersey's former capital, Burlington. Originally a Quaker settlement, the town has a number of historic homes and churches. A walking tour will take you past 33 sites dating from 1685 to 1829, some of them open to the public.

In Camden, travelers will find the Walt Whitman House, the poet's residence from 1884 to 1892, and the intriguing Campbell Museum exhibiting ladles and soup bowls dating back to 500 B.C. as well as eighteenth-century silver, pewter and porcelain. Swedesboro to the southwest has the Old Swedes Church, founded in 1703, and a seventeenth-century log cabin located on Schorn Farm outside town. Salem farther along is a treasure trove of eighteenth-century buildings, more than 60 of them. The 1754 Hancock House, which was used as a barracks during the Revolution, was attacked by British soldiers resulting in a bloody massacre. Visit the old Friends Burying Ground, too, and see the impressive 500-year-old Salem Oak.

Over to the east lie the Pine Barrens, an enormous tract of more than one million acres of scrub pine and oak trees, sand, swamps, golden-brown streams and rare wildflowers. From the highway the Barrens look unimpressive and uninviting, but travelers who are interested in some of the country's strangest folk culture will find them fascinating. The Pine Barrens have spawned many legends—of smugglers, pirates, a band of cutthroats known as the Pine Robbers, peculiar loners who lived deep in the forest, and even the "Jersey Devil," a cloven-hoofed creature said to be part bat, part kangaroo, part horse and part snake. Some tales add part dog—of varying breeds—to the list.

You can, if you wish, explore the deepest recesses of the Barrens by following its miles of sand roads, but it is not advised. Not only is it far too easy to get lost but some of the people in the Barrens—even today—do not welcome visitors. Do, however, take the time to visit Batsto, a restored bog iron village on the Mullica River, with a number of buildings to be explored including the ironmaster's mansion. The town was founded by a Swedish explorer named Mullica in the mid-1600s; its old iron works, established in 1766, supplied American munitions during the Revolutionary War. In 1874 much of the town burned, and soon after that Philadelphian Joseph Wharton bought the property as part of an estate that eventually covered nearly 100,000 acres. The State of New Jersey purchased the Wharton Tract in 1954; the Wharton State Forest is now one of four state parks in the Pine Barrens, offering fishing, hunting, canoeing and camping.

Balaban's. You'll find Rae Balaban's pleasant bed and breakfast guest house in Cherry Hill, next to Camden. There are only two rooms for guests—one single and one double—so reservations should be made well in advance. A sitting room upstairs and the downstairs family room are both available for guests' use. The large, comfortable, air-conditioned house, with terrace and beautifully landscaped gardens, is located in a fairly new custom home suburb. Decorated by both the owner and a designer, it is furnished with antiques, art and Oriental rugs. A Continental breakfast of rolls, bagels or toast, cold cereal and coffee is included in the rates. For a modest extra fee you may have a full breakfast, and your hostess specializes in delicious pancakes. For other meals, ask Mrs. Balaban's advice; you'll need a car to reach restaurants and shops but there are many in the area. Balaban's is close to many of New Jersey's most interesting attractions, one hour from Atlantic City and ocean beaches, and only 20 minutes from Philadelphia. Your hostess will also provide personal tours for a nominal fee.

Balaban's, 6 Willow Court, Cherry Hill, NJ 08003; (609) 428-6206. (Ask for specific directions when you call or write for reservations.) Rates are moderate. Children over 8 are welcome; no pets, please. No smoking upstairs. Parking is available at the house. Open from January to Thanksgiving.

THE NEW JERSEY SHORE

New Jersey's justly famous Atlantic shore has been luring summer vacationers for more than a century. But spring, autumn and even mid-winter are good times to visit, too—for then the seemingly endless miles of beaches are ideal for solitary walks along the sand sniffing the clean, brisk air, collecting shells, bird-watching or simply communing with the sea. The region's towns, both along the shore and inland, are also fun to visit. They vary widely in ambiance and size; you'll find small fishing villages, bustling resorts, historic seventeenth- and eighteenth-century settlements, and quaint seaside communities whose shady streets are lined with elaborately-ornamented Victorian houses. You'll also discover sandy barrier islands, old lighthouses, shipwrecks, pirate lore, wildlife sanctuaries, and even a Revolutionary War battleground.

The Atlantic Highlands, one of the highest points on the Atlantic seaboard between Maine and Florida, are a good place to begin a tour of New Jersey's shore region. At Navesink Twin Lights State Park there are an old Coast Guard Lifesaving Station, marine museum and, from one of the lights, a marvelous view of the region. Next head for Sandy Hook State Park jutting northward just below, with a lighthouse built in 1764 and a magnificent stand of holly trees. You might also spot all manner of waterfowl including geese, egrets and herons. Middletown, over to the west, was settled around 1665 and has a fine Dutch Colonial house that shouldn't be missed. Marlpit Hall on the Kings Highway was built in 1684; seven of its 13 rooms, furnished with lovely Dutch and English period pieces, are open to the public.

In the late 1800s, Long Branch to the south was one of the country's most popular (and wicked) resorts. Such notables as Diamond Jim Brady, Lillian Russell, Lillie Langtry and President Ulysses S. Grant frequented the place to enjoy its gambling palaces, horse racing at nearby Monmouth Park and other pleasures. Although its glory days have long since passed, Long Branch's three miles of beach and 800-foot fishing pier still attract their share of vacationers. Asbury Park a bit farther down is another well-known shore resort dating to the 1870s. A fine beach and three lakes, plus a boardwalk and large convention hall, provide a host of activities. Ocean Grove next door began in 1869 as a Methodist camp meeting ground. Both Asbury Park and Ocean Grove were originally created as refuges for pious folk who found the sinful ways of Long Branch intolerable, and even today Ocean Grove retains much of its nineteenth-century starchiness (and a great deal of Victorian charm.) A "dry" town, alcohol is banned although guests are free to bring their own for private consumption, and until as recently as 1979 the village's streets were closed to cars on Sunday.

One of the prettiest towns along the shore is Spring Lake. Founded by businessmen from Camden and Philadelphia, it is a rather posh little community with manicured lawns, tree-shaded streets and handsome, turn-of-the-century summer "cottages" adorned with broad porches. In addition to its excellent beach the town boasts a lovely spring-fed lake with swans, weeping willows and arched wooden bridges. Ten miles inland the Deserted Village of Allaire is great fun to explore. The site of a thriving iron works in the 1800s, the village now includes a number of restored buildings. In Freehold, a few miles northwest, the Monmouth Battlefield State Park commemorates a major engagement of the Revolutionary War. On a viciously hot day in June, 1778, George Washington's army defeated the British at the Battle of Monmouth; during the fight young Molly Hays carried water to the thirsty artillery and won her nickname of "Molly Pitcher." When her husband was wounded Molly stepped into the breach to swab and load cannon until the battle was over. Washington, in recognition of her bravery, enrolled her as a sergeant in the army's roster and Congress later voted her an annuity.

Back on the shore again you will come to Point Pleasant and Bay Head; from there drive on to Island Beach State Park, a splendid ten-mile stretch of sandy dunes and beaches. A narrow barrier island, the park is divided into three sections: one, at the top, for guided nature tours, the middle for swimming, and the bottom for surf-casting and a bird sanctuary. Just beyond lies Long Beach Island, 19 miles long, with Barnegat Lighthouse State Park, villages with the intriguing names of Loveladies and Ship Bottom, fabulous beaches, sailing and fishing.

Finding a place to stay along New Jersey's shore is a simple matter; accommodations are many and varied including a veritable galaxy of guest houses, many of which remain open year-round. The only difficulty you will have is choosing just the right location to suit your taste. Some of the towns along the coast are crowded and filled with activity, especially during the summer months; others are small, select and very quiet. If you are not familiar with the area, the best way to decide is to drive the length of the shore and explore; you will be certain to discover a community that appeals to you. The guest houses described here are a sampling of what you'll find along the way.

Ocean Breeze Guest House. Located in Asbury Park, Sandra R. Gill's Ocean Breeze is ideal for families. Her accommodations are all efficiencies with kitchenettes, so guests can prepare their own meals if they wish. The house, built around 1890 as a summer home, has been remodeled into individual units, each with its own private bath and entrance. A picket fence and windowboxes blooming with geraniums add charm to its exterior. There are five comfortable units in all, some two-room, others one. Three are on the ground floor. Each has been tastefully and individually decorated by Mrs. Gill with a variety of sleeping accommodations and some antiques including oak and mahogany pieces and a Jenny Lind spool bed. All include color TV and air conditioning, and all open onto porches to catch the sea breeze. Your cordial hostess provides complimentary breakfast pastries and the makings for coffee for guests' first-day stay. The house is within walking distance of restaurants and shops and is two blocks from the Boardwalk. Mrs. Gill also provides free beach passes for guests.

Ocean Breeze Guest House, 301 Third Ave., Box 230, Asbury Park, NJ 07712; (201) 774-6788. Rates are moderate, lower from Sept. 16 to June 14. Special rates are also available for weekly and monthly stays. Minimum stay is two days. Visa and MasterCard are accepted. Children and pets are welcome. Off-street parking is available. Open year-round.

The Cordova Hotel. Ocean Grove's turn-of-the-century appeal is personified in the almost-100-year-old Cordova. One of the town's best-known landmarks, the white four-story Victorian structure is now owned by Doris and Vlad Chernik; their son Eric is the manager. The European Cherniks are widely traveled, and they feel that their experience staying in every kind of hostelry from castles in Scotland to guest houses in Galilee have given them a rare understanding of the qualities most desired by visitors: a friendly atmosphere, old-fashioned hospitality, cleanliness and quiet, and reasonable rates. There are 20 rooms for guests, some with a view of the ocean, plus two efficiencies; most have double beds, four are singles and there are five twin-bedded rooms. Baths are shared; most rooms also have a wash basin. Guests are invited to gather in the spacious living room/lounge with antique oak furnishings, TV, radio and phonograph, books, card table and games. A patio outdoors has tables for barbecues, and there are three shaded porches. A Continental breakfast is included in the rates, with toast, muffins, coffee cake or bagels, orange juice, coffee, tea or hot chocolate. Also included is a Sunday barbecue, and a fully-equipped common kitchen and dining area are available for guests' use. Restaurants and shops are within walking distance; the beach is a block away. Ask the Cherniks for suggestions on local activities such as the daily events held in summer at Ocean Grove's famous 7000-seat Great Auditorium, bicycling, nearby Asbury Park, and—20 minutes away—the Garden State Art Center.

The Cordova Hotel, 26 Webb Ave., Ocean Grove, NJ 07756; (201) 774-3084. Rates are inexpensive; special rates are available for longer stays and for adjoining family rooms. Children are welcome; no pets, please, but there are kennels nearby. Smoking is permitted only on porches or in living room;

no noise after 11 p.m. Street parking is available. Open from May to September.

The Kenilworth. The Kenilworth, an exceedingly attractive Victorian frame structure built in 1883, is right on the oceanfront in Spring Lake. Formerly the Letchworth Hotel, the house was recently acquired by Lesley and Ron Mills. A British couple, Ivy and Ron Mason, are the innkeepers; the inn was renamed after Sir Walter Scott's *Kenilworth.* The immaculately-maintained house offers 25 rooms for guests: eight singles, eleven doubles and six triples. Seven have private baths; the others, with in-room running water, share seven more baths. One of the guest rooms is on the ground floor. Guests are invited to relax in the Kenilworth's two lounges and parlor or on the flower-bedecked porches with comfortable wicker furniture.

The owners' goal is to restore the century-old building to its original Victorian charm unspoiled by telephones, air conditioners or television in the bedrooms. There is, however, a color TV in the downstairs lounge. Since acquiring the house the Mills have been collecting period antiques, handmade quilts and other Victorian objects and have refurnished the lounges, hallways and several of the bedrooms. Breakfast, included in the rates, is served during the summer season and offers juices, fresh fruit, cold cereals, pastries, croissants, coffee or tea; on weekends there will also be quiche or perhaps French toast. Boxed lunches are available on request, and for special occasions such as New Year's Day, Easter, Mother's Day, Big Sea Day (June 15), Thanksgiving and Christmas, festive holiday buffets are offered. In June and September, cocktail receptions are held for guests on Sunday evenings. Other Kenilworth specials include midweek seniors packages in spring and fall, and massage-teaching and chamber music get-togethers.

There's a large private beach for swimming and sunning; guests may also use a pool and tennis courts nearby. Fishing and boating are easily accessible, bicycles can be rented for a small fee, and the lengthy, non-commercial boardwalk is ideal for jogging or walking. The town, with restaurants and shops, is only a few blocks away.

The Kenilworth, 1505 Ocean Ave., Spring Lake, NJ 07762; (201) 449-5327. (From the Garden State Parkway Exit 98, go south on Rte. 34 to Allenwood Traffic Circle, head east on Allaire Road to Ocean Avenue and turn right; go 4½ blocks.) Rates are moderate to expensive with a 20 percent discount in June and September and a 50 percent discount during winter months. Children are welcome; quiet pets are allowed off season. Parking is available at the house. Open year-round (with limited occupancy off season.)

The Normandy Inn. Beautiful Spring Lake is sometimes called the "Irish Riviera" and the Normandy is owned, appropriately, by Frank and Marcia O'Keefe. It's a handsome old place built around 1888; a former governor of New Jersey lived here before it became a guest house. Today it is filled with antique furniture and many original drawings and paintings. Each room boasts a collection of books, and several rooms are notable for their fine examples of ornamental ceiling plasterwork. Two charming Victorian parlors are ideal for reading, writing or conversation, and there are wicker-furnitured porches for enjoying the ocean breezes. The Normandy has 20 air-conditioned, tastefully furnished rooms for guests: four singles, ten doubles, five triples and one suitable for four persons. Each room has either a full private bath or lavatory. A free washer and dryer are available for guests' use.

A truly lavish Irish breakfast is served, included in the rates, with a choice of juices or fruit, Irish oatmeal or cold cereal, eggs any style, French toast or pancakes, bacon, sausage or corned beef hash, and a selection of breads! For other meals, the O'Keefes will be delighted to recommend restaurants in the nearby village of Spring Lake and elsewhere in the area. The house is just half a block from the boardwalk and beach, and it is an easy drive to a number of the region's attractions such as Allaire State Park with its Deserted Village and old steam railroad, an amusement park, Belmar Marine Basin or—for horse racing—Monmouth Park. If you'd like to explore the area by bicycle, your hosts will arrange rentals.

The Normandy Inn, 21 Tuttle Ave., Spring Lake, NJ 07762; (201) 449-7172. Rates are expensive, lower from Labor Day to Memorial Day; special rates are available for children. Children and pets are welcome. There is free parking at the house. Open year-round.

Guest Houses

The Carriage House. Another of Spring Lake's delightful Victorian structures, the Carriage House was built around the turn of the century. Your genial hosts, Marie and Tom Bradley, moved to Spring Lake from Long Island several years ago and thoroughly enjoy welcoming guests to their home. They have eight spacious, airy rooms for travelers including one single, four doubles and three extra-large rooms which can accommodate up to five people. Two rooms share a bath; the others have private baths. All of the guest quarters are air-conditioned, although it's seldom needed: several rooms have five windows and the others have three for fresh air ventilation. There is a pleasant living room with color TV, and a big, shaded front porch; the lovely grounds offer flowers, trees and umbrella tables. The Bradleys work hard at improving the house each year and keep it in pristine condition. They have painted, added new carpeting and furniture—and justifiably pride themselves on offering comfortable, sparklingly clean accommodations for their guests. Complimentary coffee is served every morning; on weekends there will be Danish pastries, too. A refrigerator on each floor is available for keeping snacks and soft drinks. Spring Lake's excellent restaurants and attractive boutiques are not far away and the ocean is only a two-block walk.

The Carriage House, 208 Jersey Ave., Spring Lake, NJ 07762; (201) 449-1332. Rates are moderate, lower from Oct. 1 to May 15 and for full-season stay (June 15–Sept. 15.) Children are welcome; no pets, please. Parking is available. Open year-round.

Moulton Guest House. The Moulton Guest House in Spring Lake is owned by Anne and Norman Goss. The three-story frame structure, built in 1915, sits on a terrace surrounded by spacious grounds. As is the norm in Spring Lake, it has a large front porch with wicker furniture for taking the air. Your hosts have eight twin-bedded rooms for guests, including three singles and five doubles, with three private baths and two semi-private. Extra cots are also available. All of the guest rooms have at least two windows for ventilation. Downstairs, guests are welcome to make themselves at home in the living room and TV room, and breakfast is served in the dining room. Included in the rates, breakfast consists of juice, cereal, toast or sometimes coffee cake, coffee or tea. The beach is two blocks away and all of the town's many attractions are easily accessible: swimming, tennis, golf, the boardwalk, shops and restaurants. Allaire State Park is about five minutes away by car.

Moulton Guest House, 120 Ludlow Ave., Spring Lake, NJ 07762; (201) 449-5177. Rates are moderate, lower from May to the end of June and for small children. Children are welcome; no pets, please. No eating is allowed in rooms except for snacks such as fruit, soda, etc. Parking is available in the rear. Open May–September.

The Billows. A number of Spring Lake's splendid old houses and hotels were originally constructed for the 1876 Centennial Exposition in Philadelphia and later transported to this pretty New Jersey seaside town. The Billows is one of these, designed as the Exposition's Portuguese Pavilion. Warren and Judy Gardner, your hosts, offer 12 rooms for guests in their unusual house: two singles, nine doubles and one triple. Most are air conditioned; seven have private baths and the others share two baths. Four of the rooms are on the ground floor. There are also, for guests' use, a living room, TV room and lobby. A Continental breakfast is included in the rates. Restaurants and shops are within walking distance as are the ocean and salt water pools for swimming; tennis and golf are easily accessible.

The Billows, 205 Atlantic Ave., Spring Lake, NJ 07762; (201) 449-7307. Rates are expensive, lower from October–May and for children. Children and pets are welcome. A private lot is available for parking. Open year-round.

The Colonial Ocean House. Located one block from Spring Lake's beautiful beach, the large Ocean House is more a hotel than a typical small guest house, but it offers the same kind of informal, friendly hospitality. The 106-year-old structure has 42 comfortably furnished rooms including 12 singles, 28 doubles and two triples with 15 private baths and eight shared baths. One of the rooms, with bath, is on the ground floor. The three-story structure with spacious wraparound porch boasts a marvelous spiral staircase brought from the 1876 Philadelphia Exposition. Some other noteworthy features are the building's high ceilings, louvered summer doors (there are also solid inside doors) on all guest rooms, and the original ceiling fans in the dining room. Your hosts are Bill and Jill Mitchell; they acquired the Ocean

House in 1979. The Taylors, whose family earlier owned it for 50 years, told them of a resident "ghost." She is—or was—Cora, a one-time chambermaid in the 1950s, and supposedly she may sometimes be heard roaming the floors. If you should chance to run into her, be nice: good help is hard to find nowadays.

The Mitchells encourage their guests to use the living room and sitting room (both with TV), a large dining room and the spacious porch. A Continental breakfast and evening tea or coffee are included in the rates. No other food is served but your hosts will gladly direct you to some of Spring Lake's fine restaurants. The boardwalk and lake are only a block away; the town's shopping district is five blocks away. There are amusement piers within a few miles, as well as may historic buildings and parks, picnic areas and Monmouth Park Race Track.

The Colonial Ocean House, 102 Sussex Ave., Spring Lake NJ 07762; (201) 449-9090. Rates are expensive, lower in June and September; reduced rates are also available for four-night stays (Monday–Thursday) and for children. Visa and MasterCard are accepted. Children are welcome; no pets, please. There is plenty of parking. Open approximately from the end of May to the middle of September.

Ashling Cottage. Also on Sussex Avenue in Spring Lake, Ashling Cottage is owned by Howard and Sheila Falk. Martha Flynn is the innkeeper. The Cottage was built in 1877 by George Hulett, who lived here with his wife Hannah until 1892. In later years the building was enlarged and became a boarding and guest house. Today there are 11 large, comfortable rooms for guests, all with queen-size beds. Two rooms share a bath; the others all have private baths. Two of the guest rooms, both with private baths, are on the ground floor. Each room is decorated individually and offers its own special appeal. Guests are welcome to enjoy the parlor, too, and the sunny glass-enclosed solarium where breakfast is served. Included in the rates, breakfast offers freshly-squeezed juice, homebaked pastries and excellent coffee. The Cottage, only a block from the beach, is just across from the town's scenic spring-fed lake.

Ashling Cottage, 106 Sussex Ave., Spring Lake, NJ 07762; (201) 449-3553. Rates are expensive, lower before Memorial Day and after Oct. 15. American Express, Visa and

MasterCard are accepted. Children are welcome; no pets, please. On-street parking is available. Open from March through December.

Conover's Bay Head Inn. Carl and Beverly Conover's comfortable guest house is in the quiet seaside village of Bay Head. It was built in 1912 as a summer cottage; framed drawings inside show the building's reconstruction in 1916 as an inn. Twelve double and triple rooms are available for guests in summer, six in winter; several have views of the water. Two of the rooms have private baths; the others share four baths. The Conovers have decorated each bedroom individually and imaginatively using antiques and country furnishings, handmade quilts, pillows and curtains, and lots of ruffles. The Geranium Room, for instance, is crisply inviting with white wicker, bright green rug, white wallpaper figured with geraniums and a geranium-red quilted spread and dust ruffle. The charming Spring Bouquet Room includes a canopy bed with off-white eyelet spread, canopy cover and curtains; the mini-print flowered wallpaper is enhanced by a larger-flowered fabric on the loveseat. Flowers, plants and books abound throughout the house.

Guests are cordially invited to share the small sitting room furnished in wicker and filled with hanging plants, and the living room with its beamed ceiling and large stone fireplace, cheerful with a crackling fire on cool days. There are three porches, shaded by blue-green awnings, for summertime rocking and on the grounds are a picnic area with umbrella tables and a garden for sunbathing. Breakfast, included in the rates, is served buffet-style in summer. You'll find juice, cereal, baked-that-morning muffins or coffee cake, coffee or tea—to be eaten in the sunny dining room or on a tray outdoors. On weekends and holidays your hostess will also whip up bacon and eggs for a small extra charge. During the cooler months a full breakfast is served on a tray in your room if you prefer.

Bay Head has a number of small specialty boutiques and antique shops for browsing, and a few restaurants; nearby Point Pleasant Beach offers amusements and a great many places to dine. The inn is a block from beach and bay; Allaire State Park with horses to ride, hiking trails and its fascinating restored village is only 20 minutes away by car.

Conover's Bay Head Inn, 646 Main Ave., Bay Head, NJ

08742; (201) 892-4664. (From the Garden State Parkway take Exit 98 to Rte. 34 to second circle; pick up Rte. 35 South and follow to Bay Head. The inn is 1½ blocks past the third traffic light.) Rates are moderate to expensive, lower from Feb.15–April 15 and Oct. 15–Dec. 15. And if you stay from Sunday to Sunday, one night is free. Children are accepted on a limited basis, in a suite with their parents during July and August only. No pets, please. There is parking available. Open from February 15 to December 15.

Bay Head Sands. Anne and Charles Copp are your hosts at Bay Head Sands. The house, built in the early 1900s, has the original fireplace and two stained glass windows. For guests there are five double and five triple bedrooms, two that can accommodate from four to seven people, and a girls' dorm. Four of the rooms have private baths; three more baths are shared. The decor is nautical, and each room is different; all except the dorm are air-conditioned and most overlook the ocean ½ block away. There are also a large living room with TV and an open porch for relaxing. A Continental breakfast of juice, toast, rolls or sweet buns, coffee, tea or cocoa is included in the rates. The boardwalk is less than a mile away and restaurants and shops are easily accessible.

Bay Head Sands, 2 Twilight Rd. (corner of Rte. 35), Bay Head, NJ 08742; (201) 899-7016. Rates are moderate, lower for longer stays and for families with children. Children are welcome; no pets, please. There is parking at the house. Open from Memorial Day weekend through Labor Day weekend.

SOUTHERN NEW JERSEY

Atlantic City/Cape May/Delaware Bay

Just beyond Long Beach Island and Great Bay, a drive along the New Jersey shore will lead you to Atlantic City, on Absecon Island. Much of the popular old resort city is distinctly seedy, but there are a number of reasons to pay a visit to the place: the prime one is simply to see it. A stroll or ride in a rolling chair along a section of the famous five-mile-long Boardwalk (America's first such ocean walkway) will provide the best introduction. People-watching is an enjoyable outdoor activity; there are also four large amusement piers, scads of souvenir shops and boutiques for browsing, salt water taffy in a multitude of flavors to buy, miles of sandy beach for swimming, and Atlantic City's newest and most popular lure—its collection of splashy casino-hotels for gambling and top-name entertainment. Not on the Boardwalk but not far away, Historic Gardners' Basin, a turn-of-the-century fishing village with shops, restaurants, an aquarium and old sailing vessels is fun to explore. And just because she's there, you really should pay a visit to Lucy, the Margate Elephant. Built in 1881, the recently-restored pachyderm, topped by an ornate howdah, stands as tall as a six-story building. Lucy is made of nearly one million pieces of wood, covered by a tin skin.

Fifteen miles north of Atlantic City you'll find the Brigantine National Wildlife Refuge with a road that follows along the tops of dikes for easy viewing. Spring and fall are the peak migration periods for thousands of geese, ducks and other waterfowl. Smithville, not far away, is a really delightful re-creation of an old South Jersey crossroads village. Its more than 30 restored historic buildings, brought to the site from all over the state, include homes, churches, a cobbler's shop and bakeshop, a mill and a wonderful old stagecoach inn. Visitors may climb aboard a rare nineteenth-century oyster boat called a "bugeye," ride on a horse-drawn trolley or a swanboat, watch authentically-dressed craftspeople at their work, and dine at the inn.

The Winchester House. If you are planning to visit Atlantic City and don't care to stay in the city itself, Winchester House offers a pleasant alternative. Located in Longport on Absecon Island just three miles south of Atlantic City, James and Mary Jane Kelly's 76-year-old house is cooled by ocean and bay breezes and is only 400 feet from the beach. For guests there are ten airy rooms including one single and nine doubles, all with private baths and water views. Winchester House, renovated in 1978 with all new furnishings, includes a large lobby and wraparound porches for relaxing and admiring the magnificent sunsets over Great Egg Harbor Bay. Complimentary coffee and tea are offered in the morning. The Kellys will be pleased to suggest some good restaurants in the area and will tell you about the variety of activities available nearby including swimming, crabbing, fishing, boating, bicycling, golf and horseback riding. The public bus to Atlantic City (the recommended way to get in and out of town) leaves every 20 minutes or so one block from the house. And across the bay you'll find Ocean City with its interesting Victorian architecture and Historical Museum.

The Winchester House, 1 South 24th Ave., Longport, NJ 08403; (609) 822-0623. Rates are expensive. Children and small pets are welcome. There is parking available. Open April 1 to October 15.

From Atlantic City, travelers have a choice of routes to follow south to Cape May. Straightest and fastest is the Garden State Parkway; Rte. 9 (which parallels the parkway) offers a much more leisurely drive, passing through rural countryside, small Colonial towns and villages. And if you haven't yet had your fill of seashore, a third option is to take the 40-mile-long Ocean Drive, called "The Flight of the Gulls." The road leads over a chain of sea islands, linked by six toll bridges, through more than a dozen beach resort towns; bays and marsh meadows lie to the west, the Atlantic to the east. Unfortunately, little of the ocean or marshes can be seen along the drive as the view is cut off by beach houses and seawalls; the best views are from the bridges. On the way you'll come to Stone Harbor and its drive-through bird sanctuary where herons, ibises and egrets spend their summers. Farther on are the Wildwoods, three neighboring beach resorts offering a multitude of family activities and amusements.

The entire town of Cape May, down at New Jersey's southeasternmost tip, is now a National Historic Landmark. You will, if you've driven the length of the coast, have seen many towns boasting fancy Victorian architecture . . . but Cape May outdoes them all. Named for Cornelius Jacobsen Mey, a representative of the Dutch West India Company who explored the area in 1620, the town has been attracting summer visitors since the late 1700s. Half a dozen presidents have vacationed here, and in the 1800s scores of wealthy Philadelphians voyaged to Cape May daily on summertime steamboat excursions.

A number of fires in the mid- and late-nineteenth century destroyed many of the old hotels and summer cottages, and on their sites arose a "new" Cape May—with a collection of extravagantly gingerbread-laced Victorian structures that is unequalled anywhere else. Many of the buildings have been painstakingly restored in recent years, and today the town's whimsical charm is greater than ever. A walking or trolley tour is an excellent way to see some of the more than 600 architectural treasures; note particularly the historic Chalfonte Hotel, built in 1876 and a survivor of the Great Fire of 1878, the Emlen Physick House and Estate with a museum of Victoriana and the Pink House, a frothy fantasy that resembles a strawberry soda.

In addition to its remarkable Victorian heritage, Cape May offers beaches for swimming, surfing and fishing, the beach Promenade for strolling, and the old downtown shopping district, now restored and turned into an inviting walking mall. And for those wise travelers who appreciate the old-fashioned charm of guest house lodgings, Cape May presents a truly splendid array of choices. Some are open year-round, and many offer not only bed and breakfast but afternoon tea as well. It is wise, however, to make reservations well in advance, especially in the peak summer season when the delightful—and very individual—houses are often booked to capacity. If you don't much care for crowds, try to come in the spring or fall, or even in the winter; local residents feel that those seasons are the best of all.

The Mainstay Inn. One of Cape May's best-known and most elegant guest houses is the Mainstay, owned by Tom and Sue Carroll. The beautifully-proportioned building with gracefully-ornamented verandas and ornate cupola is a joy just to look at, let alone stay overnight in! Built in 1872 as an exclusive clubhouse-casino for a pair of Mississippi gamblers, the handsome structure included 14-foot ceilings, elaborate chandeliers, 64 tall windows, 12-foot mirrors and the finest of furnishings. The Carrolls, while adding some modern conveniences, have carefully preserved the splendid Victorian ambiance of the place. Now a bed and breakfast inn, the Mainstay offers 11 double rooms for guests—some in the main house and others in an adjacent (and equally charming) 1870s-period summer cottage. Seven rooms have private baths and four share two full baths. All of the rooms are furnished with a grand collection of Victorian antiques, many of which are original to the house. A large, handsome drawing room and small parlor are also available for guests' use, as are the broad porches with high-back rockers, and a lovely garden for sunbathing. Guests are invited to climb up to the cupola, too, via a ladder from the upstairs hall, for a fine view of the ocean.

The Mainstay Inn

A sumptuous breakfast, included in the rates, is served in the French-windowed formal dining room in chilly weather, outdoors on the pillared veranda in summertime. You'll be offered fruit, cereal, freshly-baked coffee cake, perhaps homemade quiche or delectable fruit crepes, and coffee or tea. Also included is afternoon tea, featuring Sue Carroll's homemade cookies. Restaurants and shops are within walking distance of the Mainstay, the ocean and beaches are 1½ blocks away, and Cape May Point State Park is one mile away.

Even if you are not staying at the inn you're invited to come for a look at the ground floor—tours given at 4 p.m. on Saturdays, Sundays, Tuesdays, and Thursdays—and join the Carrolls and their house guests for tea, all for a modest fee.

The Mainstay Inn, 635 Columbia Ave., Cape May, NJ 08204; (609) 884-8690. Rates are expensive, one night free for a week's stay. Children over 12 are welcome; no pets, please. On-street parking is available. Open April 1–Nov. 1.

The Victorian Rose. The work of famed architect Stephen Decatur Button, who also designed the Mainstay, this Cape May Victorian structure was originally a tea room. In later years the building was turned into a school for girls and then a guest house called the Southern Inn. Renamed the Victorian Rose by its current-day owners, Bob and Linda Mullock, the handsome old house has been beautifully restored to its original nineteenth-century charm. Antiques abound throughout; bedrooms are wallpapered with imported Victorian prints, and the baths boast huge clawfoot tubs. The Victorian Rose offers eight tastefully appointed guest rooms, six doubles and two with two single beds; four have private baths and four share a bath. In addition there are two suites with private baths and fully-equipped kitchens, accommodating up to four persons, and a cottage with private bath and large country kitchen suitable for four adults or a family of five.

Breakfast at the Victorian Rose is served in the dining room, where guests sit around a massive antique oak table (with ten planks!). Honeymooners may, if they wish, be served in bed. Typical morning offerings include fresh fruit salad, homemade quiche and cinnamon rolls. Breakfast, and afternoon tea appropriately served in the original tearoom, are both included in the rates. Guests are also invited to enjoy the house's restored parlor with antiques and a fireplace, and a third-floor reading lounge with an ocean view. Outdoors, the verandas that surround the house offer rocking chairs and hammocks for lazy relaxation. The Victorian Rose is two blocks from the ocean and three blocks from the restored Washington Street Mall with shops and restaurants.

The Victorian Rose, 715 Columbia Ave., Cape May, NJ 08204; (609) 884-2497. Rates are moderate to expensive, lower from October to May, and one day free for a seven-day stay. Children are welcome in suites or cottage; no pets, please. Parking is available on nearby streets. Open year-round.

The Brass Bed Victorian Guest House. As you might guess, brass beds are very much in evidence in John and Donna Dunwoody's delightful bed and breakfast establishment! Situated in the heart of Cape May's historic district, the house was built in 1872 as a summer retreat for Lewis Dannenbaum, a Philadelphia businessman. Originally the structure was divided into two buildings: the main house (still virtually unchanged today) and an outbuilding for summer kitchen and servants' quarters. At some point later the two units were joined. In 1930, the property was purchased by a Philadelphia doctor and opened to the public as the Woodbine Tourist Home, one of Cape May's earliest guest houses.

The Dunwoodys bought the place in 1980 and have since restored it, taking great care to preserve its host of intriguing architectural details and many of the original furnishings. There are eight tastefully decorated double bedrooms for guests, all with brass beds and other period furniture. Two rooms have private baths; the others share three baths. Downstairs, guests are invited to use the formal parlor with its Victorian settee and rocker, marble-topped rosewood table, and a marvelous turn-of-the-century Grafonola, a windup phonograph on which John Dunwoody will, if asked, play some of his large collection of old records. The dining room with fireplace, puzzles and games is notable for its gas and electric chandelier, called a gasolier, and huge Victorian table. For outdoor relaxing there's a splendid porch, with rockers and wicker chairs.

Breakfast, included in the rates, consists of juice, fresh fruit, choice of cereals, homemade baked goods, coffee or tea. And, Donna Dunwoody adds: "Lots of good conversation!" Your hostess also offers guests a refreshing glass of lemonade on warm afternoons. The Brass Bed is 2½ blocks from the beach, and two blocks from the Washington Street Mall. Ask the Dunwoodys to tell you more about the area and its attractions, including Cape Point State Park and Nature Preserve, and horseback riding on the bay beaches.

The Brass Bed, 719 Columbia Ave., Cape May, NJ 08204; (609) 884-8075. Rates are moderate to expensive, lower off season, and one night free for a seven-day stay. Children over 12 are welcome; no pets, please. Open year-round.

The Queen Victoria. Named in honor of the British monarch who loved the sea, the Queen Victoria celebrated its 100th anniversary in 1981. The comfortable old house is owned by Dane and Joan Wells, a friendly couple who very much

The Brass Bed Victorian Guest House

enjoy making their guests feel at home. Among the special extra touches guaranteed to please are fresh flowers in the rooms, turned-down beds and piles of thick, fluffy towels. Your hosts also provide a hearty country breakfast and afternoon tea, both included in the rates. Morning offerings might be freshly-squeezed juices, fruit, a crunchy homemade granola called "The Queen's Oats," Joan's own quiche or souffle, and homebaked breads or muffins. In the afternoons the traditional English tea features a "sweet" such as homemade shortbread, and a "savory," perhaps kipper pate or cucumber sandwiches.

The recently-restored Queen Victoria has 12 pleasant rooms for guests including one suitable for three persons and another that can accommodate four. Four rooms have private baths; eight have their own sinks and share a bath. One of the rooms is on the ground floor, and there is a downstairs powder room, with shower. All of the rooms are furnished with antiques in walnut, wicker, oak and pine; beds are covered with colorful handmade quilts. In warm weather, guests are invited to enjoy the house's porch and pretty garden. When the air is nippy you'll find a fire blazing away inside the parlor, furnished with the Wells's collection of interesting "mission" pieces and—sometimes—a friendly cat. The library offers well-filled shelves of books to read, including novels and many volumes on art, history and Victorian architecture.

The Wellses supply bicycles for guests to ride and will be delighted to suggest some interesting routes to follow, such as a tour of Cape May's historic houses. Other activities available nearby are golf, horseback riding, tennis and swimming. Cape May Point State Park offers nature trails and birdwatching, and the region's beaches are fun to walk along year-round.

The Queen Victoria, 102 Ocean St., Cape May, NJ 08204; (609) 884-8702. Rates are moderate to expensive, lower for weekday stays of more than one night from Columbus Day to Mother's Day, and there is a ten percent discount for weeklong stays. A small extra fee is charged for a child in a room. Visa and MasterCard are accepted when reservations are made through Western Union. Children are not encouraged, although well-behaved youngsters are occasionally accepted. Smoking is not permitted in guest rooms or dining room. No pets, please. In summer there are a few parking spaces avail-

able on the property for a nominal charge, and free parking is offered at a nearby lot; street parking is free the rest of the year. Open year-round.

Captain Mey's Inn. Captain Cornelius Mey, the seventeenth-century explorer for whom this delightful bed and breakfast inn is named, was Dutch. And a flavor of Holland is evident not only throughout the house where you'll find a host of Dutch artifacts and a superb collection of Delft Blue, but on the grounds where in spring some 1000 tulips bloom. The antique-filled inn, built around 1890, is now owned by Carin Feddermann and Milly LaCanfora. Their ten guest rooms (nine spacious doubles and one triple) are decorated in exquisite taste, furnished with handsome period pieces including a century-old Victorian walnut bed, marble-topped dressers and Empire sofas. Lacy curtains adorn the windows, the beds are covered with handmade quilts, and there are fresh-cut flowers in every room. Three of the rooms have private baths; others are semi-private or shared. Two of the guest rooms are on the ground floor.

The Delft Blue collection is in the Victorian sitting parlor, a cozy place to relax and read on cool or rainy days. Outdoors there is a pleasant veranda offering sun, shade and ocean breezes. Spectacular hydrangeas, for which your hostesses have won prizes, are on display during the summer months. Breakfast, included in the rates, consists of homemade breads and cakes, beach plum jelly, and—another Dutch touch—cheeses imported from Holland. Afternoon tea, or perhaps a tall glass of iced tea with fresh mint from the herb garden, is also included.

Captain Mey's Inn

The house is centrally located in Cape May's historic district, within easy walking distance of the beach and mall, tennis courts, movie and open-air theaters, and a deep-sea fishing marina. Not far away are Cape May County Park, historic Cold Spring Village and horseback riding facilities.

Captain Mey's Inn, 202 Ocean St., Cape May, NJ 08204; (609) 884-7793 or 884-9637. Rates are moderate to expensive, lower from Oct. 15 to Memorial Day, and there is a 10 percent discount for week-long stays. Visa and MasterCard are accepted. Children over 12 are welcome; no pets, please. Smokers are discouraged. Parking is available on a private lot right at the house. Open year-round.

The Gingerbread House. Another of the Cape May structures designed by famed Victorian architect Stephen Decatur Button, the Gingerbread House is one of eight identical houses known as the "Stockton Cottages" built in conjunction with the long-gone Stockton Hotel. Now listed on the National Register of Historic Places, the charming 1869 "cottage" has been carefully restored by owners Fred and Joan Echevarria. Six rooms are available for guests: five doubles and a master suite with two double beds, private bath and spacious private porch. Two of the rooms, located on the first floor, share a bath; on the third floor, three rooms share one bath. The cozy accommodations are decorated with oak furniture, bright colors, plants and photographs taken by your host. Some rooms also include ceiling paddle fans, reminiscent of the movie "Casablanca."

An interesting architectural feature is the etched half-moon glass window above the front double doors; its seashell theme may also be seen in the living and dining room ceiling medallions. The large living room also has an ornate ironwork fireplace, a cheerful focal point on cool days when a fire is lit. Outdoors, guests are invited to enjoy the breeze-cooled porch with wicker furniture, and the small front lawn where flowers bloom from spring to late fall. A Continental breakfast of juice, fresh fruit in season, homebaked coffee cake and coffee or tea is included in the rates. The house is centrally located, seven houses from the beach and two blocks from the mall. Free beach passes are included with a four or more nights' stay.

The Gingerbread House, 28 Gurney St., Cape May, NJ 08204; (609) 884-0211. Rates are expensive, lower from Sep-

tember to June. A 10 percent discount is offered in season for seven or more nights' stay; in the off season one night is free for a week's stay. Visa and MasterCard are accepted. Well-behaved children over five are welcome during the summer season. No pets, please. There is public parking nearby. Open year-round.

The Abbey. A standout even among Cape May's impressive and varied collection of Victorian structures, the Abbey is an architectural prize; measured drawings of the house are recorded in the Library of Congress. With its imposing 60-foot tower, Gothic arched windows and ruby glass, the building looks at first glance very much like a church (perhaps designed by Charles Addams!), but at second glance the viewer notices unchurchlike details such as the broad porch, a great deal of typical Victorian "gingerbread" fringe, and—atop the tower—an ornate railed gallery. For privacy, a fence has been installed around the property.

The Abbey, now owned by Jay and Marianne Schatz, was built in 1869 for John B. McCreary, a wealthy Pennsylvania coal baron and politician. His one-time summer retreat is today a comfortable bed and breakfast inn still maintaining its nineteenth-century elegance. The entire house is furnished with handsome Victoriana including marble-topped sideboards and dressers, tall walnut beds, tufted velvet sofas and chairs, 12-foot mirrors and electrified gas lights. There are seven double guest rooms, some accommodating three or four persons. Four of the rooms have private baths; three share a large tower bathroom which boasts a clawfoot tub, an old "water closet" complete with an overhead water tank and long pull chain, and a chandelier and Oriental rug. Guests also have full use of two parlors (one with a stunning fruitwood and mahogany harp), the dining room and the spacious, shaded veranda. During the spring and fall a full breakfast is provided; during the summer a Continental breakfast is served on the veranda, included in the rates.

Also included are late-afternoon refreshments. Jay Schatz, by the way, is an avid collector of all sorts of hats— and can be counted on to model them for guests, often at the convivial "community" breakfast get-together.

Tours of the Abbey's ground floor are available for Cape May visitors not staying at the inn; they are given at 5 p.m. on Thursdays, Saturdays and Sundays.

The Abbey

The Abbey, Columbia Avenue, and Gurney St., Cape May, NJ 08204; (609) 884-4506. Rates are expensive; 10 percent discount for a Sunday to Sunday stay. Children over 12 are welcome. No pets, please. (You may, according to your hosts, use theirs.) There is parking available at the house. Open April–November.

The Seventh Sister Guesthouse. Stephen Decatur Button, that busy nineteenth-century architect, must have accumulated almost as much money as his wealthy patrons considering the number of structures he designed in Cape May during the late 1800s. The Seventh Sister, another of his seaside creations, was built in 1888 as one of seven identical Renaissance Revival-style "cottages" called the Seven Sisters. Of particular appeal is the beautiful central circular staircase that joins the house's three floors. Your hosts, Bob and Jo-Anne Myers, offer guests six sunny rooms, two of which include both a double and single bed; baths are shared. The comfortable rooms, most with ocean views, are decorated with original and antique wicker furniture (part of your hosts' impressive collection), live plants, and a selection of Jo-Anne's own paintings. An inviting living room with player piano and ornate coal grate fireplace overlooks the ocean, as does the spacious awninged porch with more of the classic wicker. Guests will also enjoy the large side lawn where flowers bloom in season. No food is served but the house is within easy walking distance of a number of good restaurants, as well as Cape May's lengthy list of other attractions. And the beach is only 100 feet away.

Guest Houses

The Seventh Sister Guesthouse, 10 Jackson St., Cape May, NJ 08204; (609) 884-2280. Rates are moderate, lower from September to July; five percent discount for a week's stay. Well-behaved children over seven are welcome; no pets, please. Parking is available in a lot half a block from the house for a modest fee in July and August; off season, it's free. Open year-round.

The Barnard-Good House. Tom and Nan Hawkins are the friendly proprietors of the Barnard-Good House in Cape May. Built in 1869 of Second Empire architecture, the mansard-roofed structure stands behind a white picket fence and is fronted by a large, breeze-cooled veranda. Furnished throughout with antiques, the house features a delightful re-creation of the Victorian whimsy called a "Turkish Corner." Actually more Oriental than Turkish (the Victorians were fascinated with the Orient), these "corners" were designed as conversation pieces or as cozy niches for intimate chats. Set in a bay window in the dining room, Nan Hawkins' version, in shades of salmon and blue, includes a loveseat and a lady's and a gentleman's chair under a draped ceiling. Guests love it for reading and relaxing, and often have their pictures taken there. The house's accommodations include a suite with bedroom, sitting room and private bath, and five double rooms which share two full baths and a powder room. One of the bathrooms, restored to its earlier elegance, includes a copper tub, marble-topped sink and the original "elephant trunk" toilet. The tastefully appointed guest rooms are all wallpapered with Victorian reproductions. From April 1 to June 15 and from Sept. 15 to Nov. 1 the Hawkinses offer guests a full breakfast, included in the rates. There will be fruit, unusual juices (the strawberry is a house specialty), homebaked breads such as croissants or delicious filled brioche, stratas or crepes. During the summer season a Continental breakfast (also included) is served. Activities include porch-sitting, swimming in the ocean only two blocks away, bicycling (bikes provided by your hosts), horseback riding, sailing and historic tours.

The Barnard-Good House, 238 Perry St., Cape May, NJ 08204; (609) 884-5381. Rates are expensive; one night free with Sunday to Sunday stay. No children or pets, please. Free off-street parking is available. Open April 1–Nov. 1.

Windward House. Awning-shaded porches, flowering roses and hydrangeas, and salt-tanged air are all part of the charm of Cape May's Windward House. A fine example of the seaside architecture called Vernacular Victorian, developed around 1880, the shingled cottage is owned by Owen and Sandy Miller. Its many notable features include both upper and lower porches, a long central hall, a great deal of lovely stained and beveled glass, and handsome oak paneling. The house was built by a Philadelphia lawyer as a summer home for his family. Apparently a thoughtful man, and a generous fellow at that, the Victorian-era lawyer also had the house next door (No. 28) constructed for his mistress so she, too, could escape the hot Philadelphia summers.

The Millers have seven double rooms for guests, each done in a different style. All accommodate at least three persons and all except two on the third floor have private baths. Downstairs the Renaissance Room offers a handsome antique double bed, marble-topped side bureaus, a small sitting room and air conditioning. Second-floor quarters include the Cottage Room with curved glass windows, two double brass beds, and French doors opening onto a sunporch; the Chippendale Room also opening onto the porch; the Jenny Lind Room facing the ocean and featuring a Jenny Lind double bed and settee, and the very large Eastlake Room with windows on three sides, a Victorian double bed and two single beds. On the third floor are the Empire Room and the Golden Oak Suite, which share a bath. And possibly, a ghost! More than one guest, according to Sandy Miller, has reported seeing a "presence" wandering around in one of the top floor bedrooms. Don't fear the traditional clammy chill, however: a warm and happy feeling is said to accompany the presence, thought to be a young girl—perhaps one of the maids who once lived in this part of the house.

In addition to the individual rooms, an attractive apartment with two bedrooms, living room, bath, fully-equipped kitchen, private entrance, TV and air conditioning is available for weekly, monthly or season rentals.

Guests at Windward House are encouraged to use the large living room, the parlor with fireplace, and the wide wraparound front porch. The bathing beach is half a block away as is the Victorian mall; bicycling, surf- and deep-sea fishing and historic house tours are other popular activities available nearby. The Millers provide breakfast for their guests, included in the rates, except during July and August. You'll be offered juice, homemade breakfast buns or cake, coffee and tea. For a small extra charge your hostess will also supply snacks for an afternoon social hour.

Windward House, 24 Jackson St., Cape May, NJ 08204; (609) 884-3368. Rates are expensive, lower during April and after Oct. 15. There is a 5 percent discount for a stay of seven or more nights, and there are special discounts for clubs and groups. Children are welcome, but the Millers prefer youngsters to be well behaved, well controlled and sand free! No pets, please. Parking on the grounds is available for the apartment only, except occasionally off-season. Cape May does, however, have public lot parking for a reasonable fee. Open April–November, and occasionally at other times for groups by prior arrangement.

Holly House. Another of the seven identical Renaissance Revival cottages in Cape May known as the Seven Sisters, designed by Stephen D. Button, the 1891 Holly House is owned by Corinne and Bruce Mannix. The three-story structure, with a circular staircase rising all the way to the top floor, includes five airy guest rooms, all with comfortable beds. Two baths are shared. Guests are invited to enjoy the spacious living room with the original coal grate fireplace and a piano, or relax outdoors on the porch with rockers, swing and ocean view. No meals are served, but your hosts will be happy to suggest some good places to eat in the area. Restaurants, shops, a Victorian museum, marinas, tennis courts and Cape May's other historic houses are all within walking distance. The beach, for swimming or jogging, is less than a block away.

Holly House, 20 Jackson St., Cape May, NJ 08204; (609) 884-7365. Rates are moderate, lower in winter. Children over 3 are welcome; no pets, please. No parking is available at the house, but there is a public lot not far away. Open year-round.

The Hanson House. This attractive old house, built in 1892, offers a large, cool, wraparound porch, shade trees and flowers. The semi-Victorian structure, owned by Vera and Alfred Hanson, has five double rooms for guests and four baths. One of the rooms, with bath, is on the ground floor. The house is nicely furnished with family antiques. In addition to the porch, there is a pleasant living room with Victorian decor for guests to use. A full breakfast is included in the rates, and guests may help themselves to coffee or tea at other times of the day. Restaurants and shops are one block away.

The Hanson House, 111 Ocean St., Cape May, NJ 08204; (609) 884-8791. Rates are expensive, special rates are available for longer stays. Children are welcome; no pets, please. On-street parking is available. Open year-round.

If you're heading for Delaware next, take the ferry from Cape May; it's a great way to travel, a 70-minute voyage across the bay. Before you embark, however, there are a number of interesting places to visit in New Jersey not far from Cape May. Historic Cold Spring Village, just a few miles north, is a re-creation of a typical, nineteenth-century South Jersey village. The 13 restored buildings, some from the 1700s, include craft shops, a country store and the "Old Grange" restaurant. In the town of Fishing Creek to the east you will find the remarkable Hedge Gardens, a sight not to be missed. Some 175 hedge sculptures, created by one man over nearly half a century, include such wonders as the cruise ship *Queen Mary*, Santa Claus (with reindeer), a baseball game, Biblical scenes, and animals galore. Next, investigate Cape May Court House, the county seat. There are actually two court houses in the town, a modern one, and the Old Court House—which contains one of the country's oldest court rooms still in active use. The Cape May County Historical Museum, in the old Jonathan Holmes House, displays a collection of native Indian artifacts; Revolutionary, Civil and modern war relics; whaling implements and ship models, and Cape May "diamonds." Cape May County Park has a zoo, picnic grounds and summertime band concerts.

Heading north and then west around Delaware Bay, travelers will come to the aptly-named oystering village of Bivalve. Although the region's oystering industry is no longer as thriving as it once was, Bivalve still has some operating oyster shucking houses, a shellfish research center and an oyster museum. Farther west is Seabreeze in the Delaware Bay meadowlands, where you can observe muskrats and other wildlife. The river port of Greenwich just beyond is a charming old town, founded in 1675; its historic district includes a fine collection of eighteenth-century buildings. The 1730 Gibbon House is now headquarters for the Cumberland County Historical Society. Also of interest is the Tea Burning Monument which commemorates a little-known Colonial act of rebellion against the British. The incident took place in 1774, one year after the famous Boston Tea Party. Tea from a British brig had been unloaded at the house of a Greenwich Tory; 40 of the town's citizens, following the lead of their Boston counterparts, disguised themselves as "Indians" and raided the house for the tea which was then burned in a nearby field.

Bridgeton to the east has a zoo, a number of historic eighteenth-century structures and an Indian Museum; Millville offers Wheaton Village, a re-created 1888 glass town with a museum, glass-making demonstrations and craft shops. And Holly Farm just outside of Millville is the site of the largest collection of holly trees in the United States, with a holly museum housed in a nineteenth-century farmhouse.

The Osprey. Bird-watchers please take note: the Osprey, in the historic town of Cape May Court House, caters especially to birders and nature photography enthusiasts. The 150-year-old house, situated on 5½ acres of land, is owned by Joe and Ellen Lomax. They have three air-conditioned rooms for guests, two double and one triple, with three baths. Guests may also use a pleasant living room and library. The Lomaxes have made wildlife the theme of the house, and several of their regular guests are wildlife artists. Cape May County is noted for its bird-watching opportunities, and your hosts offer expert guidance to the region's natural areas. The house is only ten minutes from the beaches for swimming, sunning and fishing, and there is a fine 18-hole golf course just across the road. Cape May and its Victorian houses are 20 minutes away. The Osprey also makes a fine base from which to explore the rest of southern New Jersey. A hearty "Scandinavian" breakfast, included in the rates, is another specialty of the house with fruit, hard-boiled eggs, cheese, bread, and coffee or tea.

The Osprey, R.D. 1, Box 231, Cape May Court House, NJ 08210; (609) 465-9857. (On Rte. 9). Rates are moderate. Children are welcome; no pets, please. Parking is available at the house. Open year-round.

Delaware

Only 96 miles long and averaging 20 miles in width, Delaware is tinier than any other state except Rhode Island. Like Rhode Island, Delaware's topography is mostly flat; they are both part of the Atlantic coastal plain. Interestingly, the two also have a similar state bird—the chicken. Rhode Island's is the domestic Rhode Island Red; Delaware's is a fighting cock, the blue hen chicken. And historically, the country's two smallest states share a tradition of proud independence. Delaware was the first state to adopt the Constitution after the end of the Revolutionary War; Rhode Island was the last.

Henry Hudson, sailing on an exploratory voyage for the Dutch East India Company, discovered Delaware Bay in 1609. (The bay, the Delaware River and later the state of Delaware were named after Lord De La Warr, a seventeenth-century governor of Virginia.) In 1631 a group of 28 Dutchmen established a whaling community in the Delaware region, near the site of present-day Lewes. They called it Zwaanendael, Valley of the Swans. Unfortunately, the entire colony was massacred a few months later by Indians. Seven years later a band of Swedish colonists arrived, landing on the banks of a river in what is now Wilmington. They were led by Peter Minuit, who had earlier served as first director general of the Dutch New Netherland colony. The Swedish colony, named Fort Christina in honor of Sweden's young queen, became Delaware's first permanent settlement. During the next few years the Swedes founded several more settlements in the region, which they called New Sweden.

The Dutch, however, felt that the Delaware territory belonged to New Netherland, and in 1651 Peter Stuyvesant established Fort Casimir on the site of present-day New Castle. The Swedes attacked and captured the fort three years later—an unwise move, as Stuyvesant immediately retaliated by seizing control of New Sweden and placing it under Dutch rule. But Dutch supremacy lasted only until 1664,

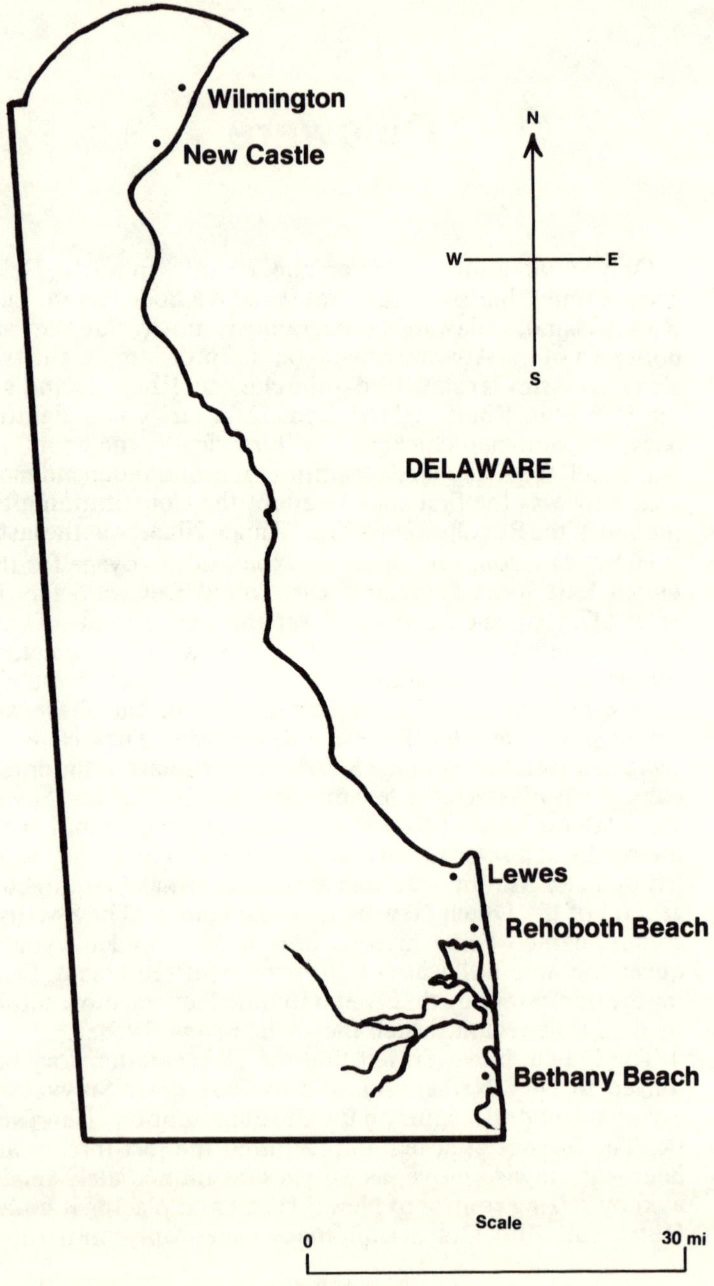

Wilmington
New Castle
N
W
E
S
DELAWARE
Lewes
Rehoboth Beach
Bethany Beach
Scale
0
30 mi

when the British—with no valid historic claim but greater military might—took over all of New Netherland, including Delaware.

England's King Charles II gave the huge territory to the Duke of York. In 1681, the Duke granted the Delaware portion to William Penn, as part of Pennsylvania. The land, called "The Three Lower Counties on the Delaware," was administered by Pennsylvania until 1704 when a separate legislature was established. In 1776, shortly after the start of the Revolutionary War, the Three Counties became "Delaware State." Although only one engagement was fought on Delaware soil during the war—at Cooch's Bridge near Newark—the state's crack volunteer regiments were widely renowned for their exceptional bravery in battle. Rooster fighting was a popular sport in those days and the Delaware troops soon became known as "The Blue Hen's Chickens," named after the particularly feisty variety of blue-feathered fowl they carried along with them as mascots.

The Du Pont family, so much a part of Delaware's history, arrived from France in the early 1800s as refugees from the French Revolution. Eleuthere Irenee du Pont de Nemours had studied with the famed French chemist and founder of modern chemistry, Antoine Lavoisier, who was, alas, guillotined by the Revolutionary tribunal in 1754. In 1802, Du Pont began to manufacture gunpowder in a mill near Wilmington, in northern Delaware's Brandywine Valley. By the middle of the nineteenth century the DuPont mills had become the largest manufacturers of gunpowder in the United States—and the family's fortunes were assured. Its mills supplied most of the explosives used in America's wars since the War of 1812. Today the DuPont corporation, now widely diversified, is the largest chemical company in the world. (Speaking of corporations, Delaware—because of its favorable corporation laws—is headquarters for more than 60,000 firms!)

A triangular chunk on the northeastern side of the lengthy Delmarva peninsula, Delaware is an odd state geographically. Bordered on the west and south by Maryland, it looks, on a map, as though it ought to belong to its larger neighbor. Indeed, for many years during the 1700s the boundaries were bitterly contested. Delaware's northern portion, which includes part of the lovely Brandywine Valley with its woods and rolling hills, curves in a small arc into Pennsylvania. The state's industrial might (including the vast DuPont enterprises) is mainly located here, in the Wilmington area. More than half of the state is used for farmland and raising livestock; chickens are the major cash crop. Bordered on the east by the Delaware River (which separates it from New Jersey), Delaware Bay and the Atlantic Ocean, the state also boasts a thriving fishing industry.

Because of its location, tucked far away from the major north-south arteries on the mainland, Delaware is often ignored by travelers. Even those who drive the length of the peninsula don't always stop to explore. They should, for diminutive Delaware offers vacationers a super-sized welcome, a delightful diversity of attractions, and a quiet charm all its own. Visitors will find fabulous gardens and mansions, fine museums, peaceful country roads, and a host of historic sites including enchanting, centuries-old towns. Along the coast are miles of tranquil marshland, soaring sand dunes and superb beaches. For sports enthusiasts there are excellent hunting, fishing, sailing and boating, canoeing, bicycling and hiking. Special events include spring and fall garden tours, arts festivals, antique shows, musical performances, and a host of Christmas carol and candlelight celebrations.

NORTHERN DELAWARE

We'll begin our tour of Delaware in Wilmington, in the north. The state's only sizeable city, Wilmington is sometimes called the "Chemical Capital of the World." In the 1600s, however, it was the site of Delaware's first permanent European settlement. Fort Christina Historical Park commemorates the landing of the Swedish (and some Norwegian) colonists on the banks of the Christina River in1638. The Swedes introduced the famous log cabin to America, and one of those simple structures is on view in the park. There's also a monument, sculpted by the Swedish artist Carl Milles. Nearby are the Hendrickson House, built in 1690 and now a museum with seventeenth- and eighteenth-century artifacts, and the Old Swedes Church. The latter, dating to 1698, is the oldest unaltered Protestant church in North America still holding regular services.

In Wilmington's Market Street Mall you'll find the 1798 Old Town Hall where the Historical Society of Delaware presents a fine display of furniture, decorative arts, glassware and silver, a wonderful doll's house, and a restored jail. Willingtown Square, also in the Mall, is an enclave of six historic eighteenth-century houses. And the restored Grand Opera House, a Neoclassic Revival-style building constructed by the Masons in 1871, is the home of Delaware's Center for the Performing Arts with a year-round schedule of musical and theatrical events.

Zoo fans will enjoy a visit to Brandywine Park and Zoo, situated on both sides of the Brandywine River. In spring the park, designed by Frederick Law Olmsted, boasts more than on hundred Japanese cherry trees in frothy bloom. The Delaware Art Museum, on Kentmere Parkway, includes a collection of 40 nineteenth-century pre-Raphaelite paintings and a room dedicated to the works of Howard Pyle, renowned illustrator and father of "The Brandywine School of Painting." Three miles northwest of Wilmington, the 200-acre Hagley Museum situated along the Brandywine River takes visitors back to the nineteenth-century beginnings of Brandywine Valley industry. Eleuthere du Pont's old stone powdermills are here, plus many other interesting restorations including a school house, a foreman's house of the 1870s, and an 1875 machine shop. An 1814 cotton spinning mill offers dioramas and working models; there are an operating waterwheel and water turbines, a stone quarry, and—high above the powder yards—Eleutherian Mills, du Pont's first residence, a lovely Georgian-style manor house built in 1803, with a French garden.

The Delaware Museum of Natural History not far away on Rte. 52 contains exhibits of mammals, birds and seashells. Youngsters, particularly, will enjoy a walk along a piece of Australia's Great Barrier Reef, and visiting a typical African watering hole. They'll also discover the largest egg in the world, the 27-pound Elephant Bird egg. The world-famous Winterthur (pronounced Wintertur) Museum and Gardens are a mile farther along on Rte. 52. The museum, housed in Henry Frances du Pont's family home, consists of more than 100 rooms containing the country's finest collection of decorative arts and furnishings from 1640 to 1840. Included are furniture, paintings, silver, ceramics, glass, textiles and prints, all displayed in appropriate settings such as a seventeenth-century room, a New England kitchen, an Empire bedroom or a Georgian dining room. The Main Museum may be viewed by reservation; a Sampler Tour of 18 rooms in the Washington Wing is available without reservation. The spectacular gardens, landscaped in the English style and covering more than 60 acres, contain thousands of species and varieties of plants. Winterthur is especially notable in the spring, when the azaleas bloom.

Nemours, the palatial estate of Alfred I. du Pont, is on Rockland Road off Rte. 141, and is open by reservation only, (302) 573-3333. Surrounded by 300 acres of formal French gardens, the Louis XVI-style chateau holds antique furniture, Oriental rugs, tapestries and paintings dating back to the fifteenth century. You'll find Rockwood, another impressive mansion, on Shipley Road off Rte. 95. A superb example of Rural Gothic architecture inspired by an English country house, Rockwood was built in 1851 by Joseph Shipley, a Quaker merchant. Now the Shipley-Bringhurst-Hargraves Museum, the house contains American, European and Oriental decorative arts from the eighteenth to the early twentieth century.

Over on the Pennsylvania side of the scenic Brandywine Valley, within a short drive from Wilmington, are two more notable attractions. Longwood Gardens in Kennett Square offer year-round flowers of every imaginable variety on the beautiful ground and in conservatories, plus fountain displays, concerts and plays. And in Chadds Ford, The Brandywine River Museum includes works by three generations of Wyeths, Howard Pyle and Maxfield Parrish.

Another short side trip will take you over to Newark, Delaware and Iron Hill Bicentennial Park. During the Revolution generals George Washington and Nathaniel Green and the Marquis de Lafayette observed British troop movements from Iron Hill. Nowadays there's a tower from which visitors can see four states—but nary a Redcoat, except in the imagination. Delaware's only Revolutionary War battle was fought near here in 1777, at Cooch's Bridge. At the foot of Iron Hill you'll find the Old Welsh Tract Church, still bearing the marks of a British cannonball.

Heading south from Wilmington travelers will come to New Castle, once a thriving river port and Colonial center of culture and commerce. Today, with its cobblestone alleys, gardens, brick walks and historic houses, New Castle is a quiet little town, bewitchingly pretty and architecturally fascinating. Peter Stuyvesant, governor of New Netherland, built Fort Casimir (no longer in existence) here in 1651 to establish Dutch influence in New Sweden. The Swedes captured the fort in 1654 but lost it again to the Dutch, who then named the town New Amstel. In 1664, when the British took over, New Amstel became New Castle. Except for a brief period during the Anglo-Dutch war, New Castle remained British until the Revolution.

In 1682 the Duke of York deeded the "Three Lower Counties on the Delaware" to Englishman William Penn as part of his Pennsylvania grant. Penn landed at New Castle a year later and took possession of the territory in a ceremony called the "Livery of Seizin'," in which the agents of the Duke of York presented him with symbolic "turf, twig, soil and water." The Delaware region was governed by Pennsylvania until 1704, when the citizens of the Three Counties demanded home rule, and New Castle became the first capital of Delaware. Following the Revolution, when Delaware became a state, the capital was moved to Dover. In the 1800s, Wilmington's emergence as an industrial and transportation center ended New Castle's growth—and left the town with its engaging, preserved-in-amber quality intact.

A walking tour will take you around the village green, said to have been laid out by Peter Stuyvesant himself, and along the waterfront Strand past a number of restored historic buildings. The Amstel House, built in 1730, is now a museum containing Colonial furnishings and arts; George Washington once attended a lively wedding party here. The Old Court House, dating to 1732, was the original Colonial capitol; the Old Dutch House (circa 1700 and thought to be the oldest dwelling in the state) is also a museum, with period furnishings. The 1804 Georgian-style George Read II House offers lovely antiques and a formal garden, and there are two eighteenth-century churches: the 1703 Imanuel-on-the-Green Episcopal Church, the site of Penn's quaint "Livery of Seizin'" ceremony, and the 1707 Presbyterian Church. In addition to the buildings usually open to the public, visitors may view even more of the town's private homes and gardens on "A Day in Old New Castle," held annually on the third Saturday in May.

The William Penn Guest House. Visitors to New Castle will be pleased to find this delightful establishment waiting for them! A brick farmhouse built in 1682, situated directly across from the Old Court House in the historic section of town, the William Penn is owned by Mr. and Mrs. Richard Burwell. Look for the small sign "Guests" outside. There are four airy, double guest bedrooms, decorated in simple, old-fashioned style with comfortable furnishings, including antiques and reproductions, and braided rugs on the old wide-planked floorboards. Two of the rooms have twin beds; two have double beds; two baths are shared. A pleasant, antique-filled living room is also usually available for guests to use. The Burwells do not serve meals, but will be happy to suggest some good restaurants within walking distance. The William Penn makes an ideal place to use as a base for exploring all of Delaware; the state is so small that all of its attractions are within a two-hour drive. But do make reservations well in advance.

The William Penn Guest House, 206 Delaware St., New Castle, DE 19720; (302) 328-7736. Rates are inexpensive. Older children are welcome (not crib-size); no pets, please. There is parking at the house. Open year-round.

CENTRAL DELAWARE

From New Castle, follow Rte. 9 south; Rte. 13 is wider and straighter, but Rte. 9 is more fun. Well off the beaten track, it passes through almost forgotten small coastal villages, and past long, lonely stretches of marshland. At Delaware City, if you're there on a summer weekend, you can take a boat out to Fort Delaware State Park on Pea Patch Island. The fort, built in 1859 for coastal defense, is being restored and has a museum with Civil War relics. The swampy, mosquito-ridden island was used as a prison camp during the Civil War; epidemics and other miseries killed some 2400 Confederate prisoners. Farther along, a short jog west of Rte. 9 leads to Odessa, once a busy grain-shipping center. The town, named for the Russian grain port on the Black Sea, has a number of beautifully-restored eighteenth-century houses, administered by Winterthur Museum. Smyrna, another exotically-named town just west of Rte. 9, also includes a cluster of historic buildings. On the coast to the east lies Bombay Hook National Wildlife Refuge through which you can drive, walk or bicycle.

Dover, a few miles south and west, has been Delaware's capital since 1777. Considered to be one of the handsomest of our state capitals, it has a richly historic core—a village green laid out by William Penn and a fine collection of eighteenth- and nineteenth-century structures. At the Visitor's Center on Federal Street you'll find maps and other helpful information, and guided walking tours for the Dover Heritage Trail start at the McDowell-Collins Store House on State Street. Don't miss the restored Old State House, built in 1792, The Hall of Records (which includes the royal charter granting the Delaware territory to James, Duke of York), and the Delaware State Museum. The museum consists of three buildings, including a 1790 Presbyterian church. On exhibit are period furnishings and costumes; military, maritime, astronomical, space and agricultural displays; turn-of-the-century shops, and an intriguing collection of Victrolas and old records, including some of Caruso's.

At Dover Air Force Base to the east you can see the awesome C5-A Galaxy, the world's largest airplane, and a rare World War II B-17 Superfort. The John Dickinson Mansion, the 1740 home of the "Penman of the Revolution," is just to the south. The restored Georgian-style plantation house, with herb and formal English gardens, offers antiques, silver and old utensils. Near South Bowers Beach farther on is the Island Field Archeological Museum, a prehistoric burial site where excavations in progress may be seen as well as interesting artifacts and a slide show.

SOUTHERN DELAWARE

From the Dover area drive south on Rte. 113 and then Rte. 1 to Lewes, site of the ill-fated seventeenth-century Dutch whaling colony of Zwaanendael. Despite the massacre of those first settlers by the Indians, the Dutch soon resettled the area, in 1659—but the town continued to have problems throughout its early years. A group of Mennonites was burned out by the British; pirates and even colonists from neighboring Maryland raided the town, and in the War of 1812 the British bombarded the place. A maritime community from the start, Lewes supplied ships with goods and pilots, and its citizens occasionally prospered through the salvaging of vessels which foundered on the treacherous sandbars beyond the harbor.

For a look at Lewes' turbulent history visit the

Zwaanendael Museum which houses exhibits on Indian, Dutch and Colonial days. The structure itself is noteworthy: a copy of the Town Hall in Hoorn, Holland, it was built in 1931 for the 300th anniversary of Lewes' founding by the Dutch. Several of the town's buildings show cannonball scars from the British attack, including the Cannon Ball House.

There's also the lightship *Overfalls,* moored on the Lewes-Rehoboth Canal, one of the last lightships to function on the East Coast. And the actual site of the 1631 Dutch settlement, recently discovered, is marked by a monument on Pilottown Road. Cape Henlopen State Park, a mile east of town, offers 1647 acres of shifting sand dunes, beaches and trails, and is a nice place for a picnic. If you're heading for New Jersey, or simply have the urge to take a sea voyage, you can ride (with or without your car) on the ferry from Lewes to Cape May. The trip across Delaware Bay takes 70 minutes, and the ferries run year-round.

Evelyn R. Pope/Guests. Located on Kings Highway in Lewes, Mrs. Evelyn Pope's guest house is, she says, "probably Victorian." Around 100 years old, the white weatherboard structure is not particularly notable architecturally, but does offer clean, comfortable weekend lodgings for travelers. There are three guest bedrooms, one with a double bed, one with twin beds, and one with a double and twin bed, suitable for three persons. One bath is shared, and there are hot and cold showers in back of the house for beach-goers to use. One of the guest rooms is on the ground floor; all are furnished simply and include fresh linen, towels, soap and paper cups. Ice cubes are also available. Mrs. Pope sometimes invites her guests to watch TV in her own private living room. Outdoors there's a front porch and a back yard with lounge chairs for fresh-air relaxing. No food is served, but there are restaurants within walking distance.

Evelyn R. Pope/Guests, 409 Kings Highway, Lewes, DE 19958; (302) 645-2382. (At Fourth Street and Kings Highway next to "Lewes Quick Wash.") Rates are inexpensive, lower for longer stays. (Mrs. Pope usually accepts guests on weekends only, but occasionally makes exceptions for return visitors.) Children are welcome; pets are discouraged but sometimes accepted. On-street parking is available. Open May–October.

Continue on Rte. 1 to Rehoboth Beach, Delaware's largest seaside summer resort. Originally created as a Methodist campground, it is now a very popular family resort town with a boardwalk, lots of daytime and nighttime activities, excellent restaurants and a sheltered bay beach. From Rehoboth Beach, Rte. 1 continues south to Bethany Beach as the Delaware Seashore State Park, a narrow strip of land about 10 miles long with water on both sides. The park offers fine beaches for swimming, surfing and fishing, and great crabbing and clamming. At Dewey Beach, children will have a great time searching for coins, old George III pennies that frequently wash up onto the sands. They're thought to be from the *Faithful Steward*, a vessel that was lost off the coast in 1785. But tales of buried pirate treasure are rife in these parts, and if the youngsters want to believe they have found Captain Kidd's booty, by all means let them!

Bethany Beach and Fenwick Island, Delaware's southernmost coastal towns, are called the "Quiet Resorts," family oriented and very relaxing. There's plenty to do, however, with beaches, bays and waterways for swimming, crabbing, fishing and boating. The Bethany Beach Recreation Program provides daily summertime activities for young people, and both resorts offer interesting shops and a variety of restaurants. For a pleasant side trip along country roads, leave the coast and head west, just meandering along on any inviting-looking route. You'll find antique shops and fleamarkets along the way, and over in Seaford travelers can take a ride on one of the country's smallest ferries. The Woodland Ferry runs for 480 feet across the Nanticoke River, and it's free. At Trap Pond State Park, 12 miles southeast of Seaford, there are swimming, fishing and rental boating facilities, and hiking trails among the pines. Nearby the Great Cypress Swamp boasts the country's northernmost stand of bald cypress.

The Pleasant Inn. Peck Pleasanton, owner of this handsome old house, advertises it as "The Most Elegant Inn in Rehoboth Beach." Established in 1928, Pleasant Inn offers ten tastefully-decorated rooms for guests, all with private

The Pleasant Inn

baths. In addition, there are two small housekeeping apartments with private entrances, and a carriage house cottage with glassed-in patio. All accommodations are air-conditioned in the summer and heated in the winter. Guests are welcome to use the inn's living room or relax on the spacious porches and large, tree-shaded lawn. No food is served, but coffee, tea and hot chocolate are available 24 hours a day at the complimentary coffee bar on the second floor. The ocean is just one block away, excellent restaurants and shops three blocks away.

Rehoboth Beach has long been a popular summer resort, offering fine beaches, superb sailing and water skiing, deep-sea and surf fishing, clamming and crabbing. In recent years, however, travelers have begun to discover what the natives have always known—that the renowned seaside community is just as enjoyable all year-round, especially in the spring and fall. It's quieter in these seasons; visitors can watch migrating Canada geese, bicycle along country roads or go horseback riding, and the ocean is comfortably warm for swimming. Even in chill December the beaches are fine for walking, and a festive Christmas Bazaar offers a splendid array of gifts for shoppers.

The Pleasant Inn, First Street and Olive Avenue, Rehoboth Beach, DE 19971; (302) 227-7311. Rates are expensive, lower off season. Visa and MasterCard are accepted. Children are discouraged, and no pets, please. Limited parking is available at the house. Open year-round.

Abbey Cottage. Carolyn and William Straile are your cordial hosts at 75-year-old Abbey Cottage in Rehoboth Beach. It is a typical old-fashioned frame beach house with a large screened-in porch on the front and a patio in the back. The Strailes have eight rooms for guests: three with two double beds each, one with a double and single bed, two with a double and two single beds, and two basement rooms each with two single beds. Three baths are shared, and there are two outside showers and dressing rooms for beach-goers. There's also a ground floor suite consisting of two rooms and a private bath. The guest rooms are simply furnished, neat and clean. No food is served, but there are numerous restaurants a short walk away. Abbey Cottage is one block from the boardwalk and ocean. Your hosts recommend bicycling, swimming and surfing, and Rehoboth Beach offers a variety of summertime entertainment including concerts performed only a few blocks from the house.

Abbey Cottage, 31 Maryland Ave., Rehoboth Beach, DE 19971; (302) 227-7023. (At the corner of Maryland Avenue and First Street.) Rates vary from inexpensive for the basement rooms to moderate for the second-floor accommodations, higher for the suite. Lower rates are offered before June 10 and after Sept. 10, and there's a 10 percent discount for weekly stays. Children are welcome; no pets, please. Street parking is available; parking on the grounds is limited to occupants of the suite. Open from approximately May 25 to Sept. 20.

The Gladstone Inn. Also located in Rehoboth Beach, this charming guest house is owned by Emma Mills. A Victorian Cottage built in the early 1900s, the three-storied structure is painted white with green shutters. There is, of course, a nice long porch for enjoying the sea air. Accommodations include one single and five double air-conditioned bedrooms on the second floor, sharing two full baths. Also available are three first-floor efficiency apartments, and a separate cottage. Guests are welcome to share the pleasant living room, with TV. Two outdoor showers are handy for washing off beach sand and salt water. No food is served at the Gladstone, but the house is only two blocks from downtown Rehoboth Beach with its many restaurants and shops. The beach and boardwalk are only two blocks away, and Rehoboth Bay, two miles south of town, offers great sailing and water skiing.

The Gladstone Inn, 3 Olive Ave., Rehoboth Beach, DE 19971; (302) 653-7301. Rates are moderate, lower from May

15 to June 15 and Sept. 15 to Oct. 1. Children are welcome; no pets, please. On-street parking is available. Open May 15–Oct. 1.

The Addy Sea. The town of Bethany Beach was founded in 1901 by a group of six businessmen, all church lay leaders who were seeking to "establish in the East a resort that shall further the work of the Christian Church all along the coast." One of them, John M. Addy, constructed the Addy Sea as one of the original six cottages built by the town's founders. Completed in 1905, the Addy Sea was unique for its day, for it boasted indoor plumbing! (Mr. Addy was a plumber.) Three generations of the Addy family operated the house as a summer hotel for almost 75 years. In 1975 it was sold to Mr. and Mrs. Leroy T. Gravatte III, who are painstakingly restoring the old Victorian "cottage" to its original turn-of-the-century ambiance. The three-story structure has been nominated for the National Register of Historic Places.

Standing only 50 yards from the ocean, the architecturally-intriguing house includes corner bay windows, gold trim shutters, ornate fretwork and marble fireplaces. Its antique furnishings include brass beds and a classic copper bathtub. There are 14 comfortable bedrooms for guests, with a variety of sleeping accommodations. All of the rooms have sinks; eight baths are shared. In addition, an adjacent cottage with two double bedrooms, living area and kitchen, is available by the week. Guests are invited to make themselves at home in the Addy Sea's spacious, antique-filled living room and parlor, and there are three breeze-swept porches for outdoor relaxation. Your hosts also provide, for an extra fee, either a Continental or a full country breakfast, served in the dining room.

If you need further tempting to lure you to Bethany Beach, perhaps the following excerpt from an old brochure will convince you (even if you're not an executive): "Every business man, having worked hard during the winter and spring, should rest his body and brain for at least a part of the summer. You will want to get away from noise, confusion and smoky atmosphere—your whole system needs recreation. You will want to go where there is no sound of trains, no ear-splitting blasts of whistles, no buzz of machinery, no scurrying and jostling on crowded streets. You will want to go where you can feel perfectly at ease, where you can have plenty of good fresh air, where birds sing, where are sunrises and sunsets beyond the skill of the artist to paint and beyond the power of language to describe, where the swishing of the waves and the bracing effect of the air will lull you to invigorating sleep. You will want to go to a place that is next to nature's heart. Bethany Beach, Sussex County, Delaware, is the charmed spot."

In case you *still* remain untouched, the brochure also includes a testimonial dated April, 1909 and entitled "The Opinion of a Traveler." Dr. Roger Williams, of Pittsburgh, "who has Roamed the World Over," wrote: ". . . Bethany Beach is highly beneficial the year round to all who are sufferers of bronchitis and many sufferers of asthma derive relief along its sandy shores. As a rest cure it possesses vast advantages over any other coast resort, for neurasthenia and all stomach derangements and its ozone laden atmosphere is a constant aid in the building up of the debilitated. The overworked visitor finds in its golden sunshine and glorious air the tonic for every ill, and the sufferers from insomnia are in the spot where relief is prompt and sure. I know of no other place as fortunately situated for the tired and weary as well as the ones who have never experienced a moment of pain. . . . Its surroundings are in keeping with the people who make it a place of tender memories, without the pang of rowdyism which is the prevailing shadow of other resorts."

The Addy Sea, Ocean View Parkway, P.O. Box 275, Bethany Beach, DE 19930; (302) 539-3707. Off season, write Suite 400, 5515 Cherokee Ave., Alexandria, VA 22312; (703) 354-8500. Rates are expensive; 10 percent discount for Monday–Friday stay and 20 percent discount for full week. The Addy Sea's accommodations are available for individual and family rental during July and August only. The house is available for group rental, at lower rates, from April to June and September and October. Visa and MasterCard are accepted. Children over 6 years old are welcome; no pets, please. Parking is available at the house. Open April–October.

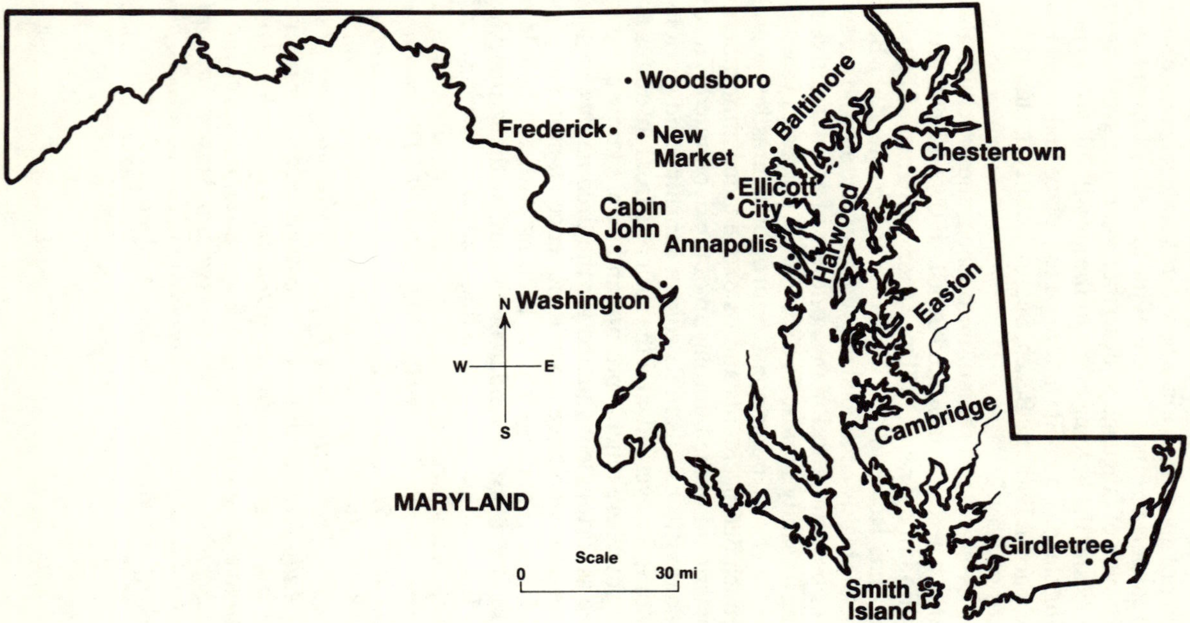
Woodsboro
Frederick
New Market
Baltimore
Chestertown
Ellicott City
Cabin John
Annapolis
Harwood
Washington
Easton
Cambridge
N
W
E
S
MARYLAND
Scale
0
30 mi
Smith Island
Girdletree

Maryland

Maryland is a decidedly appealing state, a beguiling blend of North and South. It offers travelers a great diversity of scenery, an ample selection of things to do, interesting people to meet, and a charmingly easy-going ambiance. The state's topography ranges from the flat Atlantic coastal plain in the east, divided by vast Chesapeake Bay, to the rugged Appalachian Mountains in the northwest. For history buffs (and camera enthusiasts) there are Antietam National Battlefield and Fort McHenry, and storied, picturesque towns such as Frederick, Annapolis, Chestertown, St. Michaels and Cambridge. Baltimore, with its exciting newly-renovated waterfront, includes a host of museums and historic structures to explore. Seekers of solitude will find stretches of unfrequented ocean beaches, cool mountain forests, miles of rural back roads and small, almost-forgotten villages.

Special events held throughout the state range from spring garden pilgrimages and summer seafood celebrations, horse shows and jousting tournaments to fall foliage fairs and Christmas candlelight tours. Maryland boasts more than 3000 miles of tidal coastline, including the indented shores of Chesapeake Bay, with excellent swimming, boating and fishing. Deer hunting is a popular sport in the mountain regions, duck and goose hunting on the Eastern Shore. The state also has a number of fine race tracks; for winter fun, there are even a few modest ski resorts. And antique shops abound.

Captain John Smith, who might be called Maryland's first "tourist," explored the 200-mile length of Chesapeake Bay in 1608. Smith was also something of a travel writer. In his diary he described the region as "truly a delightsome land" and added: "Heaven and earth never agreed better to frame a place for man's habitation." But settlement of the territory (except by the Indians, who were already there) did not begin for another 26 years. It's an interesting tale. A prominent Englishman, George Calvert, was Secretary of State to James I and later a member of the House of Commons. In 1625 he converted to Roman Catholicism; Catholics, however, were not allowed to hold public office in seventeenth-century England and Calvert was forced to resign his post. In gratitude for his years of service to the crown he was given the title of Baron Baltimore, along with several substantial estates in Ireland.

Some years earlier Calvert had founded a small colony in Newfoundland, as a place of refuge for Catholics. He hoped to establish a second haven in the New World where Catholics and Protestants alike could worship as they pleased. In 1632 Charles I granted him the territory that now includes the states of Maryland and Delaware; the region was named "Maryland" in honor of the king's wife, Queen Henrietta Maria. Unfortunately, Lord Baltimore died before the new colony could get under way, leaving his son Cecilius with the family title and the project. In late 1633 the second Lord Baltimore sent some 200 colonists to Maryland, under the leadership of his younger brother Leonard Calvert. More than half of the group were Protestants. Sailing on two ships, the *Ark* and the *Dove*, the expedition reached Chesapeake Bay in March of the following year. Soon after landing on the southwestern shore of the bay they purchased a crude village from the Indians and named it St. Mary's City.

The colony thrived, but religious freedom—its main reason for being—did not. Other settlements in the region, founded by Protestants and even less tolerant Puritans from Virginia, refused to accept Catholic rule. With the influx of many more Puritans from England in the next few years, trouble was assured. By the early 1650s the Catholics were outnumbered; the Protestants took over formal control of the colony and even went so far as to enact penal laws against the Catholics. In 1691 the third Lord Baltimore was removed from office and supplanted by a royal governor. The Calverts did not regain power until 1715, when the fifth Lord Baltimore—who had, perhaps expediently, converted to Protestantism—was named governor. Under his rule all faiths *except* Catholic were allowed freedom of worship.

Boundaries were further bones of contention during much of the eighteenth century. Maryland and Pennsylvania both claimed ownership of Delaware, and the often ugly border dispute wasn't settled until the Mason-Dixon Line (part of which separated Delaware from Maryland) was drawn in the late 1760s. Maryland's feisty citizens were also involved with pre-Revolutionary British baiting. As early as 1765 patriots in the town of Frederick staged a protest against the infamous Stamp Act, and nine years later England's tax on tea brought Annapolis residents to a boil, resulting in the burning of a British tea ship. No battles were fought on Maryland soil during the Revolution, but its troops were widely respected for their bravery.

In the War of 1812, the state was heavily involved in battle. Several towns were burned by the British, British soldiers attempted to capture Baltimore, and the city's Fort McHenry was savagely bombarded. During the Civil War Maryland, a slaveholding border state, was bitterly divided. Many of its citizens favored the South, and wished to secede from the Union; others strongly disagreed. President Lincoln, concerned about Maryland's proximity to Washington, D.C., sent in Federal troops to assure the state's allegiance. An angry riot ensued, but eventually the state complied and remained with the Union. Even so, a large number of Marylanders joined the Confederate Army. Southern forces invaded the state several times, and in 1862 the Civil War's bloodiest battle was fought at Antietam.

Slavery was abolished in Maryland in 1864; the great tobacco plantations, first established in the 1600s by the early colonists, were doomed by the loss of slave labor. The state rebounded rapidly, however, with mills and factories sprouting up around Baltimore and a burgeoning seafood industry along Chesapeake Bay. Today Maryland is pleasantly prosperous, with a healthy economy based on industry, farming, commercial fishing and tourism.

MARYLAND'S EASTERN SHORE

The lengthy finger of Chesapeake Bay extends all the way from Virginia to within a few miles of Maryland's northern border. The section of Maryland that lies to the east of the bay, part of the Delmarva Peninsula, is known as the Eastern Shore. It is a fairly flat region, with rich soil and a ragged tidal shoreline that meanders in and out along innumerable inlets and creeks, with marshes and small fishing villages along the way. The major industry is farming, closely followed by commercial fishing— particularly for oysters, crabs, clams and striped bass— all of which provide visitors with some of the best seafood in the world.

The region is also awash with history, dotted with quaint, pretty towns dating back to the seventeenth and eighteenth centuries. Starting at the northern end of the Eastern Shore and heading south, you'll come to Kent County, first explored by Captain John Smith in 1608. Georgetown, on the banks of the Sassafras River, was burned by the British in the War of 1812—except for one house. An elderly spinster named Miss Kitty Knight, undaunted by the enemy, threatened to die by fire rather than leave her home. The house still stands and now serves as an inn.

Chestertown, the county seat a few miles to the south, is a perfect jewel of a place. Founded in 1706, the beautiful little village was once one of Maryland's most important seaports. Wealthy merchants, involved in maritime trade in the eighteenth and nineteenth centuries, built imposing townhouses along the bluff overlooking the Chester River. Many of the handsome Georgian and Federal homes are still there, as are the town's old brick sidewalks laid out in herringbone patterns along the narrow, tree-shaded streets. At the Kent County Chamber of Commerce visitors can acquire a brochure with map for a walking tour that includes many of the town's historic structures. Most of Chestertown's fine old mansions are private residences, however, open to the public only during the annual Candlelight Walking Tour held yearly on the third Saturday of September. Even so, just seeing their exteriors is a treat.

Especially outstanding are the Wickes House with its gracious walled garden of boxwood and flowers, and the Hynson–Ringgold House, dating to 1735 and partly designed by William Buckland, a renowned early American builder-architect. Widehall, perhaps the most elaborate of the townhouses built by Chestertown's merchants, is a classic example of symmetric Georgian architecture. The Customs House, parts of which date to the early 1730s, is also noteworthy; in the eighteenth century the building was the focal point for the town's trade with British West Indies sugar plantations. Near the site, on May 23, 1774 (five months after the famous Boston Tea Party), angry citizens boarded Port Collector William Geddes' brigantine and tossed its cargo of tea into the river. The event is jubilantly reenacted each May during the Chestertown Tea Party Festival. Chestertown is also the home of architecturally interesting Washington College, founded in 1782 and named after George Washington, who served on its Board of Visitors and Governors.

The White Swan Tavern. One of the most intriguing stops on Chestertown's walking tour, the White Swan Tavern is also—happily for travelers—an operating bed and breakfast inn! Situated in the center of the town's historic district, the brick structure has been a local landmark since pre-Revolutionary days. Although the earliest records concerning the site have been lost, it is known that John Lovegrove, the "Shoemaker of Chestertown," operated a tannery there prior to 1733. Joseph Nicholson, who owned the property from 1733 to 1787, added several rooms in order to make a home for himself and his wife. John Bordley purchased the house in 1793 and enlarged it, probably for use as a tavern; between 1803 and 1853 the building was operated as such by various owners. One was the Reverend William H. Wilmer, an absentee landlord, as he was then pastor of St. Paul's Church in Alexandria, Virginia. (Reverend Wilmer was also rector of Bruton Parish Church in Williamsburg and president of the College of William and Mary.) Thomas W. Eliason, a local merchant who became Kent County's first millionaire, bought the tavern in 1853. For the next 125 years the building underwent many changes and was used by a number of small businesses.

Christian Havemeyer purchased the property in 1977,

The White Swan Tavern

with the intent of returning it to its eighteenth-century use as "a commodious tavern or Public House . . . with every attention given to render comfort and pleasure to such as favor it with their patronage." The Havemeyer family began restoration work with intensive research; archaeologist Karl de Rochefort-Reynolds and his archaeology class from Chesapeake College were invited to the site to help unearth the past. During excavation of the back yard, basement and the ground beneath the front porch and kitchen floor, more than 70,000 shards of pottery, glass and other materials, some dating as far back as the mid-1600s, were uncovered. The most treasured item, pieced together from several shards, was a "charger" (a round platter) which came from North Devon, England and is inscribed with the date 1730. The white swan motif in its center is now used as the logo for the tavern which, after three years of faithful restoration, opened once again for business in March, 1981.

Furnished throughout with antiques and period reproductions, the inn today offers a remarkably authentic eighteenth-century appearance and atmosphere, with the added comfort of twentieth-century amenities. You'll be greeted at the door by Susan D. Matthews, the innkeeper, who will show you through the elegantly austere first floor public rooms. There's also a cozy sitting room just for guests, with a TV, a desk for postcard writing and a fireplace with wood all ready to be lighted by your hostess.

The five double guest bedrooms, all named after previous owners, begin with the John Lovegrove Kitchen, located on the ground floor. The spacious room, with one double bed and one single bed, was originally the old tavern kitchen and still has its brick floor, original ceiling beams and massive fireplace, complete with black iron cooking pots. Upstairs are the Thomas Peacock Room, tucked away under a sloping "catslide" ceiling, with lacy canopied bed and a twin bed; the John Bordley Room done in beige, salmon, cream and white with twin beds and a fireplace; the Wilmer Room in cheerful reds, whites and blues with four-poster twin beds and a fireplace, and the T. W. Eliason Suite. The Eliason family owned the building from 1853 to 1977, so this room is fittingly decorated in Victorian style with greens, copper, gold and peach, with two double beds. All of the accommodations offer full private baths, central heat and air conditioning, and—a nice welcoming touch—a bottle of wine, fresh fruit and flowers.

A Continental breakfast of freshly-squeezed orange juice, pastries and coffee, included in the rates, is served on a tray in your room or downstairs in the old tavern—faithfully reproduced except for, the owners say, the sawdust on the floor and a gathering of rowdy eighteenth-century patrons! Afternoon tea (which is also available to the public) is served here on Wednesdays, Thursdays and Fridays from 4–6 p.m. for $3 per person. Tea goodies and breakfast rolls are all homemade.

Chestertown and the surrounding area offer a large selection of fine restaurants for other meals, particularly seafood. Your hostess will be delighted to recommend a few. And if you'd enjoy an hour or so of pedaling along the region's country lanes, the White Swan Tavern will supply you with bicycles. Tennis, swimming, boating, fishing and hunting are also all available nearby, as are attractive boutiques and antique and craft shops.

The White Swan Tavern, 231 High St., Chestertown, MD 21620; (301) 778-2300. (Just a few blocks west of Rte. 213, opposite the Kent County Court House.) Rates are expensive, lower in July and August. (As the Tavern is small, to avoid disappointment it's advised that you make reservations well in advance.) Well-behaved children are welcome; no pets, please. Parking is available at rear of building. Open year-round except for the last week of January and first week of February.

Hill's Tourist Home. Also located in Chestertown's historic district, Mrs. Beth Horsey's handsome old Victorian home was built between 1870 and 1880. Set on attractively wooded grounds, the house offers three comfortable rooms for guests, two with one double and one single bed and one with a double bed. Furnished in Victorian style, the rooms share one bath. No food is served, but there are restaurants within walking distance. Your hostess will be happy to recommend a few and will provide directions to Chestertown's many attractions.

Hill's Tourist Home, 114 Washington Ave. (Rte. 213), Chestertown, MD 21620; (301) 778-1926. Rates are moderate, ½ price for children under 12; weekly rates are available. Children are welcome; no pets, please. There is parking at the house. Open year-round.

Hill's Tourist Home

If you follow Rte. 20 west out of Chestertown and then south, you'll come to Remington Farms, a wildlife research and demonstration area. The 3000-acre site, in addition to being a waterfowl sanctuary, also grows food for ducks and geese, songbirds, deer and a variety of smaller animals. Farther along is Rock Hall, an old bay fishing village widely renowned for a seafood restaurant called the Chesapeake. Hardly inspiring to look at, the derelict structure nevertheless offers marvelous food, most notably owner Ginny Squibb's generously-sized crabcakes. Another spot where you can gaze upon thousands of migrating waterbirds lies just to the south: the Eastern Neck National Wildlife Refuge. A jog back up and around will bring you to Centreville with a number of historic eighteenth-century homes (two of them now housing museums) and Maryland's oldest court house, dating to1792. Just past town, Rtes. 301/50 lead onto the 4.3-mile bridge that crosses Chesapeake Bay over to Maryland's Western Shore. We, however, are continuing on south to Easton.

The seat of Talbot County, pretty Easton was settled in 1682 as a Quaker community. The Third Haven Friends Meeting House, built from 1682 to 1684, is still standing; William Penn once spoke here. Every June, the first weekend is devoted to the Delmarva Chicken Festival with a Poultry Princess Pageant and Giant Fry Pan. On the first Wednesday of August each year, Easton holds a merry Jousting Tournament and horse show. Several miles south of town are the Wye Oak State Park and reconstructed 1721 Old Wye Church, of Flemish-style architecture. The Park is the home of Maryland's official state tree, a 400-year-old white oak. There are also an old mill and a restored one-room schoolhouse to be explored.

And don't miss a visit to St. Michaels, a few miles west of Easton. In Colonial days the now serene little village was a busy shipbuilding center; during the War of 1812 the British twice attempted, with no success, to destroy the six shipyards where fast trading vessels and privateers, which were later to harass British shipping, were being built. Although shipbuilding declined in the late 1800s, the town today is the home of a thriving fishing industry. The best way to explore St. Michaels is on foot; a map of the historic district with descriptions of sites along the way is available at the Chamber of Commerce. In addition to a fine collection of Federal and Victorian houses, you'll see St. Mary's Square, laid out in 1770; St. Mary's Square Museum, a restored, furnished Colonial house with exhibits on local history; Hell's Crossing, where sailors long ago caroused in taverns and grog shops and regularly engaged in battle with other crewmen; a log house and an old footbridge, and the fascinating Chesapeake Bay Maritime Museum. The 18-acre waterfront museum complex consists of some 18 buildings, with floating exhibits including examples of Chesapeake Bay's unique fishing vessels, a boat building shop, an aquarium and a century-old lighthouse.

Hynson's Tourist Home. Mrs. Nellie Hynson graciously welcomes visitors to her comfortably homey guest house in Easton. A two-story bungalow with white aluminum siding and green roof, the house has six rooms for guests including two singles and four doubles. Two rooms, with semi-private bath, are on the ground floor; the upstairs rooms share one bath. Guests are also invited to share Mrs. Hynson's family room, with TV, and to enjoy her spacious yard—especially in spring and summer when it's bright with blooming flowers. Your hostess sometimes offers morning coffee, but no other food is served. The house is within easy walking distance of many restaurants; it is about a ten-minute walk to the center of town.

Hynson's Tourist Home, 804 Dover Rd., Easton, MD 21601; (301) 822-2777. Rates are inexpensive, lower for longer stays. Children are welcome; no pets, please, and no drinking in the house. Parking is available. Open year-round.

Guest Houses

Continuing south along the Eastern Shore, you will reach Dorchester County, rich in history, tradition and folklore, and birthplace of six Maryland governors. *Chesapeake*, James Michener's novel, was set here as were several of John Barth's works, including *The Sot-Weed Factor* and *The Floating Opera.* (Barth is a native of Cambridge.) The county hosts a number of festivals annually: in August there are the Bay County and Seafood Festivals, and in February the Outdoor Show includes concerts, a beauty pageant and a muskrat-skinning contest. Cambridge, founded in 1684 and situated on the Choptank River, is Maryland's second largest deepwater port. A walking tour of historic High Street will lead you past a number of fine old houses, many dating back to the late 1700s. The Chamber of Commerce will provide you with maps and brochures describing the county's many other sites of interest including Old Trinity Church, a tiny edifice built around 1675 and carefully restored, and a reconstructed post windmill.

East New Market, the entire town designated a historic district, offers an excellent collection of eighteenth- and nineteenth-century houses; in Secretary travelers will find My Lady Sewall's Manor with its original portion dating back to 1662. The enormous Blackwater National Wildlife Refuge, 12 miles south of Cambridge, covers more than 14,000 acres. At the peak of fall migration some 80,000 Canada geese and 30,000 ducks pause here on their way south. Blackwater is also a haven for four endangered species: the resident bald eagle and Delmarva fox squirrel, the migrant peregrine falcon and—very occasionally—the rare red-cockaded woodpecker. Not far to the south are a cluster of rustic fishing villages named Bishops Head, Hoopers Island, Toddville and Wingate; they're well worth the drive. And in the Robbins area visitors may spot spooky lights on the marshes. Called "Mysterious Lights," they are probably caused by marsh gases.

High Water. Mrs. Evelyn S. Tomey's very attractive guest house, situated on Cambridge's historic High Street, is right on the beautiful Choptank River. There's a yacht club on one side, boat marinas on the other—and you can fish, crab or boat from the house or dock! High Water, a century and a half old, is furnished in antiques and offers seven rooms for guests, sharing four baths. One of the rooms, and one bath, are on the ground floor. Your cordial hostess allows guests the run of the house, and there's a pleasant awninged porch for outdoors relaxing. Mrs. Tomey often offers coffee and refreshments; for regular meals you'll find a number of places to dine nearby, including a good home-cooking restaurant one block away. Shops, churches and many of Cambridge's other sites of interest are close by, too.

High Water, 100 High St., Cambridge, MD 21613; (301) 228-4969. (Across the street from the municipal park.) Rates are very inexpensive, lower for weekly stays. Children are welcome; no pets, please, and no cooking allowed in rooms. There is parking at the house. Open year-round.

Maryland's Eastern Shore now makes a sharp turn eastward all the way to the Atlantic Ocean and the resort town of Ocean City. If you're going in that direction, stop for awhile at Salisbury to see the Wildfowl Art Museum in Salisbury State College's Holloway Hall. The museum houses a marvelous collection of carvings of geese, ducks and other birds and tells the history of decoy and wildfowl carvings. Princess Anne, an otherwise serene old town to the south, comes to life in October with two well-attended weekend events. Olde Princess Anne Days includes an Open House and Garden Tour of historic houses and churches; the Somerset County Historical Society Antiques Show takes place soon after.

Ocean City, where deep-sea fishing is the popular sport, offers a fine three-mile-long white sand beach and a boardwalk with a variety of amusements. It's a rather crowded, noisy place in summer, and if you'd like to get off by yourself for a peaceful walk along a less-active beach, head for the Assateague Island National Seashore. A 37-mile-long stretch of sandy barrier island, Assateague is connected by a bridge to Chincoteague Island to the south. On Assateague are sand dunes, marshes and forest, with deer, birds galore and wild ponies. Actually stunted horses, the shaggy little animals are believed to be the descendants of horses which swam ashore from a wrecked Spanish galleon. Their small size is due to their steady diet of marsh grass.

For a delightful place to stay in this area, head down the coast and inland, to the small village of Girdletree.

The Stockman's. John and Joan Stockman are the friendly proprietors of this nice bed and breakfast guest house in

Girdletree. They don't regretfully, know how the town got its name; Joan Stockman says that they have asked half a dozen people there and received half a dozen different answers. The history of their turn-of-the-century country house, however, *is* known: it was built by the town banker, who later absconded with the bank's funds! Your hosts have owned the place since 1979 and are presently doing over the yard, adding a charming herb garden among other changes. They've also re-sided the house, painting it a Williamsburg blue with white trim and carefully preserving the third floor's scalloped shingles. A large, wraparound porch-veranda offers a great place for sitting and enjoying the air. The house, furnished comfortably in a mix of styles including some antiques, has two guest bedrooms. One offers twin beds, the other a queen-sized bed; two baths are shared. Guests are encouraged to use the living room and a den with TV.

A Continental breakfast with fresh local fruit in season and hot, homebaked muffins is included in the rates. Refrigerator privileges are available for guests who are carrying food along. There's a small general corner store nearby, but a car is needed to reach restaurants and other sorts of shops. Girdletree is halfway between Ocean City and Chincoteague-Assateague Islands for swimming, boating, fishing and hiking. Pocomoke State Park is nearby, and there are two interesting small museums in historic Snow Hill.

The Stockman's, P.O. Box 125, Taylor Landing Rd., Girdletree, MD 21829; (301) 632-3299. (From Rte. 12 traveling south from Snow Hill come into Girdletree, turn left at the Post Office at the second cross street, and go to the fourth house on the right.) Rates are inexpensive, lower from Labor Day to Memorial Day. Older children are welcome; the Stockmans do not have special equipment such as cribs, highchairs, etc. for very young children. No pets, please. Open year-round, but please give as much advance notice as possible during the winter months.

For an unforgettable experience and a close-up view of another world, drive southwest down to Crisfield on Chesapeake Bay; there, take a ferry out to Smith Island. The voyage takes about an hour; there are three fishing villages to explore once you get there, and the seafood is superb. Softshell crabs, crabcakes, oysters and clam fritters are only some of the mouth-watering choices at the island's restaurants. The shellfish are freshly caught by the resident watermen.

Chesapeake Bay has many islands, but Smith Island is perhaps the most distinctive. Named for Captain John Smith, the peaceful, water-surrounded haven once had a well-deserved reputation for lawlessness and heavy alcoholic consumption. Still fiercely independent, the islanders today are far tamer (and very friendly) but still tend to resent government interference with their unique way of life. Most of them speak in a sometimes difficult-to-understand dialect. Many Smith Islanders, like the inhabitants of Tangier and other bay islands, are direct descendants of the original seventeenth-century British settlers and their speech in some ways resembles that of Cornwall, with a number of colorful regional words and terms thrown in.

To reach the island, first park your car in Crisfield. The *Captain Jason* leaves the City Dock daily at 12:30 p.m. and 5 p.m.; return trips start daily at 8 a.m. and 3:30 p.m. If you'd like to stay overnight or longer, there are guest houses in the Smith Island village of Ewell, all serving meals. Be *sure* to phone or write ahead for reservations as the number of rooms is limited; your hostess will reserve a seat on the boat for you when you call. And if you have a bicycle along, by all means bring it; the island is an ideal place for short bike trips.

Pitchcroft Inn. Eloise Tyler owns Pitchcroft, the oldest house on Smith Island. Built around 1700, the well-preserved old farmhouse has been occupied ever since its construction. During the Revolutionary War an English soldier, wounded in Baltimore, died while being transported down the bay and was buried on Pitchcroft land. The house has four rooms for guests, two singles and two doubles, sharing three baths. Visitors are welcome to use the small lounge with TV, as well. Both breakfast and dinner are included in the rates, and lunch is offered for an extra fee if desired. Seafood, of course, is the specialty; the meals are homecooked and served family style in the air-conditioned dining room overlooking the water. Outdoors, guests may relax in the front yard and watch sail and crabbing boats, or take a walking or bicycling tour of Pitchcroft's grounds and the quaint town of Ewell.

Pitchcroft Inn, Ewell, Smith Island, MD 21824; (301) 425-5851. Rates, which include two meals, are moderate, ½ price for children under 12. MasterCard and Visa are accepted. Children are welcome; no pets, please. Open from May through November.

Frances Kitching's. Mrs. Kitching's attractive house is a newer one, built in 1942, with an enclosed front porch. She has five bedrooms for guests with a shared full bath upstairs and a half bath on the first floor. Guests may also use the living room and TV room. Breakfast and dinner are included in the rates, served in one of the two dining rooms. Mrs. Kitching specializes in seafood dinners, served family style.

Frances Kitching's, Ewell, Smith Island, MD 21824; (301) 425-3321. Rates, including two meals, are moderate; lower for children under 12. Children are welcome; no pets, please. Open from May until after Labor Day.

Bernice Guy's. Mrs. Bernice Guy, whose guest house is open year-round, has two rooms for visitors. One has a double bed, the other twin beds; both are located on the ground floor and share a bath. Guests are invited to share the Guys' living room, too. Breakfast and dinner are included in the rates; the homecooked dinner consists of one meat or seafood, vegetable, salad and dessert.

Bernice Guy's, Ewell, Smith Island, MD 21824; (301) 425-2751. Rates, including two meals, are moderate; ½ price for children. Children are welcome; no pets, please. Open year-round.

THE WESTERN SHORE AND CENTRAL MARYLAND

On the other side of Chesapeake Bay, Maryland's Western Shore extends from the Susquehanna River in the north down past Baltimore and Annapolis all the way to the mouth of the Potomac River in the south. At the southeastern tip is St. Mary's County, a quiet, scenic region jutting out into the bay between the Patuxent and Potomac rivers. Much of the gently rolling land is still farmed; tobacco is the leading product. Indented with hundreds of small bays, creeks and inlets, the county includes 400 miles of waterways providing visitors with some of the best fishing in the state, year-round. In season there are rockfish (striped bass), bluefish, trout, croakers, flounder and perch, as well as oysters and soft- and hard-shelled crabs. Pleasure boating, sailing, swimming and water skiing are also excellent.

Other enjoyable things to do in St. Mary's County include attending tobacco auctions, country dances, church suppers and crab feasts. There are a variety of festivals, too: Maryland Day Celebration in March, St. Mary's Summer Festival in July and August with theatrical and other events, the County Fair in September, and an Oyster Festival in October. Throughout the year the region's Amish gather at Farmers' Markets held every Wednesday in the town of Charlotte Hall, where delicious homemade preserves and other foodstuffs are sold along with antiques and other appealing items.

Called "The Mother County" of Maryland, St. Mary's dates back to 1634 when Leonard Calvert—brother of the second Lord Baltimore—led a small band of English colonists to the territory. Soon after landing they bought a village from the Indians, naming it St. Mary's, and established Maryland's first permanent settlement. St. Mary's City served as the capital of the new colony until 1694 when the seat of government moved to Annapolis. Only the foundations of the original 1676 State House remain today; the structure was torn down in 1829 and its bricks used to build Trinity Church. You can, however, explore a reproduction, built in 1934 for Maryland's 300th anniversary celebration. Near Trinity Church, at the water's edge is a stone bench that marks the spot where the colonists came ashore, and a replica of the *Dove,* one of the two ships that brought them, is docked at the wharf.

In the seventeenth century the city also boasted a large fort, a tavern, a Governor's Palace and a Council House, all long gone. It was in the Council House that one of Maryland's most fascinating women appeared before the General Assembly to demand the right to vote. Mistress Margaret Brent, an English spinster and cousin to Lord Baltimore, sailed to American in 1638. She became a wealthy landowner and, in 1647, was named executrix of Governor Calvert's will. Mistress Brent chose to turn the responsibility into an official act, and, surprisingly, the Assembly agreed. She became the colony's treasurer and shortly thereafter requested not one but two votes—one for her private status as a property holder and one for her public position. Although the demand was refused, she continued to hold great power as Lord Baltimore's agent. At some later date the local court records began to refer to her as "Margaret Brent, Gentleman"—an astonishing acknowledgement, for that time, of her unusual standing in the colony.

About 20 miles south of St. Mary's City you'll find the unique Confederate Monument. Erected to honor some 4000 prisoners of war who died at Point Lookout Prison during the Civil War, it is the only Federal monument to Confederate soldiers. Just beyond is Point Lookout State Park. Sotterly, an elegant Colonial manor house built in 1717, is situated a few miles north of St. Mary's City. Still a working plantation and family home, Sotterly is renowned for its handsome paneling; its Great Hall is called "one of the 100 most beautiful rooms in America." On the grounds are English formal gardens, an old slave house, smokehouse and "necessary" and an eighteenth-century custom house and warehouse, now housing a museum displaying farm implements.

Tudor Hall, in Leonardtown, is another handsome structure worth seeing. The Georgian mansion, its earliest section built in 1750, now serves as the St. Mary's County Library. At the Historical Society Headquarters in Leonardtown visitors can acquire a large map showing some 200 historic houses and sites around the county. St. Clement's Island, not far away, was the first landing place for the colonists in 1634; a museum with Indian and Colonial artifacts is located on a bluff across from the island.

Calvert County to the north, a peninsula beyond the Patuxent River, is noted for its 30-mile stretch of tall bluffs along Chesapeake Bay and a fun-filled festival called Cavalier Days. The event, held each May in the town of Prince Frederick, is an eighteenth-century fair with period-costumed participants and Colonial music, dramas, militia rallies, games, and arts and crafts. Also included are Irish Ceili dances, Scottish games and medieval jousting tournaments, and visitors can sample the region's seafood specialties, pastries, and Colonial stuffed ham, a piquant dish of sweet boiled ham, cabbage, kale, onions and spices—including mustard seed and crushed red pepper. Charles County to the west offers tobacco auctions at La Plata, and the restored village of Port Tobacco—originally an Indian village, colonized by English settlers in 1638.

If you continue from Charles County northward along the Potomac River you'll come to Fort Washington, across the river from George Washington's lovely Virginia home, Mount Vernon. Washington, D.C. and its suburbs lie just beyond. The territory that is now the capitol of the United States was ceded to the government by Maryland in 1788; Virginia ceded another tract on the west side of the Potomac a year later. In addition to the lengthy list of places to see in Washington itself, the Maryland side of the Potomac offers a number of interesting sites. The Great Falls of the Potomac tumble spectacularly over massive rocks, and the Chesapeake and Ohio Canal Historical Park offers fine hiking and bicycling along the tree-shaded towpaths and canoeing in the canal itself. College Park is the home of the University of Maryland, Greenbelt Park, and the NASA/Goddard Space Center with satellites, rockets and other space research displays.

The Winslow Home. Mrs. D. B. Winslow's comfortable bed and breakfast guest house is located in Cabin John, an attractive suburb of Bethesda, northwest of Washington, D.C. The house, built in 1963, is of contemporary architecture, long and low. Its lower level does not show from the street. There are two bedrooms for guests located on the main or street level: one double and one single, sharing a bath. For a modest extra fee you can request the double room with private bath. Guests are also cordially invited to share the living room and garden, the latter particularly lovely in spring when the azaleas and rhododendron are in bloom. Breakfast, served in the dining room, consists of fruit, orange juice, cereals, toast, muffins or sweet rolls, coffee, tea or milk, and it is included in the rates. If they wish, guests may prepare their own dinner in the kitchen.

Cabin John is a quiet, residential community which began as a summer cottage retreat for residents of Washington, D.C. The Chesapeake and Ohio Canal is within walking distance of the house; the Great Falls of the Potomac are just up the road. Washington is only 20 minutes away; historic Annapolis and Frederick are an hour's drive and Baltimore is 1½ hours away. If you don't have a car, the Winslows will arrange to meet you, and they'll get you to a bus or Metro for sightseeing during your stay.

The Winslow Home, 8217 Caraway St., Cabin John, MD

20818; (301) 229-4654 or (office) (202) 887-2536. Rates are moderate, free for children under 12. Children are welcome; pets may be allowed, but check with Mrs. Winslow first. The Winslows are a non-smoking, non-drinking family and prefer guests who are the same. Parking is available at the house. Open year-round.

Sweet Dreams & Toast, Inc. Liz Cooke and Eleanor K. Chastain operate Sweet Dreams & Toast, a bed and breakfast service for the Washington, D.C. area and Annapolis to the east. All of their listings have been personally inspected to assure comfort, cleanliness, attractive surroundings and interested hosts. Accommodations available include a double room and a single with loft bed, ideal for children, in a unique modern home with sundeck and indoor pool set in the woods near Chevy Chase Circle; a double room in a Georgetown townhouse, and an art-filled home just off Rock Creek Parkway with three double rooms. Breakfast is included in the rates.

Contact: Sweet Dreams & Toast, Inc., P.O. Box 4835-0035, Washington, D.C. 20008; (202) 363-4712. You'll be sent a guest application form for details and references. Return it with a $25 deposit and you will receive confirmation by mail; the balance of the fee is due at the service's office two weeks prior to your arrival. Visa and MasterCard are accepted. Rates are moderate, slightly higher for exceptional accommodations. Your deposit less a $5 service fee will be refunded with a 48-hour notice.

From the Washington, D.C. area, an hour's drive to the east will bring you to Annapolis, Maryland's capital since Colonial times and home of the United States Naval Academy. Situated at the mouth of the Severn River, historic Annapolis offers visitors a splendid collection of restored homes and gardens, excellent restaurants, antique shops and imaginative boutiques. It is a small, gracious city, its narrow streets easily explored on foot. A good place to begin a tour is at the State House, built between 1772 and 1779. The country's oldest state house in continuous use, the building also served as the first peacetime capitol of the United States; Congress ratified the Paris Peace Treaty here in 1784. Nearby are the Old Treasury Building, circa 1735, and the

1868 Governor's Mansion. St. John's College, founded in 1784, is a short walk away. On campus is the famed Liberty Tree, a tulip poplar believed to be more than 400 years old; during the American Revolution the Sons of Liberty met under its spreading branches. McDowell Hall just to the left, built between 1742 and 1789 as the Governor's Palace, is now St. John's main classroom building.

Two handsome homes designed by William Buckland are located on Maryland Avenue, one street over. The Chase-Lloyd House at No. 22 was constructed in 1769 for Samuel Chase, one of the signers of the Declaration of Independence. The Georgian-style Hammond-Harwood House at No. 19 dates to 1774. On Prince George Street you'll find the William Paca House, a faithfully restored 1765 mansion. Paca was a three-term governor of Maryland and another signer of the Declaration of Independence; his friend Thomas Jefferson provided suggestions for Paca's home. The house's magnificently-restored gardens, reached through an entrance around the corner on Martin Street, include a delightful miniature wilderness, formal flower beds and waterways.

The waterfront campus of the United States Naval Academy is just across King George Street. Established in 1845 on the grounds of an old Army fort, the Academy is an interesting place to explore. Guided tours are offered at the Visitor Information Center, or you may stroll about as you please through the approved areas and buildings. John Paul Jones is buried beneath the chapel in a large subterranean room under an elaborate marble sarcophagus. In the Naval Academy Museum you'll find more than 50,000 items encompassing 300 years of American Naval history, with a large collection of model ships. Commodore Oliver Perry's battle flag from the War of 1812 is on display in gigantic Bancroft Hall, the Academy's student dormitory housing some 4000 men and 400 women. In the courtyard outside Bancroft hall, stop for a moment to pay homage to the fiercely glowering figure of an Indian chief. Often called "the god of C" (the Academy's passing grade), the statue is popularly believed to represent the warlike chieftain Tecumseh. Actually, the bronze figure is a likeness of Tamanend, chief of the Delawares, and was copied from the figurehead of the old U.S.S. *Delaware.* In spring and fall, if weather permits, visitors may see a dress parade on campus, and during Commencement Week (called Commissioning Week) in May all manner of activities take place.

If the nautical atmosphere of the Naval Academy brings out the sailor in you, then head for the Annapolis city docks. There are boats of all sorts to look at and several choices of boat trips are available for cruises of the harbor, Chesapeake Bay and the Severn River, and longer voyages across the bay to Oxford and St. Michaels on the Eastern Shore. Sandy Point State Park, seven miles northeast of Annapolis on Chesapeake Bay, offers fine boating, fishing, swimming and picnicking. In late fall the park is the site of Chesapeake Appreciation Days, during which Maryland's oyster-dredging skipjacks—the last commercial sailing fleet in North America—compete in an exciting race.

In addition to all its other attractions the Annapolis area offers two exceptional bed and breakfast guest houses, either of which will make a fine base from which to explore the region, including Baltimore in the north, Washington, D.C. to the west, and much of southern Maryland. One of the houses is located right in Annapolis; the other is in Harwood, 12 miles south.

Gibson's Lodgings. Cary and Ayrol Ann Gibson welcome guests to their imposing old brick home, located in the Historic District of Annapolis one block from the Naval Academy Visitors' Gate. The house, about 200 years old, stands on property assigned in 1684 to Richard Hill, first Naval officer of the Port of Annapolis. In the seventeenth century a brick building referred to as "the Old Court House" stood on the site. Richard MacCubbin, a local businessman and owner of a large tobacco plantation, constructed the present house (to which later additions have been made) between 1760 and 1786.

The large, Georgian-style house has thirteen rooms for guests, ten with double beds and three with two twin beds. Twelve of the rooms share six baths; one, on the ground floor, has a private bath. All of the rooms are tastefully furnished in period style with handmade quilts and some lovely antiques; two include TV, and one even has a piano!

Breakfast is included in the rates and consists of juices, French toast or waffles, English muffins, biscuits or bagels, honey, jellies and jams, and coffee. Some 30 excellent restaurants are within easy walking distance, as are many of the town's charming specialty and antique shops. The city docks and picturesque harbor are only 50 yards from the house, and Sandy Point State Park for swimming and sailing is just a few miles away. Another pleasant side trip in Anne Arundel County is the London Town Publik House in Edgewater a few miles southeast; the eighteenth-century inn is surrounded by almost nine acres of woodland gardens.

Gibson's Lodgings, 110 Prince George St., Annapolis, MD 21401; (301) 268-5555. (The first house behind Dock Street on Prince George Street.) Rates are moderate. Well-behaved children are welcome; no pets, please. There is ample off-street parking for guests. Open year-round.

Oakwood. Situated in Harwood at the end of a winding country lane, beautiful Oakwood is owned by Dennis and Joan Brezina. Of frame construction, the main house is two and a half stories high. A two-story original wing projects from the south gable, and one-story porches extend along the east and west facades. Oakwood was built around 1840 as part of Cherry Hill Manor, formed in 1839 from 562 acres of seventeenth-century Anne Arundel Manor and 44 acres of Taylor's Search. The property was originally owned by the Harwoods, a family of strong Southern sympathies. Shortly after the Civil War Sprigg Harwood sold the place to Jacob Rogers Woollen, and it remained in the Woollen family for many years. The Brezinas purchased Oakwood in the late 1970s. After several years of diligent restoration work, they opened it for bed and breakfast guests in the fall of 1981.

There are two spacious rooms for guests: one with a queen-size bed, TV and private bath, the other on the ground floor with twin beds and a shared bath. Guests are also cordially invited to use the house's library, parlor and veranda. Breakfast, included in the rates, is highlighted by freshly-baked, homemade bread. Your host will recommend some good places to dine in the area for other meals. In addition to restoring the house, the Brezinas have been hard at work on the grounds. They've uncovered the old terraced formal gardens and have created a charming interpretative trail through the woods leading to the foundations of the stable, the spring house, butler's house and ice pond. Oakwood, lovely the

Oakwood

year-round, is especially so in the spring when the forsythia blooms in golden abandon. And there are peacocks on the lawn!

Joan Brezina, an economist with a Ph.D. from Yale who directs a computer division of the federal government, also enjoys needlepoint and refinishing furniture. Dennis, a graduate of the Naval Academy with a master's degree from Harvard in the history of science, is a writer. He also manages the day-to-day operations at Oakwood and has taken up latch hooking—resulting in a splendid 7′ x 10′ rug for the family room, with more to come. Your hosts are very much interested in the history of their old house and, through the help of several of the past owners, have discovered a great deal of information which they'll be delighted to share with you. Oakwood is now included in the Maryland House and Garden Pilgrimage which takes place each year in late April and early May. Ask the Brezinas to tell you about their frantic efforts to get ready for their first tour in 1981—including painting several 11-foot ceilings and washing both sides of 674 panes of glass!

Oakwood, 4566 Solomons Island Rd., Harwood, MD 20776; (301) 261-5338. (From Annapolis, follow Rte. 2 south for 12 miles to "4556" mailbox on right.) Rates are moderate. No children or pets, please. There is parking at the house. Open year-round.

Sharp-Adams, Inc. Sharp-Adams is a bed and breakfast organization currently offering accommodations in

Annapolis, Baltimore and a number of communities on Maryland's Eastern Shore. Headquartered in Annapolis, the service is owned and operated by Cecily Sharp-Whitehill and B. J. Adams. Their extensive (and unusual) range of lodgings includes motor and sail yachts, mansions, farmhouses, contemporary and historic townhouses, watermen's cottages, a barge and a lighthouse, and homes with private moorings for a guest's own boat. They will also arrange excursions including "moonrise" sails aboard your overnight yacht accommodation and one- or two-day trips on board a Chesapeake waterman's boat. In addition, Sharp-Adams will suggest bicycle itineraries with a box lunch and will set up guided goose and duck hunting expeditions for interested travelers.

Contact: Sharp-Adams, Inc., 8 Gentry Court, Annapolis, MD 21403; (301) 269-6232. Rates, including breakfast, are moderate. You will be mailed a reservation request form, and a deposit is required: $25 times number of locations requested.

Baltimore, Maryland's largest city, is about 25 miles north of Annapolis. Named after George Calvert, the first Lord Baltimore, the city—today a major seaport and industrial center—is situated on the Patapsco River not far from Chesapeake Bay. During the War of 1812 the British tried unsuccessfully to capture Baltimore, savagely bombarding Fort McHenry during the night of September 13-14, 1814. Francis Scott Key, a Maryland lawyer and poet, witnessed the bombardment from the British frigate *Surprise.* He had gone aboard under a flag of truce to try and arrange for the release of a friend being held prisoner by the British and was himself detained for the duration of the battle. Inspired by the sight of the American flag still flying over the fort at dawn, Key wrote "The Star-Spangled Banner." He later asked that his poem should be sung to an eighteenth-century melody by John Stafford Smith; it was named our official national anthem in 1931.

Not too many years ago Baltimore's downtown and waterfront were suffering from a severe case of urban decline. The late H. L. Mencken, famed Baltimore newspaperman and author, once pithily described the inner harbor as smelling like "a billion polecats." In the 1970s, however, the city began to transform its blighted areas into a sparkling new showcase. Charles Center, a highrise office development, was constructed first, followed by the World Trade, Convention and

Maryland Science centers. Surrounding blocks were restored by private citizens taking advantage of an ambitious homesteading program. And Maryland native James Wilson Rouse, the renowned urban developer who created Boston's Faneuil Hall Marketplace among other innovative inner-city ventures, designed Harborplace—Baltimore's splendid multi-million-dollar waterfront market complex.

Unlike Boston's markets which were developed from restored existing buildings, Harborplace, which opened in 1980, is all new. Two glass pavilions with peaked roofs, flanked by awninged terraces and waterside patios along a brick promenade, house hundreds of attractive shops and restaurants. The Pratt Street Pavilion contains an appealing collection of specialty boutiques, restaurants and cafes; the Light Street Pavilion is a festival of foods, with a changing array of peddlers' carts and kiosks offering intriguing items for sale. Natives and tourists alike come by the thousands to look, eat, buy, watch jugglers and mimes, listen to music and inhale the aromas of roasting coffee beans, sausages, spices and herbs, and freshly-baked bread, cookies and croissants.

At the eastern end of the harbor, on Pier 3, is the spectacular new National Aquarium with its 157-foot pyramidal roof. Baltimore's ebullient Mayor William Donald Schaefer, the city's number one booster, promised that the structure would be completed by July 4, 1981. When it failed to meet the deadline the Mayor, wearing a striped Victorian bathing suit and a straw boater and accompanied by a yellow rubber duck and a "mermaid," jumped into the seal pool to demonstrate his remorse. Housing some 5000 fish, mammals, birds and amphibians, the Aquarium, now completed, includes a dolphin pool, a tropical rain forest, coral reefs and a section of the Maine coastline, among other superbly-designed exhibits.

The U.S.F. *Constellation*, a three-masted frigate commissioned in 1797 as one of America's first warships, lies in the water just beyond the Pratt Street Pavilion. Also on view are the clipper ship *Pride of Baltimore* and the S.S. *Nobska*. Now a restaurant, the old steamer *Nobska* once plied its way from Woods Hole to Martha's Vineyard in Massachusetts. Paddle boats and small sail boats are available for rental, and tour boats take passengers for harbor cruises or on excursions to Fort McHenry. For a grand view of the harbor and the rest of Baltimore, take an elevator up to the observation level of the 28-story World Trade Center. And don't miss the Maryland Science Center, with fascinating science exhibits and demonstrations and a planetarium. When your feet tire of walking, plunk yourself on a bench or bulkhead along the harbor and enjoy the scene. If you listen carefully perhaps you'll hear snatches of the local consonant-dropping accent, with Baltimore pronounced "Ballamer"—in the state of "Merlin."

After you've explored Harborplace to your heart's (and stomach's) content, you may enjoy seeing some of Baltimore's other sights of interest—and there are many. The Museum and Library of Maryland History includes extensive exhibits of silver, furniture and paintings, and the original manuscript of "The Star-Spangled Banner." The Peale Museum, America's oldest museum building and Baltimore's first city hall, has historical displays and portraits; the Baltimore Museum of Art houses European, American and Oriental paintings and sculpture. Historic sites include monuments galore, Fort McHenry, the Star-Spangled Banner Flag House and 1812 War Museum (the flag is a replica; the actual banner is in the Smithsonian in Washington, D.C.), the Edgar Allen Poe House, the writer's home from 1832 to 1835, and Westminster Presbyterian Church Cemetery, Poe's burial place.

To cover the city properly you'll need a car, and self-guided auto tour tapes are available for rental. Ask for details at the Tourist Information Center at the Hilton Hotel or main office at 110 W. Baltimore Street. If you don't care to drive, bus tours covering historic points of interest leave from the Convention Center. One of the most noticeable things about Baltimore is its spic-and-span neatness; even today many owners of the city's typical nineteenth-century brick row houses come out each morning and scrub their steps! It is also a city of neighborhoods, with great ethnic diversity. Greek, Italian, American Indian, Jewish and many other ethnic festivals are held throughout the summer along the Inner Harbor.

A few miles west of Baltimore, the historic old mill town of Ellicott City on the Patapsco River offers a large state park and the Baltimore and Ohio Railroad Station Museum, the first passenger terminals in the country. Here in 1830, "Tom Thumb," the famous steam locomotive, raced a horse-drawn railroad carriage along the original 13-mile section of track . . . and lost. The town itself was founded in 1772 by three Quaker brothers as a site for their gristmill, and many of the original log cabins and stone houses have been preserved. To the southeast, the Savage Mill complex on the north bank of the Little Patuxent River offers 15 restored nineteenth-century historic buildings, now housing shops and restaurants. Columbia, a modern planned city just south of Ellicott City, is a cluster of villages surrounding a lake and a town center with gardens, fountains, and a wide range of restaurants, shops and cultural events.

Hayland Farm. Louis and Dorothy Mobley's Hayland Farm in Ellicott City is a large, contemporary stone ranch-style house set on 4 acres in the middle of 500 acres of rolling countryside. Summer visitors will revel in the 25-by-50-foot outdoor pool behind the house. The Mobleys have two pleasant rooms for guests, sharing one bath. One has a queen-size bed, the other has bunk beds—ideal for a family traveling with children. The accommodations are nicely furnished, and the beds boast hand-crocheted afghans. Guests are welcome to join the Mobleys in the living room and music room or relax on the spacious screened porch. A complete breakfast is included in the rates, and other meals, offering fresh vegetables from the garden, will be provided on request for a reasonable fee. You'll need a car to reach restaurants, shops and local points of interest. Baltimore is only a short distance away, and Annapolis and Washington, D.C. are both within an easy drive.

Hayland Farm, 5000 Sheppard Lane, Ellicott City, MD 21043; (301) 531-5593 or 596-9119. (A map with directions will be sent when you make your reservation.) Rates are moderate. Children are welcome; no pets, please, and no smoking in the bedrooms. Plenty of parking is available. Open year-round.

WESTERN MARYLAND

Frederick County, west of Baltimore and northwest of Washington, D.C., is a pleasantly rolling region with meandering country roads, historic houses and sites, orchards and farm markets, antique shops, covered bridges and small, pretty villages. Frederick, the county seat, is particularly attractive. Even though its 33-block Historic District attracts visitors by the thousands, the town manages to retain a quiet serenity, a comfortable, lived-in quality that doesn't seem at all "touristy."

Originally called Fredericktown, named after Frederick Calvert, the sixth Lord Baltimore, the village was founded by English and German settlers in 1745. Wagon trails heading West over the mountains stopped here for supplies; later the town became a major crossroad, part of the Old National Pike. Francis Scott Key lived in Frederick, and so did Civil War heroine Barbara Fritchie.

According to legend, when Confederate Gen. "Stonewall" Jackson occupied the town Mistress Fritchie not only flew the Stars and Stripes in defiance but also personally challenged the offending general and his "rebel hordes." Poet John Greenleaf Whittier described the scene in dramatic verse: "Up from the meadows rich with corn,/Clear in the cool September morn,/The clustered spires of Frederick stand/Green-walled by the hills of Maryland." . . . "Up the street came the rebel tread;/Stonewall Jackson riding ahead." Leaning from her window Fritchie confronted him: "'Shoot, if you must, this old gray head,/But spare your country's flag,' she said" . . . and Jackson gallantly responded. "'Who touches a hair of yon gray head/Dies like a dog! March on!' he said."

True or not, it's great stuff and you can visit a reproduction of Barbara Fritchie's home, with a museum, on W. Patrick Street.

Other historic Frederick structures include the 1763 Trinity Chapel and the 1799 Roger Brooke Taney Home and Francis Scott Key Museum. Taney, who swore in Abraham Lincoln as President, was chief justice of the Supreme Court from 1835 to 1864. A number of interesting buildings are located around Court House Square, including the Ross/-Mathias Mansions dating to 1815 and 1817, with an old carriage house and slave quarters out behind; the Ramsey Home, once visited by Abraham Lincoln; the William Tyler Page Home (Page was the author of "The American's Creed"), and Dr. Tyler's Home, built in 1790. In 1765, during the American Revolution, Court House Square was the scene of the first protest against the hated British Stamp Act; an effigy of the stamp distributor was burned.

Francis Scott Key and Barbara Fritchie are buried in the Mt. Olivet Cemetery at the south end of Market Street. Rose

Hill Manor, north on Market Street, is a beautiful eighteenth-century mansion that is now a children's museum with garden, old carriages and farm implements. Schifferstadt on Rosemont Avenue, a superb example of German Colonial architecture, was built by Joseph Brunner and his son Elias in 1756. Monocacy Battlefield, where Union Gen. Lew Wallace's band of 5000 men managed to delay Confederate Gen. Jubal Early's 23,000 soldiers for 24 hours during the Civil War, is located three miles south of Frederick. The battle, which took place on July 9, 1864, allowed General Grant time to reinforce threatened Washington, D.C.

121 Record Street. This delightful bed and breakfast guest house is a special pleasure to describe, for its owner, Miss Elaine A. Heiberg, is a long-time personal friend. She's a superb hostess, warm, witty and great fun to know; you'll like her! Situated on Court House Square in the center of Frederick's Historic District, 121 Record Street was built around 1820. William Tyler Page, author of "The American's Creed," was born a few doors up the street, but lived here during his boyhood years. From 1963 to 1980 the house was owned by educator Eleanor Johnson, who initiated and for many years published *My Weekly Reader*, an excellent newspaper for grammar school students that is still in use today. Miss Heiberg, who purchased the property in 1980, opened her home to guests in 1982.

A handsome three-story brick Federal-style structure, 121 Record Street is currently painted off-white. Beyond the gracious front door you'll discover an elegant entrance hall, formal high-ceilinged double drawing rooms, a large dining room with Williamsburg mural wallpaper, a country kitchen and a sunny garden room. The house also includes five working fireplaces. In the rear is a lovely perennial garden, shielded from the street by a long white board fence.

For guests there's a charming two-bedroom suite, one easy flight up, that includes a spacious bedroom with twin beds, a sitting-room with fireplace, a private bath, and a roof terrace with view of the garden. The tastefully decorated rooms, furnished mainly in antiques, also include fresh flowers in season or plants, and a telephone. Musically-minded guests will enjoy the pleasant sound of a carillon in the park half a block away, and choir practice or music from services in several nearby churches can be heard on occasion. Breakfast, included in the rates, consists of fresh fruit in season, English muffins, hot breads or toast (depending on the mood of the innkeeper) and coffee or tea.

Elaine Heiberg is of Norwegian descent, born in Minnesota, and you will note many colorful Scandinavian touches in her house. If you're interested in genealogy, do ask about her remarkable family book which traces the Heibergs back for many centuries. Elaine is also an enthusiastic collector of newspapers and periodicals—always *intending* to go through them, clip interesting articles and toss the rest out. As this seldom happens, you will most likely find the Garden Room pleasantly full of reading material!

121 Record Street is two blocks from Frederick's main downtown shopping street, which has several fine restaurants, antique and gift shops, art and jewelry stores, clothing stores and a unique hardware store (in existence since 1796 and still operating in the old tradition). Churches of many denominations are within walking distance, and many of Frederick's historic houses are just a few steps away. For other activities in the area your hostess suggests visiting nearby New Market for antiques and some of the marvelous orchards within a 15-mile radius. Her favorite is the Catoctin Mountain Orchard in Thurmont, where in season visitors can pick their own strawberries, raspberries and cherries and buy freshly-picked peaches, nectarines, grapes, apples and other fruits.

121 Record Street, Court House Square, Frederick, MD 21701; (301) 694-6458. (Record Street, on one side of Court House Square, is only one block long; the house is on the corner of Record and West Second Street, two blocks west of Market Street, Rte. 355.) Rates are moderate. No children or pets, please. On-street metered (except Sundays) parking is available on two sides of the house; free parking (with some time restrictions) is available a block away. The house is generally open year-round, but please be sure to call or write ahead for reservations as space is limited.

Spring Bank Farm Inn. Spring Bank, a stately brick Italianate house now owned by Beverly and Ray Compton, is located in the small community of Harmony Grove just north of historic Frederick. Constructed in the 1800s for George Houck, a local banker and gentleman farmer, the residence was described in a nineteenth-century book on the region as containing "... all the modern improvements that judiciously-expended wealth could obtain or refined taste suggest." The Comptons first saw Spring Bank while bicycling in Frederick County, and purchased the old house in 1980. They immediately began the difficult (and costly) job of restoration. Their goal was to return the residence to its original splendor, reproducing the period as exactly as possible, and open it as a Victorian bed and breakfast inn. To date the Comptons have completed the first floor, converting the billiards room, dining room and former kitchen into three double guest rooms. As time and money permit, they plan to add more guest rooms on the second floor and hope to convert the enormous cellar into an eighteenth-century tavern.

The spacious guest accommodations feature 12-foot ceilings with deep plaster mouldings, 9-foot windows, heart-of-pine floors, stenciled walls and antique furniture and linens. One room has a private bath; two share a bath and powder room. Guests are welcome to share the Comptons' elegant double parlor with bay window seats, marbled fireplace, Oriental rugs, warm brass decorations and antiques. A library in the parlor contains books on Maryland's history, gardening, aviation and antiques. Included in the rates is a hearty Continental breakfast of fresh fruit, freshly-baked breads and coffee or tea, served in your room on a tray with antique china, silverware and fine linens.

Guests at Spring Bank are also invited to explore its ten acres of grounds on which stand four brick outbuildings: a carriage house, smokehouse, outhouse and gas house. Frederick, three miles away, offers a host of historic houses and sites, fine shops and restaurants, and New Market to the east is called "The Antiques Capital of Maryland." Swimming, hiking, picnicking and cross-country skiing are available at nearby state and national parks. Baltimore, Washington, D.C., Harpers Ferry and even Gettysburg are all within easy driving distance.

Spring Bank Farm Inn, 7945 Worman's Mill Rd., Frederick, MD 21701; (301) 694-0440. (North of Frederick, turn east from Rte. 15 onto Rte. 355; Spring Bank is ¼ mile ahead on the left.) Rates are moderate; one night free with a full week's reservation. Children over 12 are welcome; no pets, please, and no smoking in the house. There is parking available. Open year-round.

The Rosebud Inn

The Rosebud Inn. You'll find the inviting Rosebud Inn in rural Woodsboro, eight miles north of Frederick. Originally the residence of Dr. George F. Smith (founder of the Rosebud Perfume Company in 1895), the grand old house is now owned by Al and Alice Eaton. Built in 1920, the 2½-story hip-roofed brick Colonial Revival home boasts large porches supported by fluted columns, two fireplaces with massive marble mantels, hardwood floors, gracefully arched windows and a dining room with oak paneling and beams. A number of beautiful stained-glass doors and windows feature a rose motif, the trademark of Dr. Smith's company. The Eatons, who opened the house as a bed and breakfast inn in 1981, have painstakingly restored the house and its grounds.

For guests there are five attractively furnished rooms, with comfortable poster beds and air conditioning. Three of the spacious rooms have private baths; two share a bath. Guests are welcome to make themselves at home in the cozy parlor and living room, on the porch and in the garden. Alice Eaton is of German descent, and throughout the inn you'll note a strong European flavor intermingled with Colonial and Victorian touches. Your hostess feels very much at home in Woodsboro, she says, as it reminds her of the little town in Germany where she grew up.

A Continental breakfast is included in the rates. The friendly Eatons will gladly suggest some good restaurants in the area for other meals—and there's a barbecue grill out back for guests who would like to arrange a cook-out. Things to do in Woodsboro include a visit to the Eatons' own Blue Spruce Gift Shop; the Holweck Furniture Company, which makes exquisite dollhouses; and the Circuit Rider Shop for antiques. Right next door to the inn you'll find the Rosebud Perfume Company, still operated today by Smith family members. The company specializes in Rosebud Salve, Strawberry Lip Balm and perfumes. On Tuesdays the Woodsboro Livestock Sales offer (in addition to livestock) vegetables and other produce, and a Flea Market. Frederick and New Market are only minutes away, and the Catoctin Mountains offer all manner of outdoor activities.

The Rosebud Inn, No. 4 North Main St., Woodsboro, MD 21798; (301) 845-2221. (Specific directions will be provided when you make your reservation.) Rates are expensive, lower for stays of seven or more days. Visa and MasterCard are accepted. Well-behaved children are welcome; no pets, please. No *drugs allowed, and only limited smoking. There is parking at the house. Open year-round.*

New Market, about seven miles east of Frederick, is a tiny gem of a town. Not quite half a mile long, it has only one street and a handful of narrow lanes. Beyond the herringbone-patterned brick sidewalks are charming old houses in a variety of architectural styles, dating from the late 1700s to the mid-1800s. Founded in 1793, New Market was created to serve the needs of travelers; conveniently located between Baltimore and Frederick, the town was a stopping-off place for drovers. After the old National Pike (a section of which ran right through the center of New Market) was built in the early 1800s, the town became a rest and supply stop for Westward-bound pioneers in Conestoga wagons.

Now, almost 200 years later, the village still appears much as it did in those long-gone days. Modern visitors, however, come to New Market for a different reason—to shop or browse in the more than 40 antique and craft shops housed in its historic old homes and one-time hotels or taverns. In them you'll find eighteenth- and early nineteenth-century furniture, hooked rugs, clocks, country primitives, antique jewelry, quilts, old books, tools and toys, china and glass, brass and copper, and countless other irresistible items. And New Market's two-century-old tradition of providing hospitality to weary travelers still exists at the Strawberry Inn, where overnight guests are offered a warm welcome, comfortable bed and breakfast.

The Strawberry Inn. Jan and Ed Rossig are your hosts at the inn, a white clapboard Victorian built in the mid-1800s and beautifully restored. There are five air-conditioned double rooms for guests; two are large enough to accommodate three people. One room is on the ground floor. All have private baths and are individually decorated with great taste and charm, furnished in antiques and period reproductions including patterned wallpaper and gleaming brass beds. Guests are cordially invited to use the antique-filled downstairs parlor, with a fireplace where a cheerful blaze will warm cold feet on chilly days or evenings.

Breakfast at the Strawberry Inn is served in the handsome bay-windowed dining room or on a tray brought to your room. There'll be fresh fruit in season (strawberries, if available), freshly-baked muffins and jelly, and a pot of coffee, tea or cocoa, all included in the rates. For other meals, your hosts suggest Mealey's Restaurant, located just across the street in what was once an old hotel. The town also has a pleasant tearoom serving sandwiches, soups and desserts on weekends, and nearby Frederick offers a choice of many fine places to dine.

The Strawberry Inn

The Strawberry Inn, 17 Main St., Box 237, New Market, MD 21774; (301) 865-3318. (From Frederick, take I-70 East about seven miles to Exit 60; follow signs to New Market.) Rates are moderate. Children over 5 are welcome; no pets, please. Parking is available at the house. Open year-round.

Western Maryland's Catoctin Mountains, a spur of the Blue Ridge, formed the first barrier faced by Westward-bound pioneers in the 1700s. Today the beautiful mountains are a lure for sports enthusiasts, for they offer outstanding fishing and hunting. Catoctin Mountain park and Cunningham Falls State Park together cover more than 10,000 acres, with hiking trails, campgrounds and picnic sites. Camp David, presidential mountain retreat since the days of Franklin D. Roosevelt (when it was called "Shangri-La"), is located in Catoctin Mountain Park—it is not, of course, open to the public.

Antietam National Battlefield lies to the southwest, near the West Virginia border. On Sept. 17, 1862, General McClellan's Union Army met and checked General Lee's Confederate troops here, forcing Lee to move back across the Potomac. More than 23,000 men were killed or wounded in the savage battle. Stop at the Visitor Center for information; then follow the roadways past some 300 tablets, battlefield maps and monuments. Hagerstown, 11 miles to the north, offers a number of interesting historic sites including the early eighteenth-century home of the town's founder, Jonathan Hager, and the Miller House, headquarters of the Washington County Historical Society, with a three-story spiral staircase and early nineteenth-century garden. Fort Frederick State Park, a few miles west, is the site of a British fort built in 1756 during the French and Indian War.

Maryland at this point narrows down to a mere passage between West Virginia and Pennsylvania and then widens again to the west. You'll come to Cumberland next, where George Washington's first military headquarters may be visited. Follow the Fort Cumberland Trail, a walking tour through the downtown historic area, and view The Narrows, a picturesque gap in the mountains that later became the transportation gateway to the West. Over in the far western reaches of the state, in mountainous Garrett County, travelers will discover more than 70,000 acres of state forests and lovely Deep Creek Lake. Summertime activities include hiking, boating, water skiing and swimming. In the fall there are hunting and autumn foliage festivals, and in winter the scenic region offers excellent skiing—downhill and crosscountry.

West Virginia

A ruggedly beautiful region of brooding mountains, peaceful valleys and swift-running rivers, West Virginia is a vacationer's delight. There are ancient limestone caverns to explore, and covered bridges, old grist mills and spectacular waterfalls to photograph. Twisting, scenic roads lead to historic sites and picturesque mountain villages. Sports enthusiasts will find excellent hunting and fishing, golfing, swimming and hiking, skiing and whitewater rafting. For shoppers and collectors West Virginia boasts some of the finest arts and crafts in the country—colorful handmade quilts, wood carvings, glass, pottery and metalwork. More than 450 fairs and festivals held throughout the year present craftspeople demonstrating their age-old skills, the mountain music of dulcimers, banjos and fiddles, and lavish displays of home-cooked country foods. And the state's friendly citizens welcome visitors with genuine mountain hospitality.

West Virginia's average elevation is 1500 feet, highest of any state east of the Mississippi River. The ridged mountains of the Allegheny Plateau cover more than one third of the state; Spruce Knob, at 4860 feet above sea level, is the highest point. To the west the mountains decrease in height and the land slopes gently down toward the Ohio River Valley. So formidable is the mountainous terrain that few Indians ever settled there; most came only to fish, hunt, and gather salt from the region's salty springs. Fortunately for today's travelers, West Virginia's numerous attractions are easily accessible via a fine network of highways and well-maintained secondary roads.

Until the Civil War, West Virginia was a part of Virginia. European explorers first roamed the region in 1669; the first permanent settlement is thought to have been established in 1731. Shortly thereafter, Scotch-Irish, Welsh and German pioneers began to immigrate to the territory. During the latter part of the 1700s the settlers often came into conflict with hostile Indians and with the French, who also had claims to

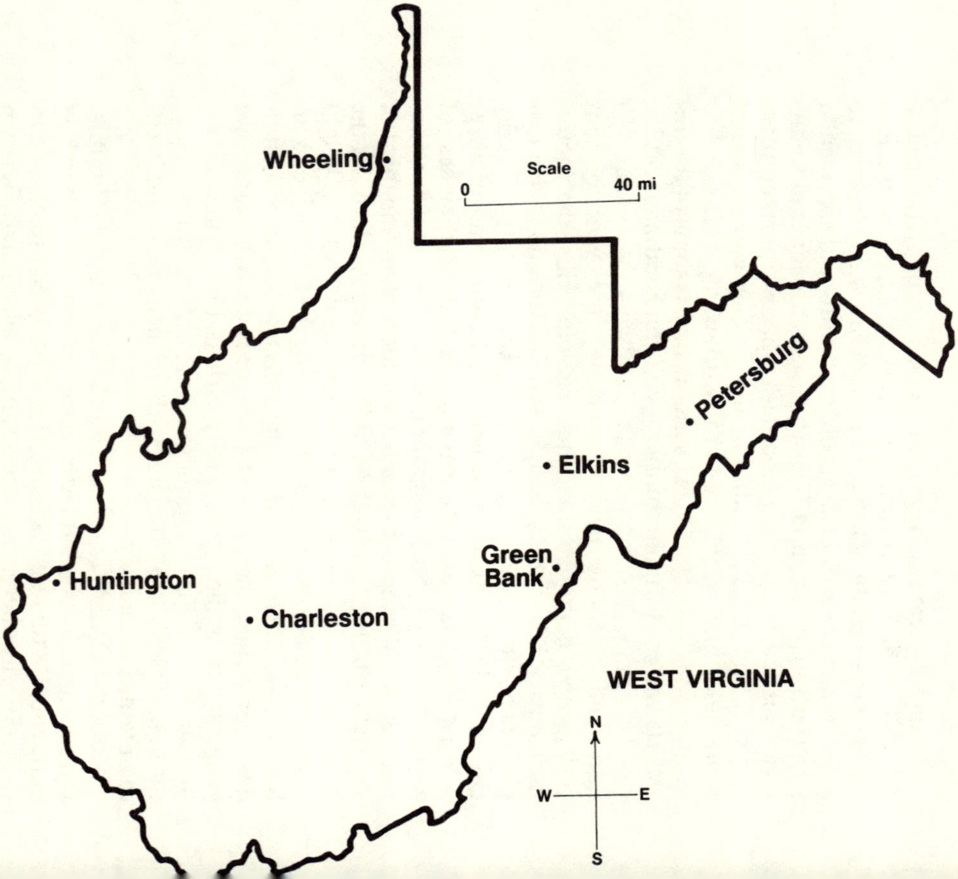
Wheeling
Scale
0
40 mi
Petersburg
Elkins
Green Bank
Huntington
Charleston
WEST VIRGINIA
N
W
E
S

the land. The frontiersmen who braved the wilds of West Virginia became farmers; their small patches of hard-won land were quite different from the vast slave-worked plantations of eastern Virginia—and eventually dissension arose between the backwoodsmen and the elegant proprietors to the east. The western settlers felt that although they paid the same taxes, they were not properly represented by the government and did not receive equal benefits. In 1783, in fact, they unsuccesfully tried to create a new state called "Westsylvania."

As the Civil War approached, the split between the two regions widened; many of the westerners sympathized with the North and when Virginia seceded in 1861 a number of representatives from the northwestern counties met to declare independence from the rest of the state. In 1863 West Virginia was formally admitted to the Union as a state in its own right. During the war more than 32,000 of the new state's citizens fought for the North; only 8000 joined the Confederate forces.

West Virginia's industrial growth began after the Civil War, with oil and particularly coal as its major resources. Today it is the nation's leading source of bituminous coal, with an incredibly rich coal region that extends over more than two thirds of the state's total area. West Virginia is also a productive agricultural state and a major producer of chemicals and glass. Tourism is big business nowadays, too, and one of the state's greatest lures for visitors is its remarkably extensive, well-designed park system offering a wide range of recreational facilities.

In addition to the vast Monongahela National Forest, West Virginia includes 14 "vacation" state parks, 8 day-use parks, 9 state forests, a number of public hunting and fishing areas, and 11 natural areas and historic sites. As traditional guest houses are scarce in West Virginia, you might want to consider staying at several of the parks as you travel around the state. All offer overnight accommodations, ranging from campsites to cabins and luxurious lodges. The cabins are completely furnished and equipped for housekeeping. They include deluxe and standard models with open fireplaces and tiled showers, one-room economy cabins, and rustic versions—the last equipped as in pioneer days with gas lamps, wood-burning stoves and fireplaces. Many of the deluxe cabins are open year-round; others are seasonal.

Guest Houses

Lodge facilities may be found at Blackwater Falls, Cacapon, Canaan Valley, Hawks Nest, North Bend, Pipestem, Twin Falls and Tygart Lake State Parks; most are open year-round. Rates for both cabins and lodge accommodations are moderate, and there are restaurants at many of the parks. For complete information write to the West Virginia Department of Natural Resources, Division of Parks and Recreation, State Capitol-SP, Charleston, WV 25305.

EASTERN WEST VIRGINIA

The state of West Virginia is shaped roughly like an egg, but over in the east the state extends in a ragged panhandle into Maryland and Virginia. Harpers Ferry, at the junction of the Shenandoah and Potomac rivers, is the scene of John Brown's famous raid. An ardent abolitionist, Brown hoped to free the slaves through armed force. On Oct. 16, 1859, with a band of 18 equally determined men, he seized the U.S. Arsenal at Harpers Ferry and won control of the town. The local militia, aided by a company of U.S. Marines under the command of Col. Robert E. Lee, counterattacked, wounding and capturing Brown. He was charged with murder and treason; during his trial he offered an impassioned defense, but was convicted and hanged. During the Civil War, Harpers Ferry, strategically important to both the South and North, changed hands many times. Harpers Ferry National Historic Park includes a self-guided walking tour of the restored old town and the fort where John Brown made his last stand.

If you'd like to experience an exciting whitewater raft or canoe trip on the Shenandoah River, Blue Ridge Outfitters in Harpers Ferry will arrange it. In June and September the town presents the Mountain Heritage Arts and Crafts Festival, with some 150 men and women demonstrating quilting, pottery throwing and a host of other crafts. During Old Tyme Christmas, held the first and second weekends in December, Harpers Ferry celebrates the holiday season in nineteenth-century style with traditional decorations, the lighting of a Yule log, a living Nativity Scene and caroling.

John Brown was jailed, tried and hanged in Charles Town to the south. Visit the Jefferson County Courthouse with the original courtroom, scene of the trial; a pyramid of stones not far away marks the site of the John Brown Gallows.

Charles Town, founded in 1786, was named for George Washington's brother Charles. His house and the home of Bushrod Washington, George's grandnephew, are located here as are a number of other handsome eighteenth- and early nineteenth-century houses. Historic Shepherdstown, north of Harpers Ferry on the Potomac River, is West Virginia's oldest continuously settled community—established around 1730. In 1787, the town was the site of the launching of the first steamboat, invented and designed by James Rumsey.

To the west is Berkeley Springs State Park, site of the country's oldest spa. The springs issue from the base of a steep ridge and provide about 2000 gallons of clear, sparkling water per minute—at exactly 74.3 degrees Fahrenheit. Two types of baths are available: the conventional bathtub, and the Roman baths, individual sunken pools lined with tile or marble. By all means try one—you'll be in good company. In the 1700s George Washington and his family regularly visited the springs.

Also interesting is the Castle, a massive stone mansion built in 1887 on a hill overlooking Berkeley Springs. The Norman-style "castle" includes a large stone-walled ballroom, wide carved staircase, and a tower room. Prospect Peak nearby offers a fabulous view of the Potomac and Great Cacapon valleys and glimpses into three states. Cacapon State Park, not far away, has an 18-hole championship golf course, swimming, boating and fishing, horseback riding and tennis. The park's accommodations include two lodges: the large 50-room Cacapon Lodge overlooking the golf course, open year-round, and the much smaller Old Inn Lodge. The latter, a rustic structure of rough-hewn logs with a veranda, stone chimneys and hand-wrought iron hardware, is done in a Colonial theme. Its 11 rooms, available during the summer months, are small and low-ceilinged, warmly paneled in knotty pine and chestnut. Baths are shared.

Down near Petersburg to the south travelers will want to explore the fascinating Smoke Hole Caverns. The Seneca Indians once used the caverns to smoke and preserve venison; their slow-burning wood fires sent clouds of smoke swirling out into the valley, causing the settlers to name the place Smoke Hole. During the Civil War the caverns were utilized by both Confederate and Union troops for storing ammuni-

Hermitage Motor Inn

tion, and later by mountain moonshiners who made illicit corn whiskey.

The Hermitage Motor Inn. In Petersburg, the historic old Hermitage—a hostelry since stage coach days in 1881—offers accommodations both in the inn and in an adjacent motel unit. The large main house was built in the early 1840s, using slave labor; its bricks were dug and fired on the premises. The first legal record of the place, in 1841, described it as a "red brick building with necessary outbuildings." During the Civil War the house was taken over by officers of the Federal troops occupying Petersburg. In 1881, then owners John and Mary Cunningham converted the house into a hotel. Around the turn of the century John Ed Taylor came to Petersburg to run the Riverside Tannery and purchased the hostelry. As he and his wife had nine daughters, Taylor needed more space—for them and for lodgers—so added extensively to the original building. It was during Taylor's ownership that the inn became known as the Hermitage, and therein lies a tale.

A frequent guest, Dr. Hay B. McCuskey, and I. B. (Ike) Wilson, a friend, decided to change the name of the place from the Taylor Hotel to a more appealing one. After dark one night in 1904 they took the "Taylor House" sign down, sneaked out to the old smokehouse to find paint and a brush, created a new sign—"The Hermitage"—and had it back on the post by midnight!

A later owner added the third floor and installed central heating and plumbing; the motel unit was built in the 1960s. James and Diane Roby purchased the Hermitage in 1980 and a year later added a heated pool out back. In the inn there are six rooms for guests: two with twin beds, three with double beds, and one with a twin-sized bed. One of the double-bedded rooms shares a bath with a twin-bedded room, an ideal combination for families. The other rooms have private baths. One, rented by the week, also has a kitchen. The comfortable accommodations include wall-to-wall carpeting, matching spreads and drapes, color TV and a telephone. The motor lodge, situated behind the inn, offers four rooms, all with private baths.

Visitors may find the room numbers in the inn somewhat confusing, as they seem to follow no logical sequence. They were, however, designated according to when the room was put into service for travelers: for example, No. 18, now part of the Robys' private quarters, is on the ground floor; No. 12 is on the third floor. Room No. 1 is called "the jury room" as it was once used by the circuit judge, attorneys and juries when court time came each year; it served as headquarters, and juries were at times "locked up" for the night. When plumbing was first added to the house Room No. 6 was the only one with private plumbing and quickly became the most sought after. When plumbing was installed in all the rooms, No. 6—because of its small size—became obsolete and was used for storage and as a retreat for afternoon naps. The Robys remodeled it in 1981 and now offer it to single visitors.

Guests are invited to use the inn's spacious lobby, decorated with crafts that are for sale, the broad first- and second-floor porches, and the surrounding 2½ acres of land with heated pool and health spa. An outbuilding still standing was originally a sample house where traveling salesmen displayed their wares. And visitors will particularly enjoy browsing through the Hermitage Book and Craft Shop, presenting a large selection of West Virginia books and fine handmade crafts, both functional and decorative. You'll find pottery, paintings, prints, pewter, stained glass, tin, leather and wood, and charming folk toys.

No food is served at the inn but several restaurants are within easy walking distance, others within a short drive.

Tennis courts, a nine-hole golf course, boating and fishing are all easily accessible, too.

The Hermitage Motor Inn, 203 Virginia Ave., P.O. Box 1177, Petersburg, WV 26847; (304) 257-1711. Rates are moderate. MasterCard and Visa are accepted. Children are welcome; pets are allowed with a $10 deposit. Parking is available in a lot to the rear. Open year-round.

Smoke Hole Lodge. This rustic lodge, located about 12 miles south of Petersburg, is the ideal retreat for travelers who *mean* it when they say they'd like to "get away from it all"! Set deep in the mountains on a remote 1500-acre tract in scenic Smoke Hole Valley, Smoke Hole Lodge is accessible only via a four-wheel vehicle. If you're not driving one, your cordial host, Edward W. Stifel III, will transport you from town in the lodge's own pickup or antique jeep station wagon. It's a bumpy, more-than-an-hour-long ride and by the time you arrive you'll know you have left the world of superhighways and neon signs far behind. Also electricity and telephones: the place runs on kerosene, wood and bottled gas.

The lodge, which sits on a low bluff 20 yards from the South Branch of the Potomac River, consists of two buildings in an "L" shape, joined by a common porch. It is of log and frame construction and dates from the mid-nineteenth century. The main building was originally a one-room schoolhouse; the second structure is a typical pioneer's cabin, moved from its original location three miles away. Tradition has it that a "giant" Indian stagecoach robber was tortured to death in the cabin—but fear not, no ghostly manifestation has ever appeared. There are four double bedrooms for guests and two dormitories, one with four beds and one with five, and five bathrooms (with hot water). Two of the bedrooms share a bath. One of the rooms and a bath are located on the ground floor. All of the accommodations are simple but comfortable. A spacious living room where guests gather in late afternoon for a social hour and good conversation features a large fireplace where, in spring and fall, a blazing log fire is lit. Three hearty, family-style meals are served daily in the dining room overlooking the river. And the lodge is never crowded; normally not more than eight guests will be staying at one time.

Smoke Hole Lodge, as owner Stifel emphasizes, is not a resort. There are no tennis courts, golf courses or the like.

Guests entertain themselves by fishing, swimming, tubing, hiking or simply reading or loafing. (Fishermen must have a valid West Virginia license, which may be purchased at several locations in Petersburg.) Trail rides are available if requested in advance. Youngsters (and adults) will enjoy the Stifels' dogs, ducks, chickens, geese and several cows. The area abounds with deer, and you *might* see an occasional bear!

It's suggested that you bring along any special-purpose equipment you may need such as fishing gear, binoculars and hiking shoes, and a flashlight and raincoat are advised. (The last is particularly comforting, your host points out, if you ride in or out in the back of the lodge's "Super Truck" during a rainstorm.) Otherwise, just plan to come and experience the mountains and their many moods . . . in spring when the redbud blooms, in summer when the forest is cool and green, or in spectacular autumn.

Smoke Hole Lodge, P.O. Box 953, Petersburg, WV 26847. There is no phone, so you'll have to write for reservations. (In case of emergencies, there is radio contact with the outside world. If necessary, a helicopter can land on the lodge's level bottom land, and there is an airfield in Petersburg. Emergency phone messages from outside may be given to Alt's Grocery in Petersburg, (304) 257-4774, and will be relayed.) Rates, which include three meals a day and round-trip transportation from Petersburg and back, are expensive; 10 percent off for groups of 8 to 14 and for stays of 5 or more nights. No charge for children age 4 and under. Reservations are accepted only for two or more nights. Reservations and deposits (minimum deposit of two nights' lodging per person is required) must be received at least two weeks in advance of your expected arrival date. Guests should be prepared to leave Petersburg (where you may leave your car) for the lodge at 5 p.m. Children and pets are welcome, but they must not harm the farm animals. The lodge is open from April 1 through October 31.

Blackwater Falls and Canaan Valley State Parks are both located a bit northwest of Petersburg, near Davis. At Blackwater the beautiful falls of the Blackwater River plunge from a height of five stories into a deep, boulder-strewn gorge. Numerous observation points afford panoramic views of the amber-colored falls and half-mile-wide canyon;

stairways and boardwalks lead to the base of the falls. Spring wildflower walks are a popular attraction; in summer the park offers swimming, boating, horseback riding and golf. Blazing fall foliage lures countless visitors, and in winter there's an outstanding sled run. The 55-room lodge of natural stone and wood, perched on the forested rim of the gorge, is open year-round. A hiking trail from the lodge leads to another lovely cataract, the Fall of Elakala, only 100 yards away. Canaan Valley State Park is situated in a mountain valley, surrounded by mountain peaks rising to more than 4200 foot. The park includes complete winter ski facilities, with lifts and snow-making equipment. Vacation cabins and the 250-room lodge are open year-round.

For a look at more of West Virginia's limestone caves, head for Franklin to the south and Seneca Caverns, the state's largest, once a refuge for the Seneca Indians. Only a few miles from Spruce Knob, the state's highest point, the caverns lie 2500 feet below sea level. The deepest room is 165 feet below the earth. Traveling between Franklin and Elkins to the northwest, you'll pass through more of the immense Monongahela National Forest. Elkins, a commercial and rail center, is a good place to stay while exploring the forest region. The town hosts the Mountain State Forest Festival each October, when autumn color is at its height.

Marian's Guest House. In Elkins, Marian D. Channell welcomes guests to her home, a large, well-maintained frame house built in the early 1900s. There are six spacious guest rooms, furnished with some antiques, and sharing 2½ baths. There's also a powder room on the ground floor. Guests may make themselves at home in an air-conditioned lounge with TV on the second floor, or relax on the porch in summer. No food is served, but there are restaurants within walking distance. Shops and activities are easily reached; two ski resorts (including superb Snowshoe) are within a short drive and hiking trails are within five miles. Scenic and historic areas are all around.

Marian's Guest House, 731 Harrison Ave., Elkins, WV 26241; (304) 636-9883. (On routes 33 and 250, half a block from junction with Rte. 219.) Rates are inexpensive, lower for longer stays. Children are welcome; no pets, please. There is parking at the house. Open year-round.

Heading south from Elkins and then east and south via routes. 250 and 92, you'll come to Green Bank. Don't miss taking a ride on the Cass Scenic Railroad a few miles out of town. There are eight-mile (1½-hour) and 22-mile (4½-hour) trips available daily throughout the summer and on fall weekends. Either will provide an unforgettable ride into one of the most remote and breathtaking areas in the country. The steam-powered railroad, the last remaining segment of the lumber railroad network that once crisscrossed the county, terminates just below Bald Knob, at 4842 feet the second highest point in West Virginia. The National Radio Astronomy Observatory at Green Bank is another interesting site to explore; free tours are offered in summer and on weekends in the fall.

Seneca State Forest is just to the south, and Hillsboro, where Pearl Buck's house may be visited, is a bit beyond. The Pearl S. Buck Birthplace Museum displays memorabilia of the late Nobel Prize–winning author, who was born in the old farmhouse. Locust Creek Bridge, lone survivor of Pocahontas County's picturesque covered bridges, stands a few miles south. If you continue in a southward direction you'll come to famous White Sulphur Springs, West Virginia's most renowned spa. The springs were popular as long ago as the 1770s, and the elegant Greenbrier Hotel has been welcoming visitors from all over the world since 1913.

Harris House Lodging. In Green Bank, Harris House is a beautiful old place, a century old, with a handsome hand-carved stairway and many antiques. There are also a number of original oil paintings brought from Paris by the owners, Mr. and Mrs. Virgil B. Harris. All of the seven guest rooms are carpeted and have two comfortable beds; two rooms are on the ground floor. Two baths are shared. There is also a pleasant living room with cable TV for guests to use. Outdoors, the nicely-maintained grounds include a lawn and a patio, for stretching your legs, reading, sunning or picnicking. No food is served at Harris House, but your hosts will provide coffee or tea upon request. Guests have the use of a refrigerator for keeping soft drinks and snacks. You will need a car to get to restaurants, and there are several good places to eat within five miles. The Harrises will be pleased to offer suggestions on interesting places to visit in the region, including the National Radio Astronomy Observatory one mile away and the Cass Scenic Railroad.

Harris House Lodging, Box 182, Green Bank, WV 24944; (304) 456-4105. (Routes. 92 and 28, between the Post Office and Exxon Station, corner of Wessley Chapel Road; 10 miles south of Rte. 250 at Bartow.) Rates are inexpensive, lower for longer stays; children free. Children are welcome; no pets, please. There is parking at the house. Open from May 1 through January 31.

CENTRAL AND WESTERN WEST VIRGINIA

Morgantown, near the Pennsylvania border in northcentral West Virginia, is the home of West Virginia University. Its two campuses are linked with the downtown area by a computer-directed personal rapid transit system. The steep-hilled town is also a major producer of handblown glass; visitors are invited to tour two of the local manufacturers—Seneca Glass and Bailey Glass. And surprising as it may seem, Morgantown has two Chinese restaurants! Of the two, I highly recommend the Hallelujah, located on the fringe of town in a very ordinary-looking house.

Grafton to the south is noted as the birthplace, so to speak, of Mother's Day. Anna Jarvis of Grafton began the tradition in 1908 on the anniversary of her mother's death; in 1914 the day was made official via a proclamation by President Woodrow Wilson. Tygart Lake State Park, with a 13-mile-long lake winding through wooded valleys, is two miles away. The park includes a handsome 20-room lodge with restaurant, closed in winter. Continuing south you'll come to Philippi, where the first land battle of the Civil War was fought. For photographers there is an unusual two-lane covered bridge, part of Rte. 250, that spans the Tygart River.

West Virginia's capital, Charleston, is situated about 150 miles southwest, on the Kanawha River. The capitol building, one of the country's most beautiful, was designed by Cass Gilbert, architect of the United States Treasury Annex and United States Supreme Court building. Its majestic dome 293 feet high, is the largest state capitol dome in the nation—five feet higher than the United States capitol. Hanging 180 feet above the ground floor rotunda is a magnificent chandelier weighing 4000 pounds and made of 10,080 pieces of hand-cut Czechoslavakian crystal. Every four years the chandelier is lowered by hand crank, and each piece removed and cleaned for the Governor's inauguration. Another highlight of the building is the exquisite outer reception room of the governor's office, of Colonial Georgian design painted white with gold trim and carpeted in blue. At night the capitol is spotlighted and the imposing statue, "Lincoln Walks at Midnight," at the front entrance is cast into shadow—a memorable sight.

The Governor's Mansion stands next to the west wing of the Capitol, facing the river. Of red Harvard Colonial brick, the elegant Georgian-style structure has a two-story portico supported by four Corinthian columns. The state rooms of the mansion are open to the public on Thursdays and Fridays from 9:30 to 11:30 a.m. In Charleston you'll also want to visit the Cultural Center with exhibits, a museum, theater and craft shop, and Sunrise, a 16-acre estate with two mansions housing a children's museum, planetarium, art gallery and botanical center.

From Charleston, follow the river southeast to Gauley Bridge, at the junction of New and Gauley rivers. Guided whitewater raft and float trips can be arranged through North American River Runners. Hawks Nest State Park offers spectacular views of the New River Gorge and has a 31-room modern lodge, open year-round, built on the edge of the gorge. A rustic museum in the park displays early pioneer and Indian artifacts, and visitors will particularly enjoy taking a ride on the aerial tramway that links the lodge with the marina and boat dock on the lake below.

As coal plays such an important role in West Virginia's economy, perhaps you'd like to see a real coal mine. In Beckley, south of Gauley Bridge, travelers can visit the Beckley Exhibition Coal Mine where in summer months motorized coal cars take passengers 1300 feet through underground tunnels. The Appalachian Arts and Crafts Festival is held in Beckley each August, and from June to September the outdoor musical dramas "Hatfields & McCoys" and "Honey In the Rock" are performed nightly except Monday at the Cliffside Amphitheatre. Twin Falls State Park, 25 miles southwest, offers a 20-room guest lodge and deluxe family vacation cabins, open year-round. The park also includes a nine-hole golf course, swimming, tennis, game courts, and an old restored pioneer home and farm.

Two more state parks, Bluestone and Pipestem, are located southeast of Beckley. Bluestone, which has 25 deluxe cabins (closed in winter), boasts an 1800-acre lake and a 20,000-acre public hunting area. Pipestem is virtually a resort, with two golf courses, indoor and outdoor pools, lighted tennis courts, bike rentals, horseback riding and cross-country ski trails. It also offers two lodges: 113-room Pipestem, open year-round, and smaller Mountain Creek Lodge, accessible only by a 3600-foot aerial tramway and open from April to October.

West on the Kentucky border, the coal town of Williamson is close to Tug River Valley where the fierce mountaineer family feud of the Hatfields and McCoys took place. In Huntington, on the Ohio River to the north, visit the Huntington Galleries which display eighteenth-to twentieth-century European and American paintings and sculpture, pre-Columbian art and contemporary mountain crafts. The *Camden Queen* takes passengers on hour-long river cruises, and three glass manufacturers in the vicinity offer tours, including the famed Blenko and Pilgrim firms. Farther north at Parkersburg you can book passage on a sternwheeler (on summer and fall Sundays) out to historic Blennerhassett Island in the Ohio River.

Archeological excavations have shown that the island was inhabited by Indians as early as 12,000 B.C. White settlers came around 1785, and a bloody massacre occurred in 1794. Four years later Harman and Margaret Blennerhassett, exiled Irish aristocrats, arrived and erected a splendid mansion, called at the time the most beautiful in the West. Its rooms were filled with fine furniture and paintings, Oriental carpets and alabaster lamps; the garden included both exotic and native flowers and shrubs. This "paradise in the wilderness" was short-lived. In the early 1800s the Blennerhassetts became involved with Aaron Burr. Burr, who had killed Alexander Hamilton in a duel, came to the island in 1806 and attempted to persuade Blennerhassett to join him in his ill-fated scheme to set up a separate republic in the Southwest. The plot was uncovered, and both men were tried for treason. Although they were acquitted, Burr and Blennerhassett were ruined financially; the Blennerhassett mansion burned to the ground a few years later. The island, now a state park, is included in the National Register of Historic Places.

North Bend State Park, about 20 miles east of Parkersburg, is located in the broad valley of the North Fork of the Hughes River. In the park you'll find swimming, fishing, tennis, golf, hiking trails and a special trail and playground designed for the handicapped. Deluxe cabins and a modern 30-room lodge are open year-round; the lodge overlooks the river's famed horseshoe bend.

In West Virginia's far northwest the state juts sharply upward in another narrow panhandle, between Pennsylvania and Ohio. Follow the lush Ohio River Valley northward to Moundsville and the Grave Creek Mound and Museum. One of the country's most impressive, the ancient Indian mound is 79 feet high and 900 feet around. At the Fostoria Glass Company in town visitors may watch handcrafted glass being produced.

Farther north is Wheeling, where the last battle of the American Revolution was fought—at Fort Henry. The fort no longer exists, but there's a bronze plaque marking the site. During the war Fort Henry's defenders fought off many attacks by the British and the Indians. In the final onslaught, in 1782, they ran out of ammunition. A young woman named Betty Zane, sister of the fort's commander, Col. Ebenezer Zane, volunteered to run to the family's cabin 150 yards outside the garrison for more powder. Managing somehow to survive the enemy's vicious gunfire, she carried the powder back in her apron and saved the fort.

West Virginia became a state in Wheeling's Independence Hall-Custom House, where at a meeting in 1861 the delegates voted Virginia's secession from the Union to be unlawful and declared their independence. The building, now restored, may be toured. The city also welcomes visitors to Oglebay Park, a wooded and handsomely landscaped area of 1460 acres with a wide range of recreational facilities. Once the elegant country estate of Col. Earl W. Oglebay, the park includes many of the original buildings such as Mansion House, now a museum. There are golf courses, a swimming pool and a lake, tennis courts, ski slopes and a riding academy, a children's center and a fine children's zoo.

INDEX

Note: Guest houses which serve breakfast, either included in the rates or for a small extra charge, are starred. (*)

East Woods Press Books

Backcountry Cooking
Berkshire Trails for Walking & Ski Touring
Best Bed & Breakfast in the World
Campfire Chillers
Campfire Songs
Canoeing the Jersey Pine Barrens
Carolina Seashells
Carpentry: Some Tricks of the Trade from an Old-Style Carpenter
Catfish Cookbook, The
Complete Guide to Backpacking in Canada
Creative Gift Wrapping
Drafting: Tips and Tricks on Drawing and Designing House Plans
Exploring Nova Scotia
Free Attractions, USA
Free Campgrounds, USA Revised
Fructose Cookbook, The
Grand Strand: An Uncommon Guide to Myrtle Beach, The
Healthy Trail Food Book, The
Hiking from Inn to Inn
Hiking Virginia's National Forests
Honky Tonkin': Travel Guide to American Music
Hosteling USA, Third Edition
Inside Outward Bound
Interior Finish: More Tricks of the Trade
  from an Old-Style Carpenter
Just Folks: Visitin' with Carolina People
Kays Gary, Columnist
Making Food Beautiful
Maine Coast: A Nature Lover's Guide, The
Mid-Atlantic Guest House Book, The
New England Guest House Book, The
New England: Off the Beaten Path
Ohio: Off the Beaten Path
Parent Power!
  A Common-Sense Approach to Raising Your Children In The Eighties
Race, Rock and Religion
Rocky Mountain National Park Hiking Trails
Sea Islands of the South
Southern Guest House Book, The
Southern Rock: A Climber's Guide to the South
Steppin' Out: A Guide to Live Music in Manhattan
Sweets Without Guilt
Tar Heel Sights:
  Guide to North Carolina's Heritage
Tennessee Trails
Train Trips: Exploring America by Rail
Trout Fishing the Southern Appalachians
Vacationer's Guide to Orlando and Central Florida, A
Walks in the Catskills
Walks in the Great Smokies
Walks with Nature in Rocky Mountain National Park
Whitewater Rafting in Eastern America
Wild Places of the South
Woman's Journey, A
You Can't Live on Radishes